HUNGER OVERCOME?

Andrew Warnes

Hunger Overcome?

Food and Resistance

in Twentieth-Century

African American Literature

The University of Georgia Press | Athens and London

© 2004 by the University of Georgia Press

Athens, Georgia 30602

All rights reserved

Designed by Mindy Basinger Hill

Set in Sabon by Bookcomp, Inc.

Printed and bound by Thomson-Shore, Inc.

The paper in this book meets the guidelines for

permanence and durability of the Committee on

Production Guidelines for Book Longevity of the

Council on Library Resources.

Printed in the United States of America

07 06 05 04 03 C 5 4 3 2 1

07 06 05 04 03 P 5 4 3 2 1

Library of Congress Cataloging-in-Publication Data

Warnes, Andrew, 1974–

Hunger overcome? : food and resistance in twentieth-century African

American literature / Andrew Warnes.

    p. cm.

Includes bibliographical references and index.

ISBN 0-8203-2529-5 (alk. paper) — ISBN 0-8203-2562-7 (pbk. : alk. paper)

1. American literature—African American authors—History and criticism.

2. American literature—20th century—History and criticism.   3. African

Americans—Intellectual life—20th century.   4. African Americans in literature.

5. Food habits in literature.   6. Hunger in literature.   7. Food in literature.

I. Title.

PS153.N5W346 2003

810.9'3559—dc22   2003017585

British Library Cataloging-in-Publication Data available

Contents

Acknowledgments

HUNGER OVERCOME?'S JOURNEY from an idea to a book has been long and sometimes hard, but it has always been helped along the way by friends and colleagues, whose advice and support has been invaluable. While any errors in what follows are my own responsibility, they are undoubtedly fewer in number thanks to the close readings and careful responses of fellow scholars Dennis Flannery, Mick Gidley, Richard Godden, and Jay Prosser. The contribution of these writers has not been simply editorial: like Rachel Farebrother, Colin Winborn, Ben Caines, and John MacLeod, they have also encouraged me to read in new ways, to draw new connections, and to expand the applications of African

American literature, as *Hunger Overcome?* hopes to, beyond U.S. borders and out into the world.

As with much of its subject matter, *Hunger Overcome?* is the child of its transatlantic crossings. Whether reaching the States wrapped in an envelope or attached to an e-mail, the book has benefited greatly from the responses of Derek Krissoff, Jason Galie in Brooklyn, and, at a very early stage of the project, Darra Goldstein.

My own life, my own friends and family also make *Hunger Overcome?* what it is. My father, Tony Warnes, has given unwavering support of all kinds throughout the life of this project. Equally influential has been my mother, Jill Warnes, a teacher, who has not only enabled countless children and adults to read and write, but who also persevered, even when I seemed determined to burn our kitchen down, in teaching me how to cook. Her constant opposition to injustice of all kinds, and her insistence that the issues concerning *Hunger Overcome?* are in no sense only academic, motivates all of this book.

Finally, I dedicate this book to my wife, Sue. It, like happiness, could not exist without her.

HUNGER OVERCOME?

I lived in Master Hugh's family about seven years. During this time, I succeeded in learning to read and write. In accomplishing this, I was compelled to resort to various stratagems. I had no regular teacher. . . . From this time I was most narrowly watched. If I was in a separate room any considerable length of time, I was sure to be suspected of having a book, and was at once called to give an account of myself. All this, however, was too late. . . .

Colonel Lloyd kept a large and finely cultivated garden, which . . . abounded in fruits of almost every description, from the hardy apple of the north to the delicate orange of the south. This garden was not the least source of trouble on the plantation. Its excellent fruit was quite a temptation to the hungry swarms of boys, as well as the older slaves, belonging to the colonel, few of whom had the virtue or the vice to resist it. Scarcely a day passed, during the summer, but that some slave had to take the lash for stealing fruit. The colonel had to resort to all kinds of stratagems to keep his slaves out of the garden.

—FREDERICK DOUGLASS, *Narrative of the Life of Frederick Douglass* (1845)

Introduction

HUNGER OVERCOME? explores the literary responses that Zora Neale Hurston, Richard Wright, and Toni Morrison have made to the startling existence of food shortage within one of the wealthiest countries in the world. It calls attention to these writers' tendency to view hunger as an avoidable condition imposed from above, and to their association of this physical void with the equally solvable and equally debilitating emptiness of illiteracy—a condition that, as Henry Louis Gates Jr. has argued, *Narrative of the Life of Frederick Douglass* and other slave autobiographies depict as a prerequisite of racial subordination.[1] And it contends that, no less than the slave narrators of the nineteenth century, these leading twentieth-century authors link cooking and writing together because they, too, identify both as cultural processes by which inequalities resulting from racial injustice can be eroded and even, eventually, overcome.

Hunger and illiteracy are most clearly linked whenever narratives by Hurston, Wright, and Morrison portray the ministration of hunger's cure: cooking. These moments, when resourceful cooks replenish a nutritional absence that characteristically implicates both racism and capitalism, often allude to that pivotal episode—featured also in the autobiographies of James Gronniosaw and even Malcolm X—when the mental chains of illiteracy are broken through secret self-education. These writers all draw a profound connection between cooking and writing, insisting on the capacity of both processes to replenish two disabling voids—hunger and illiteracy—that external forces have invested with special prominence throughout African American history.

The narratives of former slaves refer repeatedly to slave traders' and slaveholders' attempts to monitor, regulate, and circumscribe both the literacy and the diet of their human property. Olaudah Equiano, in his *Interesting Narrative* of 1789, recalled watching the crew of his transatlantic slave ship gorge themselves on fish before tossing the leftovers "into the sea again . . . rather than give any of them to us to eat" (58–59). Yet Equiano's early initiation into the nutritional control slavery demanded finds a parallel in the elaborate apparatus that Douglass's owners placed between him and the sating of his hunger for words. For Douglass, the "bread of knowledge" and bread itself coalesce: just as he and other slaves are living "in the midst of plenty, yet suffering the terrible gnawings of hunger," so "their minds [are] . . . starved by their cruel masters."[2] Nor are the autobiographies of slaves restricted to decrying slaveholders' circumscription of cooked foods and written words. Equally often, they refer to acts of resistance—to moments of food theft and foraging, to surreptitious self-education, and to other individual rebellions that challenged such circumscription. By characterizing cooking and writing as volatile practices that held out a promise to slaves and a threat to slaveholders, occasioning "stratagems" through which plantation codes could be transgressed and consolidated, *Narrative of the Life of Frederick Douglass* furnishes a rich supply of such acts of everyday resistance. And what these acts suggest is that, within the plantation, the almost constant ability of slaveholders to control access to foods and words coincided with the occasional ability of slaves to disrupt this calculated distribution. Douglass's first autobiography suggests that if slaves could reassert their humanity by appropriating "white" foods and "white" books, then slaveholders could deny it by withdrawing such materials and so returning their property to what they saw as an animalistic diet and an animalistic illiteracy. If slaveholders could abject their African property by banishing them from their Edenic orchards, then slaves could launch Brer Rabbit–like forays that, by lifting "the hardy apple" and "the delicate orange" from predestined white mouths, reaffirmed their own humanity. If every food slaves secretly ate and every word they secretly read eroded the edifice of plantation life, then every withdrawal by slaveholders of these materials rebuilt it.

It is this politicization of food, this transformation of a necessary human activity into a forum in which white supremacist ideology can be affirmed and challenged, that distinguishes many African American views of cooking from those forwarded in the cultures of other U.S. racial or ethnic groupings. That is to say, Douglass's account of the possibilities food opens for disciplinary control and defiance—possibilities that abide due to the continuing problems of African Americans in twenty-first century America—exemplifies the distinctive politicization that operates within black culinary culture. Admittedly, Irish and Native American histories of famine, not to mention the controversies still surrounding the causes of such catastrophes, reveal that the African American is not the only national subculture in which food has become intensely politicized. But what distinguishes this particular culinary culture from those of other social groupings is that historical experiences of what Doris Witt terms *Black Hunger* neither arose from westward U.S. expansion nor prompted a wholesale immigration but occurred within the secured borders of existing states. As Douglass's autobiography reminds us, hunger was as normalized and integral to the status of slaves as illiteracy. If to be a slave was to be unlettered, then it was equally true that it was to be hungry, or at least it was to be dependent on unreliable and often vindictive slaveholding authorities for one's nutritional welfare. In a striking conjunction of hunger and labor productivity, many African Americans experienced malnutrition even as they contributed to the development of a national harvest that has proven to be among the most dependable in the world. Slaves and sharecroppers experienced food shortage while producing food surfeit.

The astonishing imbalance between the intense labor activity and the nutritional want experienced by the sharecropping and, later, the proletarian descendants of slaves is illustrated by the three narratives on which this book focuses: Zora Neale Hurston's *Their Eyes Were Watching God* (1937), Richard Wright's *Black Boy (American Hunger)* (1944), and Toni Morrison's *Tar Baby* (1981). By dramatizing the discrepancy between the economic contributions and the economic earnings of African Americans, these narratives establish adequate nourishment as another achievable social goal that, like universal literacy, has been denied African Americans because of a toxic blend of white supremacist ideology and unrestrained capitalism. None of these three texts merely represents hunger. Each text also surrounds its representations of want with images of that American harvest to which black labor has generously, if sometimes involuntarily, contributed. These images of a pervasive and apparently inexhaustible abundance show that the hunger endured in the course of such labor was preventable.

The similarities of these representations are all the more striking because, in other respects, these writers are so different. The need for a new way of reading the work of these writers, for developing an approach that acknowledges their underlying agreement without disregarding the singularity of their individual achievements, shapes the rest of my introduction. For instance, all three writers agree that black hunger has helped maintain American racial hierarchies, but their work treats food preparation in different ways: Hurston's and Morrison's prose often celebrates cooking, while Wright's, never reflecting his own culinary prowess, paints the process instead in an unremittingly functional, artless light. To reach a theoretical basis that accommodates these differences, I consider two contradictory appraisals of the respective merits of cooking and writing in African American culture. First, I examine Booker T. Washington's and W. E. B. Du Bois's views on the teaching of cooking and writing to the recently freed, and argue that theirs and other black political dialogues did not escape those Western, patriarchal assumptions that have historically undervalued the "female" culture incarnated in the culinary arts. I then turn to other black voices: to Abby Fisher, author of *What Mrs. Fisher Knows about Old Southern Cooking* (1881), and to Jessica Harris and Ntozake Shange, who publish what I call "talking" recipes, that is, recipes that represent both cooking and orality in writing and thereby affirm the vernacular tradition in its many forms. From this prefatory discussion, gender, class, and other aspects of identity arise and are considered as potential determinants of African American writers' decisions to celebrate or shun, forget or memorialize, black culinary forms.

My discussion of *Their Eyes Were Watching God*, *Black Boy (American Hunger)*, and *Tar Baby* does not focus on those novels exclusively but rather uses them as guides to examine a wider range of topics, including folklore collection, urbanization, orality, and utopianism. This discursive approach is also reflected in the historical compass of the book; while broadly chronological, it occasionally interrupts its journey from the publication of *What Mrs. Fisher Knows about Old Southern Cooking* in 1881 to that of *Tar Baby* a century later with excursions into the histories of colonialism and postcolonialism and of American slavery and freedom. Thus the first chapter charts colonial literature's promotion of the orange to a symbol of America's fertility, indeed, of its fragile, Edenic perfection, before considering the reformulation of such literary utopianism that Hurston achieves in her references to Florida's abundance of citrus groves. The second chapter relates Wright's memories of childhood hunger to the fields of literature, sociology, and biopsychology; the third chapter retraces the popularization of the Tar Baby folktale during the late nineteenth century and then relates it to Toni Morrison's eponymous novel.

I adopt this broad thematic and historical approach to prepare for the book's conclusion, which suggests that the positions these African American novelists reached resonate far beyond the U.S. borders and could potentially encourage a global reacknowledgment that *all* hunger is now akin to that endured by Olaudah Equiano; that *all* hunger—whether that of Colombian coffee farmers ruined by plummeting prices or of Ghanaian cocoa farmers who have never tasted chocolate—could be remedied by the "fish" that we in the West toss "overboard." This is a simple point, admittedly, but so too were the immorality of slavery and of segregation. The ultimate motive of this book is to reveal that, having helped defeat slavery and abolish de jure segregation, the writing and rhetoric of African Americans might now be used as a new kind of weapon, one that provides the will to renew the fight against hunger.

Booker T. Washington and W. E. B. Du Bois

Despite isolated exceptions, such as the male-dominated world of French gastronomy, the belief that the skill of writing is superior to that of cooking remains firmly entrenched in the Western world. Cooking has been reduced to an inartistic functionalism in those cultures forged by the Judeo-Christian separation of the body and soul. This separation, supported and secularized by Cartesian philosophy, has led to a suspicion of bodily functions and actions and an elevation of cerebral work over its manual equivalents. Assumptions regarding the insignificance, mundanity, or even vulgarity of the culinary arts have also found support in lingering patriarchal prejudices against cultural practices associated with women. These gender prejudices are further supported by the suspicion, articulated by Socrates in the Platonic dialogues, that cooking is a decadent, corrupted science. According to this view, the science of cooking pursues not progress but pleasure, and fraudulently adorns "the mask of medicine, and pretends to know the foods that are best for the body."[3] As these cultural formations continued to influence Western thought, the supremacy of oratory and, later, of writing over cooking became embedded in Western cultures, in a manner that contrasts sharply with, for example, the Chinese valorization of the *ch'i* of food explored by Jack Goody and, more recently, E. N. Anderson.[4]

The African American literary tradition, which includes many writers who loved to cook, provides a striking adjunct to the Western prioritization of writing. Ntozake Shange has written a recipe book, Maya Angelou is writing a recipe book, and the Black Panther Bobby Seale, having spent the 1960s cooking for hungry schoolchildren, spent the 1970s cooking for his restaurant's clientele. Similarly, in a *1973 New York Times Book*

Review article, Toni Morrison describes a picnic and vaunts the power of cooking to unify her family, noting that "we were all there. All of us, bound by something we could not name. Cooking, honey, cooking under the stars."[5] In the very different circumstances of postwar France, Richard Wright once cooked an expatriated African American meal for C. L. R. James. And a famous 1966 photograph, taken in Istanbul, in which the apron-clad James Baldwin hovers over a meal he is preparing for Bertice Redding, reveals that the author of "Everybody's Protest Novel," despite his attacks on Wright, shared his onetime mentor's taste for culinary experimentation.[6]

Yet, notwithstanding this preponderance of intellectual cooks and culinary writers, the African American tradition has never been entirely free of those dismissals of cooking strewn so liberally throughout Western cultures. For example, the idea of writing's cultural supremacy numbered among the few views that Booker T. Washington and W. E. B. Du Bois held in common. Although Washington and Du Bois often disagreed about the merits of teaching writing and cooking skills to black students, they concurred on the relative positions of these activities in a received hierarchy of cultural endeavor. For all their differences, both Washington and Du Bois accepted the prevailing characterization of cooking as a functional, inartistic practice and of writing as a passport to political awareness, high culture, ambition, and upward mobility. Indeed, the acceptance of this familiar binary opposition often led Washington and Du Bois to invoke cooking and writing simultaneously to typify the choice between the vocational and the academic that faced black education leaders. Oppositional differences between Washington and Du Bois proceeded from their shared endorsement of this fundamental binary opposition: whereas the former advocated the vocational route encapsulated by the apprenticeship of cooking, the latter favored literary education as a means of enlightening and uplifting the individual. Washington tended to think of cooking, which fed families and sometimes paid wages, as an end in itself. He regarded writing as a means to an end at best, and at worst as a bourgeois practice that could prematurely arouse in his students professional aspirations that American society was not ready to fulfill. Washington eschewed writing for purposes other than the immediately

practical—recipes, engineering manuals, or legal documents—as too rarefied to assist in the business of racial uplift. Washington banned the
excessive teaching of "rhetoric" at Tuskegee Institute and prescribed only
"good, simple, direct English" for his students.[7]

By contrast, Du Bois felt that the seemingly impractical field of writing
held untold, latent value; it held the inestimable capacities, if not of a
strictly economic uplift, then of one effected via the less measurable fields
of politics and culture. The basic binary opposition between cooking and
writing receives stronger support in Du Bois's writings than in Washington's. While the conflict between Tuskegee and the National Association
for the Advancement of Colored People (NAACP) subsided slightly after
Washington's death, Du Bois clearly remained mindful of old, unsettled
scores when he defended writing's "glorious world of fancy and imagination, of poetry and art, of beauty and deep culture" in a 1930 commence-
ment address at Howard University. From this defense of the aesthetic
strata of literature, Du Bois proceeded to dismiss as antiquated the fabled
culinary talent of black people, which Washington's Tuskegee had done
much to demystify, theorize, and teach. "Our success in household arts
is due not to our effective teaching so much as to the mediaeval minds
of our women who have not yet entered the machine age. Most of them
still seem to think that washing clothes, scrubbing steps and paring potatoes were among the Ten Commandments."[8] Such snobbery adds gender
prejudice to the concerns Cornel West recently expressed regarding Du
Bois's "inability to immerse himself in black everyday life." For West,
black vernacular culture's occasional and "ritualistic explosion of energy
frightened this black rationalist." By confirming Du Bois's dismissal of a
culinary practice that Washington valued, this snobbery also reveals that
at the root of these contradictory figures' assessment of cooking and writing lay a disagreement about the perceived usefulness these activities held
for the emergent African American classes. Both men proceeded from a
binary opposition between "functional" cooking and "academic" writing. They differed only insofar as Washington prioritized the practical,
whereas Du Bois, though not blind to the virtues of apprenticeship, tended
to prize the scholarly path he himself had trod. It is tempting to suggest
that, if an ideal graduate of Tuskegee might have been Abby Fisher—

whose pioneering cookbook I discuss shortly—then an ideal Du Boisian graduate might have been Phillis Wheatley, who escaped the manual work of the plantation to engage in the cerebral work of poetry, and who shared what West characterizes as Du Bois's "Enlightenment world-view."[9] At the very least, in a Tuskegee address of 1910, Booker T. Washington seemed to consider his entire female audience potential cooks as he commanded them to

> Study the soil. . . . Now you think I mean you have got to get a book and sit down and bury yourself in it for two or three hours when I say I want you to make a study, but I mean . . . find out what will grow in the community where you will reside. . . . [M]ake a study of the best methods of cooking that food. You know what I mean when I say "cooking." Sometimes girls get so mixed up on this subject of Domestic Economy that they forget all about cooking. I am talking about cooking, not about Domestic Economy.[10]

Although Washington is here typically contemptuous of the theoretical designation "Domestic Economy" in particular and of intellectualism in general, his own mastery of prose suggests this contempt is directed not at writing per se but at the idea that it is a suitable field of study for ordinary black women. Though more sympathetic to the value of "female" cooking than Du Bois, Washington effectively confirms the supremacy of writing by characterizing it as the province of an elite to which black people (and particularly black women) had no hope of belonging en masse. Writing remains, in Washington's vision, a signifier of "deep culture," and its supremacy is as secure in his works as in those of Du Bois. The thought of Du Bois and Washington thus remained drenched in a contemporary cultural view that prioritized a litany of intellectual pursuits from which cooking had been disqualified on the grounds that such a "female" and manual craft was inadequately cerebral. Both men largely endorsed the prevailing belief that the written word constituted the ultimate durable marker of a social group's achievement—an achievement for which Washington felt his contemporaries remained unprepared, but which Du Bois insisted could be drawn within reach. Throughout their disagreements, neither of these robust thinkers suggested that a marker of the cultural achievement of black people might already exist in the form of the foods they cooked for their own enjoyment and, often, for that of whites. The comparably sexist yet otherwise divergent appraisals of cooking these figures offered reveal that both men remained unwilling either to acknowledge the decisive contribution women had already made to African American literature or to consider the possibility that foods might likewise sustain meaningful cultural creativity. Neither the industrial nor the cultural objectives advocated in the progressive ideologies of Washington and Du Bois, respectively, include the artistry of cooking. Both men endorsed the prevailing view of writing as a supreme cultural endeavor: both allow its prioritization over cooking and other manual activities to pass unchallenged.

A scholarly exploration of food cannot satisfactorily proceed from these hierarchical precepts. Before beginning our analysis of African American literary treatments of hunger and cooking, we must recognize that, contrary to Du Bois's explicit dismissal and Washington's implicit belittlement, foods, as a field of academic inquiry, are no less ripe for study than words. The belief that audiences interpret foods as fruitfully and endlessly as they interpret words—the idea that foods can fatten, satisfy, give energy, convey love, and kill—forms the basis of Doris Witt's cultural history of soul food, *Black Hunger*. The present volume can be seen as one response to Witt's call for critics to recognize "that food is simply central to African American literature" (8). What follows in this book, then, is an interpretation of novels *and* an interpretation of foods, in which I intersperse close readings of text with readings of the social functions and cultural connotations of oranges, molasses, barbecue, and other foods and culinary styles. This said, it is equally important that we do more than merely upend the hierarchical ladder construed by Washington and Du Bois. Our task is not to reverse their terms, to affirm that cooking belongs on a higher rung than writing. Rather, cooking and writing must be liberated from the competition into which Washington's and Du Bois's remarks place them and seen, instead, as the three novelists represented in this study see them: as reciprocating practices able to serve each other. To reach a methodological position from which to advance the book's key arguments, we must turn to other African American cultural practitioners who have been interested less in the respective merits of cooking and writing than in the formal interaction and reciprocity of these processes. We must turn, in short, to those recipe writers like Jessica Harris and Ntozake Shange, for whom cooking and writing have not existed within some suppositional hierarchy but have remained recognizable as discrete yet reciprocal cultural activities.

Signifying Dishes, Talking Cookbooks

More often than not, recipes published by African Americans since the 1960s are suffused with a textual atmosphere of orality.[11] By addressing readers individually, by importing phrases from the black vernacular, and by relentlessly apostrophizing and abbreviating, myriad African American cookbook writers nowadays present their recipes less as acts of writing per se than as transcripts that capture the fleeting spontaneity of speech. In part inspired by the longstanding influence of the vernacular tradition over canonical black writing and specifically activated by the publication of Vertamae Smart-Grosvenor's *Vibration Cooking: Or the Travel Notes of a Geechee Girl* in 1970, this authorial simulation of orality is now the preferred approach of the African American recipe writer. The following argument—which identifies this collision of speech, writing, and cooking as a useful metaphor for the treatment of food in much African American literature—is prompted by Rafia Zafar's analysis of *Vibration Cooking* and by her description of the recipes it contains as "signifying" dishes that, like the "signifying" literary texts investigated in Henry Louis Gates's *The Signifying Monkey,* enact "the cultural, expressive, and historical agenda of the African American" tradition.[12] Since the publication of *Vibration Cooking,* this agenda of orality has become yet more prominent, to the point where what I call the "talking" recipe has come to dominate the African American cookbook archive. Cookbook writers from such radically different cultural backgrounds as the former Three Degrees singer Sheila Ferguson and the novelist and poet Ntozake Shange nowadays attempt to achieve the impossible, and find a way to make their recipes "talk" to the reader. Just as Smart-Grosvenor peppered her prose with phrases like "you supposed,"[13] so Sheila Ferguson's *Soul Food* (1989) is suffused with vernacular formulations. Ferguson's recipe for "Scrambled Eggs 'n' Brains" exemplifies this approach:

Now listen, folks, I have got to admit that I have never put a single brain into my mouth. I am extremely open-minded about food but I figure this way: I've gone this long without eating anybody's brains, so I can certainly go a little while longer. . . . But this is a most typical dish from the deeeep deeep South and lots of people like it. So, here's how it's made. . . .

Now what do you think you do with the poor things? You place them in a colander and pour boiling water over them to rid any traces of blood and membrane which remain. (You want to sort of clear the mind, so to speak.) . . . When the fat is hot, but not smoking, you just throw your old brains right on in there. Lower the heat but don't stop stirring them around, oh no, or they might decide to clump up or stick to the pan. Well, now that your brains have been nicely browned, oh about 10 minutes in all, pour in your already beaten-up eggs and scramble it all up there together. (9)

Deeeep deeep, to sort of clear, you just throw, oh no, oh about 10 minutes in all—all these unorthodox formulations are dedicated to capturing the oral sensibility on paper, to creating a new mode of recipe production that retains emphasis on the oral channels by which African-American cookery has been disseminated historically. A similar approach emerges in "Pig's Tails by Instinct" and other recipes Ntozake Shange includes in *If I Can Cook / You Know God Can* (1998):

Obviously, the tails have gotta be washed off, even though the fat seems to reappear endlessly. When they are pink enough to suit you, put them in a large pot full of water. Turn the heat high, get 'em boilin'. Add chopped onion, garlic, and I always use some brown sugar, molasses, or syrup. Not everybody does. Some folks like their pig extremities bitter, others, like me, want 'em sweet. It's up to you. Use a large spoon with a bunch of small holes to scrape off the grayish fats that will cover your tails. You don't need this. Throw it out. Let the tails simmer till the meat falls easily from the bones. Like pig's feet, the bones are soft and suckable, too. . . . There's nothin' wrong with puttin' a heap of tails, feet or pig's ears right next to a good-sized portion of Hoppin' John, either. (9)

Shange here crowds her recipe with improvised pointers that indicate the continuing influence of the vernacular tradition. Characterized by hyphenation, abbreviation, and a direct address to the reader, Shange's literary aesthetic is intensely personal and conversational, determined to transcribe the speech of the cook as much as his or her method.

Shange and Ferguson are not the only African American writers to build on Smart-Grosvenor's example by imbuing their written recipes with this deliberate oral atmosphere. The first recipe offered by *Barbeque'n with Bobby*—a cookbook that the former Black Panther Bobby Seale conceived while a "political prisoner" in 1969 (ix) and eventually published in 1988—arrives in the form of a quotation from Seale's uncle. Rendered in a literary vocabulary tailored to capture black speech, the transcribed words of Seale's uncle insist that "[w]hen you make bobbyque, you don't put no sauce on it till it's done. Da base makes it tenda. Taste good right down to da bone" (3). Seale's efforts to freeze his uncle's speech into publishable prose are signaled by his use of the double negative and by the coinages "da" and "tenda," which seek to capture pronunciation in print. Alongside Seale's introduction of a playfully self-aggrandizing coinage ("bobbyque"), such literary strategies place *Barbeque'n with Bobby* alongside *If I Can Cook / You Know God Can* as another cookbook whose recipes represent orality and cooking simultaneously.

A concern with orality is often also a concern with the shift toward mass literacy. For African Americans, this shift was delayed by racist legislation during slavery and segregation and began only with the tentative establishment of black schools and colleges during the Reconstruction Era. From *The Domestication of the Savage Mind* (1977) to *Food and Love* (1998), Jack Goody turns repeatedly to examples of this epochal shift to printed culture. Goody often speaks in terms of profit and loss and often balances what a given society gains from the advent of mass literacy against what it loses. And what a given society gains, to summarize Goody's position, is access to those metropolitan discourses that can nurture national cohesion and stratification, while what it loses is the influence of those familial and regional traditions disseminated via oral channels. When discussing educational developments in precolonial and colonial India, *Food and Love* contends that this society witnessed mass literacy's general propensity to "divide internally as well as unify . . . externally"—to erode the roles of smaller familial and regional units in cultural production and to ferment, instead, national identification (185–87). This cautious balancing of advantages and disadvantages develops views set out in *The Domestication of the Savage Mind,* which likewise couches the shift toward mass literacy in positive and negative terms. Goody's explanation of the development of international cuisine in industrial Britain invokes not only imperialism and improved transportation but also mass literacy, because this latter phenomenon enabled cookbooks to record and so to retain an expanded culinary vocabulary of previously unsustainable breadth. Yet Goody concurrently recognizes the threat that print posed to "regional cooking," whose "attraction" in the age of mass literacy is "precisely that it is tied to what grandmother did ('les gaufres de mémé') . . . rather than to the recipes that are diffused by writing" (140). *The Domestication of the Savage Mind,* like *Food and Love,* thus views the shift to literacy as one that dissolves or at least destabilizes a foregoing vernacular tradition even as it anticipates the expansive culinary enterprises of the future. It views the shift to literacy as monumental, to the point where this transformation even lays the foundations for a definition of the recipe itself.

> The point about a recipe or a receipt that emerges from . . . dictionary definitions and literary usages is their essentially written character. The recipes are collected in one place, classified, then serve as a reference book for the doctor or the cook, for the sick or the hungry, as in Dryden's line, "The Patients, who have open before them a Book of admirable Receipts for their Diseases." For recipes, once collected, have then to be tried. . . .
>
> The recipe or receipt, then, is a written formula for mixing ingredients for culinary, medical or magical purposes; it lists the items required for making preparations destined for human consumption. (136)

By acknowledging the longstanding association of cooking with vernacular culture, Goody's work in general is enormously useful to the present discussion. But by partially endorsing Washington's and Du Bois's views on the supreme usefulness of writing, his definition of a recipe is problematic. Goody's definition frames the following pages because, by negotiating the problems it raises, we can better understand the interaction between cooking and writing in the novels of Zora Neale Hurston, Richard Wright, and Toni Morrison.

Principal among these problems is Goody's characterization of the recipe as an intrinsically written genre, one not so much transformed as actively created by the arrival of mass literacy. The corollary of this characterization—that there can be no such thing as an oral recipe—is energetically, emphatically refuted by many different African American writers. It is refuted by the simulation of orality effected in *Barbeque'n with Bobby,* because this simulation strongly suggests that one of Seale's key authorial duties is the collation of recipes that already exist in oral form. It is also refuted by the belletristic prose of Hurston, Wright, and Morrison, who all depict illiterate cooks who nevertheless follow tried and tested culinary practices that are nothing if not recipes. As we will see, when Ondine cooks in *Tar Baby,* the fact that Morrison's server never consults a cookbook hardly means her actions are instinctive or haphazard; it is clear she is following a recipe in her mind.

The implicit recognition of the existence and vitality of the oral recipe is also a hallmark of the work of Jessica B. Harris, one of the most prolific of current African American cookbook writers. Indeed, in cookbooks issued in the 1980s and 1990s by Harris—who, as a professor of English, divides her time between writing recipes and teaching writing—the remarkable hold of the oral sensibility seems to grow firmer still. But Harris's consistent desire to honor orality also complicates the ways in which its simulation operates within written texts, whether these texts take the form of recipes or novels. Harris's cookbooks transform the authorial fabrication of orality from an implicit motive behind the recipe text into an ambition that it foregrounds, articulates, and celebrates. In support of her conscious summoning of orality, Harris introduces her cookbook of the African Diaspora, *Iron Pots and Wooden Spoons* (1989), with an excerpt from an 1880 *Harper's* magazine article by Charles Gayarre. In it, Gayarre insists:

> The Negro is a born cook. He could neither read nor write, and therefore he could not learn from books. He was simply inspired; the god of the spit and the saucepan had breathed into him; that was enough. (xxiii)

That an author who expresses pride in her racial identity should introduce her celebratory affirmation of the foods of the African Diaspora by invoking an essentialist view that relegates the fabled culinary expertise of

African Americans to the level of basic instinct demands critical attention. We can begin to comprehend this astonishing editorial decision only by realizing that, here, Harris is confirming neither Gayarre's essentialism nor his subsequent depiction of cooking as an acceptable replacement for the literacy skills that apparently remained beyond the reach of African Americans. What Harris finds useful in Gayarre's observation is, instead, its revelation that African American cooking traditions were maintained in the absence of mass literacy. The realization that earlier disseminators of African American cooking traditions necessarily operated via conversational channels indicates that, if Harris's work is to continue rather than destabilize these traditions, she must achieve an accommodating literary voice in which the rich legacy of orality remains apparent.

A Kwanzaa Keepsake (1995), Harris's guide to celebrating the African American holiday of Kwanzaa, can be interpreted as a cookbook that seeks, in form and content, to surmount the transformations inherent in writing and to remain "true" to a foregoing oral tradition. Lending weight to Anne Bower's recent insistence that cookbooks are never as "innocent of narrative force" as they appear, one can say that this celebration and defense of orality is the particular "force" behind A Kwanzaa Keepsake.[14] Throughout A Kwanzaa Keepsake, Harris pays tribute to what she calls the "juking and jiving, talking and testifying, speechifying and signifying, preaching and teaching" of the vernacular tradition. Harris's desire to protect and maintain the centrality of such oral practices leads her to emphasize griots, gifted speakers, whom she terms the "true masters of the word, . . . [who savor] each nuance of language. . . . Think of the sermons of unknown ministers or the songs of the minstrels of Mali." This celebration of the "unknown" oral practitioner lends shape to the subsequent celebration of such published and therefore "known" griots of industrial America as Maya Angelou and Ntozake Shange, who, for Harris, merely "capture our ephemeral words from the air and place them on paper for the future" (23). The somewhat misleading depiction of the African American literary canon as one that not only sustains but is practically identical to an ongoing oral tradition systematically mutes the transformations wrought by publication, obscuring the shift to mass literacy that Jack Goody considered able to "divide internally" and "unify . . .

externally." Harris associates *A Kwanzaa Keepsake* with this reduction of literary practice to mere transcription and presents her holiday manual as a commemorative work that merely records preexisting oral texts. This inaccurate representation, which disguises the mediations and manipulations Harris engages, culminates with her inclusion of several sections of entirely blank pages titled simply "Family Recipes." The authorial silence that these sheaves of whiteness embody is explained by the following invitation:

> One of the aims of Kwanzaa is to bring together families and friends in productive ways. To this end, each night will conclude with a project. . . . On the first night of Kwanzaa Umoja, family unity, is saluted with the creation of a cookbook of family favorites. Most of us know only too well that we never ask for the recipe for something until it is too late. When grandma's gone, we wish we knew how to make her beaten biscuits. When Aunt Dorcas moves away, we wish we had watched exactly how she fluted the edges of her pies. . . . Begin this first night of Kwanzaa by making a conscious effort to write down the favorite recipes of your family. . . . Start by using the blank pages in this book. Then, collect the recipes on sheets of paper to be kept in a file folder or a blank book. . . . Keep the project growing and developing. It will help to keep the family together and it will preserve your traditions for another generation. (45)

This prescriptive attempt to solicit audience participation, which simply delegates responsibility for transcription from writer to reader, is the ultimate expression of the deference *A Kwanzaa Keepsake* as a whole pays to the vernacular tradition. And, as the ultimate tribute the book pays to orality, these white pages can also be seen as the ultimate expression of Harris's ambivalence regarding the act of publication. The blank pages that the invitation introduces confirm that the entire form of *A Kwanzaa Keepsake* has been determined by certain assumptions concerning publication, some of which support, and some of which contradict, the recipe definition posited in *The Domestication of the Savage Mind*.

On one level, Harris's ingenious formula for preserving familial tradition reveals that Goody's definition, and the notions of profit and loss that it associates with the cultural shift to mass literacy, retains enormous resonance for her. After all, *A Kwanzaa Keepsake* is not an actual conversation: it *is* a cookbook. Harris's preference for this textual form effectively concedes that, as Goody maintains, advantages are indeed bound up in publication, which facilitates the archiving and popularizing possibilities *A Kwanzaa Keepsake* repeatedly characterizes as a switch from the "unknown" to the "known." Motivating the production of these blank pages is an equally profound apprehension of the loss of those familial formulas that Goody terms "les gaufres de mémé," but Harris specifies as "grandma's . . . beaten biscuits" and the "pies" of "Aunt Dorcas." Guarding against the melancholia inspired by the vanishing of such recipes, Harris abandons these pages to the reader as a ghostly space on which the actual ghosts of family and friends can be memorialized. In this sense, these silent white pages endorse Goody's definition: they draw from the archiving opportunities he identifies as a key advantage of publication while striving to avoid the homogenization he identifies as a key disadvantage of publication. Although other critics ascribe homogenization to quite different factors—for George Ritzer, this cultural phenomenon gains a new synonym in *McDonaldization* and is understood broadly as capitalistic globalization—Harris and Goody prioritize literacy, which, for them, brings to a given society a certain loss as well as gain.

Even as the blank pages of *A Kwanzaa Keepsake* reiterate Goody's notions of profit and loss, they refute his concomitant characterization of the recipe as an intrinsically written genre. These silent white pages also speak to a position implied throughout Harris's cookbook oeuvre, namely, that, contrary to Goody's claims, there *was* and *is* such a thing as an oral recipe. Through her simulation of orality and her attempts to involve readers in her transcriptive processes, Harris characterizes the shift to writing less as a revolution, able to conceive the recipe from scratch, than as an evolution, which merely alters the formal qualities of extant oral texts. For Harris, this undiminished vernacular template exerts enormous influence over and lends shape to the production of a written version that she presents as merely derivative of speech. An aesthetic of transcription guiding *A Kwanzaa Keepsake* in this way refutes Goody's suggestion and asserts simply that recipes predated cookbooks.

By accepting aspects of Goody's definition while challenging its exclusive focus on script, Harris's response to the transition to published culture offers a more fruitful understanding of the interrelation between cooking and writing than the hierarchical, formal competition premised by Du Bois and Washington. For Harris, cooking and writing, at least in an African American context, must be understood in terms of their relation to a third creative process: speech. The simulation of speech achieved in A *Kwanzaa Keepsake* manifestly associates the culinary proficiency of African American cooks with a corresponding conversational proficiency, linking the two as reciprocal elements of a vernacular tradition, which future black literary production must honor. Harris's simulation of speech implies that African American writing, rather than follow the hierarchical formulations of Du Bois and Washington, should honor a spoken form. As the expressive vehicle through which recipes were and are transmitted, this spoken form does not so much compete with culinary traditions as it complements and maintains them. Central to Harris's aesthetic, then, is a literary form that seeks to sidestep the pitfalls Goody identified in order to pay tribute to a vernacular culture in which vernacular foods and vernacular words are deeply linked.

To move toward the African American literary canon explored later in this book, let us compare this culinary situation with the following eighteenth-century anecdote:

> [My Master] used to read prayers in public to the ship's crew every Sabbath day; and then I saw him read. I was never so surprised in my life, as when I saw the book talk to my master, for I thought it did as I observed him to look upon it, and move his lips. I wished it would do so with me. As soon as my master had done reading, I followed him to the place where he put the book, being mightily delighted with it, and when nobody saw me, I opened it, and put my ear close down upon it, in great hopes that it would say something to me; but I was sorry, and greatly disappointed, when I found that it would not speak. This thought immediately presented itself to me, that every body and every thing despised me because I was black. [15]

This anecdote about the enigmatic, magical relationship between writing and speaking, taken from the autobiography of James Gronniosaw, is deceptively naive. Henry Louis Gates recently cited it in his preface to *The Norton Anthology of African-American Literature*, recasting it as an unconscious statement of intent to which the black literary canon repeatedly aspires. Gates uses Gronniosaw's anecdote as a springboard from which he launches his analysis of the significance of orality in much subsequent African American literary production. Gates's argument, which develops ideas theorized in *Figures in Black* (1987) and *The Signifying Monkey* (1988), holds that African American writers have frequently implored audiences to read not only with their eyes but also, figuratively, with their ears, thus producing "talking" books able to consummate Gronniosaw's impossible vision. Gates observes that the trauma of the Middle Passage, which was surely a linguistic as well as human atrocity, coupled with educational inequalities resulting from slavery and segregation, compelled African Americans to fashion a compensatory oral culture of particular vibrancy, durability, and resilience. Severed from the native tongues of their ancestors and prevented from acquiring literacy in English, African Americans created a vernacular tradition. Originally defined against social inequities, this tradition became so desirable, flexible, and useful in its own right that such eminently literate academics as Gates now seek to protect it. Thus, Gates suggests that, while "all of the world's literatures have developed from an oral base," these origins in speech retain particular influence over "our literary tradition, [where] the oral . . . is never far from the written."[16] Perhaps the most notable manifestation of this deliberate conservation of orality can be found in the anthology's accompanying CD, which contains work songs, blues lyrics, raps, speeches, and other texts that Gates sees as key influences on the African American literary tradition.

A Kwanzaa Keepsake among myriad "talking" cookbooks amply substantiates Gates's claims regarding the vernacular tradition, but materials offered throughout *The Norton Anthology of African-American Literature* also substantiate them. Prose and poetry in which the vernacular is simulated, together with statements about the correct literary rendition of black speech, such as Hurston's "Characteristics of Negro Expression" (1934), generously pepper the anthology's 2,665-page tour of African American literature. Poets proclaim an intense identification with singers, momentarily puncturing the usually impermeable boundaries between script and performance: James Weldon Johnson's "O Black and

Unknown Bards" (1908) murmurs a tribute to those illiterate and therefore "unknown" slaves who composed spirituals such as "Go Down,
Moses" and "Roll, Jordan, Roll." [17] Along with Johnson's explicit poetic tribute to oral practitioners is his implicit respect for those poets
whose work refashions orality into the metropolitan sphere of literature
by borrowing from such vernacular forms as the blues, rap, spirituals, and
sermons. *The Norton Anthology of African-American Literature* sam-
ples much poetry, including the dialect verse of Johnson, Claude McKay,
Langston Hughes, Sterling A. Brown, and others, to demonstrate the enduring influence orality holds over African American poetic practice. The
restrictions of space, however, force *The Norton Anthology* to exclude
much important vernacular verse. One such omission is Paul Laurence
Dunbar's 1896 poem "Possum":

> Ef dey's anyt'ing dat riles me
>   An' jes' gits me out o' hitch,
> Twell I want to tek my coat off,
>   So's to r'ar an' t'ar an' pitch
> Hit's to see some ign'ant white man,
>   'Mittin' dat owdacious sin—
> W'en he want to cook a possum
>   Tekin' off de possum's skin

> W'y dey ain't no use in talkin',
>   Hit jes' hu'ts me to de hea't
> Fu' to see dem foolish people
>   Th'owin 'way de fines' pa't.
> W'y, dat skin is jes' ez tendah
>   An' ez juicy ez kin be;
> I know all erbout de critter—
>   Hide an' haih—don't talk to me!

> Possum skin is jes' lak shoat skin;
>   Jes' you swinge an' scrope it down,
> Tek a good sha'p knife an' sco' it,

Den you bake it good an' brown.
Huh-uh! honey, you's so happy
    Dat yo' thoughts is 'mos' a sin
When you'se settin' dah a-chawin'
    On dat possum's cracklin' skin.

White folks t'ink dey know 'bout eatin',
    An' I reckon dat dey do
Sometimes git a little idee
    Of a middlin' dish or two;
But dey ain't a t'ing dey knows of
    Dat I reckon cain't be beat
W'en we set down at de table
    To a unskun possum's meat![18]

The work of one of the earliest published African American poets
whose oeuvre extensively simulates orality, "Possum" initiates a discourse about the best way to write black speech, a discourse to which
Zora Neale Hurston, Richard Wright, and Toni Morrison made particularly valuable contributions. In tandem with this formidable trio, such
interwar poets as Sterling A. Brown also inherited from Dunbar a new
sense of poetic possibility that delegated aesthetic responsibilities to a
fictionalized black persona whose conversance in the vernacular amply
compensated his or her illiteracy. Apparent in the development of this
new and profoundly egalitarian poetic model was an inquiry into how
best to capture in print the speech of this innovated folk mouthpiece.
"Possum" displays many of the conclusions that Dunbar reached in the
course of this inquiry. Intense abbreviation, the coining of new words
such as "unskun," and spellings such as "owdacious" that reflect the
spoken vernacular attempt to consummate Gronniosaw's vision and figuratively draw the reader's ear closer to the page. Some of Dunbar's innovations have not stood the test of time: later African American poetry
rarely substitutes "ez" for "is" and does not use such coinages as "w'y"
and "w'en," which merely delete the silent "h" of "why" and "when."
Other formulations, however, have been reused so frequently by later

African American writers that, as elements within a vocabulary tailored to the literary reproduction of the vernacular, they have acquired canonical status. *Dat, dey, git,* and *jes*—like Dunbar's consistent trimming of the gerund ending *-ing* to *-in'*—appear in many works included in the *Norton Anthology* as well as in *Their Eyes Were Watching God, Black Boy (American Hunger),* and *Tar Baby.*

These coinages also reemerge in *Barbeque'n with Bobby*: "When you make bobbyque, you don't put no sauce on it till it's done. Da base makes it tenda. Taste good right down to da bone." That is to say, Dunbar's inquiry into how to write the vernacular not only influenced the official black canon, as sanctioned by academics like Henry Louis Gates, but also bequeathed its ready-made and improvisational lexicon to cookbook writers who seek to simulate oral recipes. These interconnections become clear when we recognize that "Possum" is as concerned with cookery as Dunbar's better-known "Dinah Kneading Dough" (1899) and that the recipe at its heart energizes its every line. "Possum skin is jes' lak shoat skin; / Jes' you swinge an' scrope it down, / Tek a good sha'p knife an' sco' it, / Den you bake it good an' brown"—by delivering a southern recipe in the vernacular, "Possum" clearly anticipates postwar recipes produced by Smart-Grosvenor, Seale, Shange, Ferguson, and Harris. Indeed, if Dunbar's and Seale's recipes were placed, anonymously, side by side, one would automatically recognize both as belonging to the same literary tradition and might even struggle to identify which had been produced in 1896 and which in 1988. The fact that Dunbar's poetic recipe and *Barbeque'n with Bobby* so evidently belong to the same literary tradition effectively overhauls our view of this tradition. It demonstrates that if "food and life exist simultaneously" in *The Black Family Dinner Quilt Cookbook,* as Sally Bishop Shigley argues, then many cookbooks by African Americans perform a similar dual function by incorporating recipes that "talk" to the "listening" reader.[19] It reveals that issues negotiated in *A Kwanzaa Keepsake,* whose blank pages result from anxieties surrounding the transformation of conversations into books, revisit the same complex relationship between speech and transcription that "Possum" and Gronniosaw's autobiography negotiate. By juxtaposing these traditions of oral poetics and talking recipes, we can trace the impulse to use writing to capture vernacular foods and vernacular words—culminating in the meal scenes of *Their Eyes Were Watching God, Black Boy (American Hunger),* and *Tar Baby*—back to the beginning of the African American literary tradition. Yet, while the simulation of orality evident in Dunbar's "Possum" establishes it as the first talking recipe by an African American, the lines at its heart are by no means the first recipe, as the next chapter demonstrates. Rather, the origins of African American cookbook publishing reach back even further than the publication of "Possum," to the late nineteenth century, when the Gilded Age culture's fascination with African American cooking led to the publication of such pioneering cookbooks as *What Mrs. Fisher Knows about Old Southern Cooking* (1881).

What Mrs. Fisher Knew

In 1880, having traveled to California by means that remain unknown to us, a middle-aged African American woman from South Carolina stepped inside the hall of the San Francisco Mechanics' Institute Fair. Into this gathering of artisans, who evidently tolerated the idea of interracial competition, Abby Fisher brought the pickles and preserves she had made following the same oral recipes that had gained her a diploma at the previous year's State Fair in Sacramento. This time around, Abby Fisher's pickles and preserves merited not only acknowledgment but also acclaim. Sampling her submissions for the categories of "Pickles and Sauces" and "Jellies and Preserves," the Institute Fair judges pronounced them the best on display. Nor did Fisher's success end here. No less impressed than these judges by this exceptional woman's culinary expertise, the Women's Institute of San Francisco and Oakland commissioned a cookbook for local publication. The resulting 1881 edition of *What Mrs. Fisher Knows about Old Southern Cooking* established Fisher as one of the first African Americans to publish a collection of recipes.[20]

Like that of Phillis Wheatley—the first African American to publish a collection of poems—the achievement of Abby Fisher was particularly astonishing because she probably had been born a slave. This, at least, is the most plausible conclusion we can draw about her birth from the meager details we have of her life in South Carolina before the Emancipation Proclamation of 1863. As Karen Hess speculates:

In . . . 1880, precisely during the period when Mrs. Fisher must have been occupied with her cookbook, the census records list Abby C. Fisher, then 48 years
of age, as living at 207½ Second Street in San Francisco. Her profession was
given as "cook," and under race she was listed as "*mu.*," that is, mulatto, born
in South Carolina of a mother who was also born in South Carolina and a
father who was born in France. . . . In 1832 or thereabouts, when Abby Fisher
was born, any relationship involving a man born in France and producing a
child designated as mulatto was almost certainly that of slaveowner and slave.
Any other scenario would be torturous, especially in South Carolina plantation
society. I think it safe to say that she was born a slave.[21]

Thus, like *Poems on Various Subjects, Religious and Moral by Phillis
Wheatley, Negro Servant* (1773), *What Mrs. Fisher Knows* can probably
be included in that archive of cultural documents authored by men and
women to whom state laws and plantation codes had once assigned the
status of a commodity. The preface of *What Mrs. Fisher Knows* reveals,
however, that in one crucial respect this pioneering publication was even
more remarkable than Wheatley's poetry volume.

> The publication of a book on my knowledge and experience of Southern Cook-
> ing, Pickle and Jelly Making, has been frequently asked of me by my lady friends
> and patrons in San Francisco and Oakland, and also by ladies of Sacramento
> during the State Fair in 1879. Not being able to read or write myself, and
> my husband also having been without the advantages of an education—upon
> whom would devolve the writing of the book at my dictation—caused me to
> doubt whether I would be able to present a work that would give perfect sat-
> isfaction. But, after due consideration, I concluded to bring forward a book of
> my knowledge—based on an experience of upwards of thirty-five years—in the
> art of cooking Soups, Gumbos, Terrapin Stews, Meat Stews, Baked and Roast
> Meats, Pastries, Pies and Biscuits, making Jellies, Pickles, Sauces, Ice-Creams
> and Jams, preserving Fruits, etc. The book will be found a complete instructor,
> so that a child can understand and learn the art of cooking. (v)

Unlike Wheatley's *Poems on Various Subjects, What Mrs. Fisher
Knows* can also be included among those works conceived by illiterate African Americans but transcribed by literate white Americans. The

preface of *What Mrs. Fisher Knows* suggests that its author was not only likely to have been born a slave but was also, to paraphrase Gronniosaw, someone to whom writing refused to speak. It reveals that, unlike those twentieth-century African American cookbooks that are presented as transcripts, *What Mrs. Fisher Knows* actually is a transcript.

This textual status is of prime importance to any reading of *What Mrs. Fisher Knows*. On one level, the fact that *What Mrs. Fisher Knows* is transcribed calls into question Zafar's treatment of Fisher as its solitary author and reveals that the text's tendency to "keep out the world beyond her kitchen" is attributable less to "Fisher's efforts," as Zafar suggests, than to those her transcribers undertook.[22] On another level, this textual status further discredits Goody's exclusive emphasis on the written status of the recipe, since such absolute terms would imply that the transcriptive processes from which *What Mrs. Fisher Knows* resulted were exhaustive enough to conceive its recipes from scratch. This emphasis is incompatible with the fact that this cookbook's recipes pertain to what its full title terms "southern cooking" and are, as such, manifestly attributable to its South Carolina–born author rather than to its Californian transcribers. The example of *What Mrs. Fisher Knows,* and the need to reaffirm Fisher's original contributions to it while acknowledging their remodeling in the hands of her transcribers, urges us to rework the approach both of Zafar and of Goody, to reach an understanding of the recipe less beholden to its occasional textual status as script.

Fisher's preface also reveals the transcriptive processes that commit her spoken words to paper to be particularly interventionist and transformative. "Upon whom would devolve the writing of a book of my dictation," "after due consideration," "I concluded to bring forward a book of my knowledge"—this is literary English, so aggressively styled into formality as to leave little remnant of the black vernacular speech in which Jessica Harris, for one, delights. Indeed, Fisher's confession of illiteracy is itself rather studied, and effectively asks the reader to believe that an illiterate woman would describe her husband as being "without the advantages of an education." This implausible contention, which anticipates the string of equally implausible and equally formalized phrases found in the recipes of *What Mrs. Fisher Knows,* opens a paradox. It reveals that *What Mrs. Fisher Knows* differs from such "talking" cookbooks as *A Kwanzaa Keepsake* not only because it actually is a transcript but also because the model of transcription behind it strives to extinguish all semblance of orality from its text. Put another way, if *A Kwanzaa Keepsake* is a cookbook that works hard to present itself as a transcript, then *What Mrs. Fisher Knows* is a transcript that works equally hard to present itself as anything but.

An explanation of these differences lies in the issues of collaboration and conflict, of authorial ownership and control, which arise from the production of *What Mrs. Fisher Knows*. The preface indicates that Fisher's ownership and control over her cookbook had been severely tested by her illiteracy, which forced her to call upon transcribers who, given the interracial inequalities then prevailing in the American publishing industry, almost inevitably would be white. In turn, Fisher's dependency on these Californian collaborators situates her cookbook not only as a signifier of racial progress but also potentially as an example of the intense and anxious fascination with blackness that influenced much contemporary white American cultural production. The Gilded Age, in which *What Mrs. Fisher Knows* appeared, witnessed an increasingly conspicuous commodification of African American cultural materials for white bourgeois consumption. Such commodification was epitomized by the marketing and publishing phenomenon of Joel Chandler Harris, who, through his recounting of black vernacular folktales under titles such as *Legends of the Old Plantation* (1881) (discussed in my chapter "The Blossoming of Brier"), enjoyed spectacular popularity. It was also exemplified by what Doris Witt terms the white cultural impulse "for African American women to be the ever-smiling producers of food, to be nurturers who themselves have no appetite and make no demands"—a yearning that encouraged several food companies in the 1880s and 1890s to incorporate caricatures of smiling African American cooks into their advertising.[23] The launch of the Aunt Jemima trademark by the Quaker Oats Company in 1889 marked an apotheosis in this commercialization of black caricature, although the appearance in 1893 of the "Rastus" logo—a waiter dubbed the "Cream of Wheat Cook," who advertised breakfast cereal—arguably had equal importance.[24] Smiling, inoffensive, childish, and deferential, these caricatured creatures were part of contemporary capitalism's response to the increased bourgeois interest in black culture—a response that effectively fed the new consumerist appetite by carving this culture up into manageable mouthfuls of stereotype. Logos like Rastus and Aunt Jemima yielded no trace of lynchings, destitution, disenfranchisement, or any other key determinant of African American social experience immediately after Reconstruction. Their purpose was, instead, wish fulfillment—of negotiating and containing the volatile mix of fear and fascination that surfaced when the contemporary white American gaze fell on black culture.

I suggest that this attempt to manage black cultural artifacts, to contain them within some digestible format, is equally discernible in the interventions of Abby Fisher's transcribers. These transcribers bracketed almost a fifth of the recipes of *What Mrs. Fisher Knows* into a section marked "Miscellaneous," thus indicating that the prevailing vocabulary of white American culinary culture was inadequate when faced with Fisher's multiethnic, unclassifiable recipes. That the "Miscellaneous" section served as a sanctuary for the experimentation and hybridity that were integral to Fisher's culinary practice is demonstrated by the appearance within it of a raft of recipes more redolent of twentieth-century American cookery than its nineteenth-century European or Euro-American counterparts. Whereas "Yorkshire Pudding" and "Rice" belong under a familiar, English category titled "Puddings," recipes for "Stuffed Tomatoes," "Beef a la Mode," and "Terrapin Stew" appear in a "Miscellaneous" section that duly emerges as the ragbag assortment of an emergent national cuisine. Even succotash appears in this section; Fisher's transcribers' mistranslation of this unique Native American dish as "Circuit Hash" enabled them to place it alongside "Corned Beef Hash" despite the many differences between the two dishes (69).

This need to contain and control Fisher's culinary practice can also be detected in the absence of the vernacular from recipes like the following:

OCHRA GUMBO.

Get a beef shank, have it cracked and put to boil in one gallon of water. Boil to half a gallon, then strain and put back on the fire. Cut ochra in small pieces and put in soup; don't put in any ends of ochra. Season with salt and pepper while cooking. Stir it occasionally and keep it from burning. To be sent to table with dry boiled rice. Never stir rice while boiling. Season rice always with salt when it is first put on to cook, and do not have too much water in rice while boiling. (22–23)

Here editorial transcription, although less obviously manipulative than that which produced the cookbook's staid preface, still results in a precise list of step-by-step instructions entirely lacking the informalities of speech. The effort not only to transcribe but also to translate Fisher's speech, which eliminates the definite article along with the hesitation and sheer verbosity characteristic of speech, betrays a desire to sculpt this recipe into a conventional methodology inherited from such stalwarts of the Victorian cookbook canon as Mrs. Beeton. What "Ochra Gumbo" witnesses is an aggressive molding of Fisher's speech to fit a canonical cast whose essential shape remains in no way disturbed by its carefully managed accommodation of a former slave. By so vigorously reassuring the implied white reader that the cookbook canon will change Abby Fisher rather than the other way around, "Ochra Gumbo" emerges as another gesture of containment, which, like Rastus or Aunt Jemima, effectively reinstates white authority by carving African American culture into digestible mouthfuls. Admittedly, we must remain cautious here. We must also entertain the possibility that the decision of Fisher's transcribers to convert her speech into standard American English resulted from a benevolent desire to circumvent the negative connotations of the demotic and, in the process, to avoid exactly those forms of caricature that Aunt Jemima encapsulated. Yet this possibility is hardly incompatible with a reading of "Ochra Gumbo" that sees, in its standardization of speech, telltale traces of the anxiety Fisher's transcribers felt on realizing the ingredients and processes of this problematic recipe were not only immensely gratifying but also, and inescapably, black.

After all, this recipe imports from Africa not only its central ingredient but also both parts of its name. As Karen Hess observes, "Okra is native to Central Africa and was brought to the New World by way of the slave trade. *Okra* is derived from *nkru-ma,* its name in the Twi language of Ghana, according to Jessica B. Harris. *Gumbo,* its other name in English, comes from *kingombo* from Angola."[25] When filtered through the dogmatically Manichean racial ideology of contemporary dominant American culture, which flattened the countless black Americans engaged in domestic labor into the silenced Aunt Jemima logo, such provenance identified okra as a hazardous signifier of irrepressible Africanism. Potentially, "Ochra Gumbo" amounted to an emphatically African American handling of an emphatically African ingredient— amounted to irrefutable evidence of the black cultural autonomy that Aunt Jemima denied and that would have threatened the comforting reliance on white assistance enshrined in Fisher's dependency on white transcription. In these terms, then, to describe a vernacular food through vernacular language, to add the further spice of the black demotic, would have been tantamount to adding nitroglycerine to an already volatile mix. To defuse the autonomous blackness of "Ochra Gumbo," Fisher's transcribers were obliged to describe its vernacular ingredients through nonvernacular words. We can thus understand the formalization of Fisher's speech as the product of an intricate interracial arbitration in which her Californian transcribers appeased white hungers for plantation and other southern cooking while easing any menace that the indulgence of such exoticism posed to the cherished racial order.

Let us compare this dispiriting situation with an example of how okra has been handled by a more recent African American cookbook writer, Ntozake Shange:

Fried Okra

Wash 1 pound of okra real well, like all other vegetables, in cold water. Then chop the top thick ends off. Discard. The rest of the okra is fine for cookin'. Chop your lovely fresh okra into slices 'bout an inch wide, including the cute little ends. They'll fry just fine. Now, you can make you a batter of 1/2 cup of cornmeal, 2/3 cup milk, and 1 egg to dip the okra in before fryin'. Or you can simply dip the okra in some milk, run it through flour or cornmeal fast as lightning, then fry. Butter is great, but you'll need a lot of it to get the okra the right color brown. So try some regular household oil like Crisco or Mazola. Before you put your okra in to fry, make sure water sizzles in the grease. Make sure that you've got a good, heavy fryin' pan, so the okra doesn't stick to the bottom and burn on one side, gettin' stuck to the metal. . . . There, we've got a batch of fine fried okra.[26]

Many more differences than similarities exist between this talking recipe and Abby Fisher's "Ochra Gumbo." The differences reach beyond the simple fact that Fisher's recipe is beholden to the selfsame official English vocabulary, authorized by dictionaries, so deliberately abandoned in Shange's vernacular instructions. Such linguistic devices as Shange's consistent abbreviation of the gerund merely signal a far more encompassing and abiding switch in the general compositional approach adopted by African American writers of cookbooks and of novels. The trimming of the gerund and Shange's complementary use of the inclusive "we" announce a more ambitious declaration, that the African American provenance of okra both as a word and as a food will no longer be smuggled behind a master narrative designed to silence the vernacular. In the process of issuing this declaration of cultural independence, "Fried Okra" retrospectively recasts the way we read *What Mrs. Fisher Knows* in general and "Ochra Gumbo" in particular. For example, Shange's consistent and conscientious desire to supply a supplementary justification for every order issued in the course of "Fried Okra"—"make sure that you've got a good, heavy fryin' pan" immediately prompts the explanation "so the okra doesn't stick to the bottom"—illuminates the contrasting didacticism of "Ochra Gumbo," its failure to explain why cooks should "never" stir but "always" season rice. In the same way, the resurgence of joy ("lovely fresh okra") and metaphor ("fast as lightning") into "Fried Okra" reveals the sheer pleasure of cooking; although surely a key motive behind Fisher's decision to enter Californian culinary competitions, this delight is utterly absent from the starched wording of "Ochra Gumbo." By this transformation, "Fried Okra" not only redirects attention to the oral recipe, which Jack Goody excludes from his definition. It also gives this talking recipe a critical role in restoring the sympathetic collaboration between words and foods, which Shange sees as central to the African American cookery tradition. In other words, via this return to orality, Shange, like Harris, presents black culinary expertise less as the secret knowledge of an isolated writer than as a public archive in which all who are conversant in the vernacular can participate. If *What Mrs. Fisher Knows* is very different from what her transcribers knew, then talking recipes such as "Fried Okra" assume that the expertise of writer and reader overlap.

I realize that these differences appear to place *What Mrs. Fisher Knows* in an antithetical relationship with twentieth-century texts such as *A Kwanzaa Keepsake* and *Tar Baby,* which strive to capture the vernacular in print. But the importance of these differences lies in their ability to lead us to a more fruitful understanding of Abby Fisher's curious relationship with later black literary traditions. These differences ultimately indicate that the relationship between *What Mrs. Fisher Knows* and "talking" books like *A Kwanzaa Keepsake* and *Tar Baby* is understood best, not as antithetical, but as problem and solution. They indicate that *What Mrs. Fisher Knows* can be seen as a cautionary tale concerning authorial control, which illustrates the problem Shange, Hurston, Morrison, and many other African American writers negotiate. The problem *What Mrs. Fisher Knows* presents to later black writers relates to the apparent incompatibility of the African American recipe and standard American English. Behind this simple linguistic injunction—a warning later writers have consciously or unconsciously heeded—Fisher's failure to retain control over her words as well as her foods points to the future importance the vernacular attains within black literary production. That Shange and Harris, not to mention Hurston and Morrison, realize that both African American cookery and orality belong to a single vernacular tradition that future writing must honor suggests that *What Mrs. Fisher Knows* is not only not incongruous with this tradition but also initiates its ongoing inquiry into the simulation of speech.

To conclude this discussions, let us return to a recipe from *What Mrs. Fisher Knows*:

JUMBERLIE — A CREOLE DISH

Take one chicken and cut it up, separating every joint, and adding to it one pint of cleanly-washed rice. Take about half a dozen large tomatoes, scalding

them well and taking the skins off with a knife. Cut them in small pieces and
put them with the chicken in a pot or large porcelain saucepan. Then cut in
small pieces two large pieces of sweet ham and add to the rest, seasoning high
with pepper and salt. It will cook in twenty-five minutes. Do not put any water
on it. (57–58)

This text can be read as the problem that the later simulation of conversation solves and as the call to which subsequent African American
literature, whether culinary or belletristic, responds. The displacement
of the vernacular, the transcriptive effort to force Abby Fisher's speech
to comply with the semantic rules of standard American English, here
produce a recipe for a now famous southern dish that is Othered by its
saturation in formality. Here the removal of the vernacular is so striking,
and results in a formulaic list so utterly removed from its immediate oral
source, that "Jumberlie" seems to speak to a future need for black writing
to proclaim, rather than disguise, African American cooking, speech, and
other elements within a vernacular tradition.

What is more, the recipe not only ushers us toward the problem but simultaneously points us in the direction of the solution. While the recipe,
like *What Mrs. Fisher Knows* as a whole, does not present itself as a
transcript, the volatile orality suppressed by such rigorous transcription
suddenly explodes in the title: "Jumberlie—A Creole Dish." Apparently
unbeknown to Fisher's transcribers, this title renders the name of the
dish, jambalaya, in a coinage that unintentionally mirrors the vernacular
and wonderfully retains their subject's South Carolinian lilt. "Jumberlie" becomes a moment of linguistic crisis—becomes the epiphany when
fingers slip, wires cross, and the vocabulary at the fingers of Fisher's
transcribers finally fails to accommodate the spoken language of their
subject. In this sudden and unexpected resurgence of orality in the text
of *What Mrs. Fisher Knows,* Fisher's transcribers were clearly forced to
fall back on those literary devices that have since been deployed deliberately by Shange, Hurston, Morrison, and many others. Although the
circumstances surrounding their production were drastically different, the
improvisational coining of "Jumberlie" by Fisher's transcribers involuntarily anticipated the refashioning of a new vernacular vocabulary that,

at the close of the twentieth century, culminates in "talking" books like *Tar Baby* and cookbooks like *A Kwanzaa Keepsake.* Whether voluntary or involuntary, whether conscious or unconscious, these new coinages redirect our attention back to speech. Effectively, they subordinate script to speech, reminding the reader that the words he or she is reading are preceded by words that may not be found in the dictionary but that have long been exchanged, in the kitchen, by the conversing vernacular cook. In this sense, then, *What Mrs. Fisher Knows* not only helped to initiate the tradition of African American cookbook publishing. It not only embodies the problems that this and other African American literary traditions have since encountered. It also anticipates the prime motive that lends shape to this future canon, as it, albeit involuntarily, forces audiences to read not only with the eyes but figuratively with the ears. To the griots, the "unknown" cooks and storytellers of the nineteenth century whom Jessica Harris celebrates, must now be added the name of this "known" publishing phenomenon, the unlettered recipe writer Abby Fisher.

Our journey through these artifacts of late-nineteenth-century American culture thus ends with a text whose transcriptive ethos supports the supremacy of writing that Washington and Du Bois asserted. This text nevertheless retains the trace of an alternative sensibility calculated to prize the reciprocation between vernacular foods and words. *What Mrs. Fisher Knows* marks a moment when the old question of how best to capture African American speech, which evidently concerned Gronniosaw, collided with the new question of how best to capture African American cooking. This collision blurs the boundaries between foods and words—intertwining the etymology and botanical lineage of okra, for example—and at the same time blurs genres, as high and low culture unite to recapture the vernacular sensibility. Throughout *Hunger Overcome?* I pay close attention to this attempt to recapture the vernacular. In the following pages I read *Their Eyes Were Watching God, Black Boy (American Hunger),* and *Tar Baby,* not as rarefied literary documents permanently divorced from the culinary traditions studied here, but as contributions to a broad African American cultural discourse attuned to the same pressures, the same uncertainties regarding literacy and orality, that lend shape to the works of Sheila Ferguson, Ntozake Shange, Jessica Harris, and Bobby Seale. When we view cooking and speech as elements within a vernacular tradition that future writing must honor, both emerge from African American cookbook and literary production as connected activities; in this new light, both enable the transmission of those recipes that abate hunger.

Eatingville

ONE OF THE MOST ASTONISHING ASPECTS of Zora Neale Hurston's literary career is the fact that she completed *Their Eyes Were Watching God* (1937), her richest novel, in only seven weeks. In September 1936, after arriving in Haiti to continue the ethnographic research that led to the publication of *Tell My Horse* (1938), Hurston delayed her fieldwork by only this time in order to write, from beginning to end, her novel of Floridian love and labor. While many writers have enjoyed similar flowerings of intense creative activity, the most compelling explanation for Hurston's prolificacy is that her senses, intellect, and literary imagination had been stimulated by the Caribbean, and specifically by her touring Kalico Beach, the Gonâve Gulf, and other beauty spots in Haiti. Home not only to unparalleled acts of black resistance and revolution but also to an ecology not yet ruined by deforestation, Haiti offered a profusion of guava and orchids that apparently stimulated Hurston's memories of the flora of her home state—of Florida's jasmine and bougainvillea, its chinaberry trees, Cape jasmine blooms, lemons, grapefruit, tangerines, and oranges. At the very least, *Their Eyes Were Watching God* enfolds Janie and Tea Cake within a fecund landscape that is not only recognizably Floridian but also powerfully reminiscent of a Caribbean ecology. Janie and Tea Cake's later movement toward the Everglades, their visiting Palm Beach and Fort Lauderdale en route, and their eventual arrival in a fertile "muck" frequented by Seminoles and "Bahaman workers" speak to the south-facing, tropical perspective of *Their Eyes Were Watching God,* which sometimes seems to want to detach Florida from the mainland United States, drag it downward, and place it into the Caribbean archipelago. [1]

If the natural beauty of the Caribbean sharpened the natural beauty of Florida, as captured in Hurston's rapid writing of *Their Eyes Were Watching God,* then its lushness and sheer unbridled fertility surely encouraged the novel's description of Eatonville as a town in which foods abound and no one goes hungry. As I show in this chapter, Hurston's fictionalized Eatonville indeed warrants its near-homophone, "Eatingville": it is a town from which the chronic undernutrition then devastating lives throughout the South almost magically disappears.

Ever since Wright's *New Masses* review attacked *Their Eyes Were Watching God* as a form of "minstrelsy" that "carries no theme, no message, no thought," Hurston's decision to exorcise contemporary hardships from Eatonville has been read as proof of her abnegation of authorial responsibility. [2] Critics have charged that, rather than tackle reality, Hurston chose to massage the sensibilities of her white patrons, to efface Jim Crow conditions, in order to secure publishing success. Hazel Carby has recently echoed Wright's argument, describing Eatonville as a "mythic space" that effects a "displacement of the urban and [of] issues of black American migration" and which "denies the transformative power of both historical and urban consciousness." [3]

There is some truth to these criticisms. In its absence not only of hunger but also of poverty, racial violence, disfranchisement, discrimination, and debilitating labor, Eatonville is exceptionally unlike and exceptionally preferable to African American life in the contemporary South. But these criticisms also seem based in a belief that social realism is the only valid option available to the black southern writer: they assume that Hurston's novels should mirror social conditions and complain that the reflection it transmits is neither accurate nor complete. By contrast, this chapter proceeds from the more rewarding reading Susan Willis advances in *Specifying: Black Women Writing the American Experience* (1987), which rejects such residual naturalist assumptions in favor of a view that positions Eatonville as the product of a "utopian fantasy" (56). The Greek terms *outopia* (no place) and *eutopia* (good or fortunate place) aptly describe Eatonville; its remarkable absence of hunger, racism, and violence qualify it not only as more "fortunate" than other places in the South but as so much more fortunate that it loses its position on the Florida map and becomes "no place."[4] Willis's reading reveals that criticizing *Their Eyes Were Watching God* for being unrealistic is a little like criticizing Francis Bacon's *New Atlantis* (1624) for being fanciful. If we associate Hurston's "Eatingville" with traditions of literary utopianism, it emerges as the product, not of a glossing of the truth, but of a systematic inversion of reality, which can itself be read as a form of social criticism. Utopianism involves more than mere fantasy: it is also an inherently progressive literary method that, by picturing the achievements of an imaginary society, can critique the failures of real society and reveal how to correct them. As Krishan Kumar suggests, the scientific and agricultural achievements listed throughout *New Atlantis* are all "ultimately, in the foreseeable future, realizable" and were cataloged by Bacon to inspire his English readers to redouble their efforts to reduce disease and stabilize the nation's harvest.[5] A similar emphasis on the political uses of literary utopianism emerges in Terry Eagleton's analysis of the genre, which highlights its concern "with that which is encoded within the logic of a system which, extrapolated in a certain direction, has the power to undo it." Utopianism, for Eagleton, is "a way of interrogating the present which unlocks its dominative logic by discerning the dim outline of an alternative already implicit within it."[6] In this light, we can adopt a new approach to Hurston's Eatonville, one that attributes the town's idealized aspects to a calculated negation that systematically "unlocks" the "alternative" implicit within the Jim Crow South. Hunger becomes satiation, violence becomes peace, and racism becomes black autonomy, as Hurston effects an exhaustive negation of the real South calculated to reveal the path by which it can be reformed. Put another way, if we must speak of mirrors, then we must also emphasize that *Their Eyes Were Watching God* "mirrors" southern society only in the sense that a reflection inverts the reality before it, transforming left into right and right into left.

This interest in Hurston's negotiation of literary utopianism lends shape to my discussion throughout this chapter. The first part of the chapter focuses on the actual and literary history of the orange and other citrus fruits since the Colombian encounter. A fruit that European and Euro-American literatures associate with both utopia and America, the orange—often described in very different terms in African American literature—offers an entry point to Hurston's idealization of Eatonville. It epitomizes the pleasure of eating, the cornucopian fertility of Florida, and the possibility of gaining useful and adequately paid labor, eventually becoming a metaphor for the racial uplift attained in Eatonville itself. The chapter's second part attends to the architect of Eatonville's progress—Joe Starks—and offers new ways of reading Janie's famous rejection of her patriarchal, egomaniacal husband. But if these discussions focus on Hurston's use of literary utopianism as a mode of social criticism, the final part of this chapter, which explores her representations of barbecue, shows how *Their Eyes Were Watching God* and *Tell My Horse* also employ utopianism to celebrate unity in the African Diaspora. Had Hurston adopted literary realism, her fictional treatment of Florida and ethnographic treatment of Haiti and Jamaica would arguably have been forced to dwell on shared experiences of racism, discrimination, poverty, and malnutrition. But by adopting literary utopianism, Hurston switched her work's emphasis from economic absence to cultural presence, thus enabling a new and more positive concentration on the symmetry between black Floridian and Maroon Jamaican folk practices, and particularly between the former's hog roasts and the latter's jerked pigs. As we turn to colonial and postcolonial histories of North America in the following discussion, we reach an approximation of Hurston's early synthesis of the diaspora and of her attempt to link the tranquil island I call Eatingville with Haiti, Jamaica, and other islands to the south.

The Orange in Colonial and African American Literature

By comparing *Their Eyes Were Watching God* with *New Atlantis* (1624) in the following argument, I do not intend to identify any broader correspondence between the biographical backgrounds or political ideologies of Zora Neale Hurston and Francis Bacon. My discussion instead focuses on the formal strategies by which *New Atlantis* systematically negates many of Elizabethan England's social problems, inverting its unreliable harvests, religious schism, and intermittent violence. This model of utopian manufacture, this transposition of social weakness into fantasized strength, of threat into security, and of hunger into satiation, anticipates the way three of the most pressing problems facing interwar African American society—racist violence, malnutrition, and poverty— become the most remarkable *absences* of Hurston's Eatonville. Only in this formal affinity do Eatonville and Bacon's Bensalem reveal their shared debt to what Zygmunt Bauman characterizes as the "galvanising feeling of deprivation and the chastening squeeze of omnipresent and stubborn realities" motivating utopian ideals.[7] In Eatonville and Bensalem alike, those fantasized aspects that most obviously solve such "stubborn realities" also make these new worlds most utopian: it is the contrast between lived and desired experience, the promise of peace to the threatened and food to the hungry, that makes these fictional paradises paradisiacal.

Any comparison between these authors is inevitably complicated by the diverse social differences between them. Bacon was an author who gained his position within the Elizabethan elite not just through his seemingly limitless creative energy but also through his class, gender, and racial status. Socially, Hurston was the opposite of such a man: her genius was notoriously devalued by publishers, and "even the eminent Franz Boas," alleges Houston A. Baker, produced a preface to *Mules and Men* that simplified Hurston's work by invoking "Uncle Remus as the prototype of the Afro-American tale-teller."[8] Any comparison of these writers must consider that, together, the now-familiar shibboleths of cultural difference—gender, class, race, region, religion—weave a web of social power in which the white male Elizabethan Bacon occupies the center and the female African American Hurston the margin. Only Thomas More's *Utopia* (1551)—a vision of a perfected society that, notoriously, retains slavery—seems further removed from Hurston's Eatonville than Bacon's island of Bensalem. What possibly could connect the Eatonville described by Hurston as a "raw, bustling frontier" with what Paolo Rossi terms Bacon's "unfinished picture of an ideal scientific community"?[9] How can an Elizabethan's dream of a seafarer's sanctuary, located somewhere in the Pacific Ocean, compare with the geographically pinpointed landscape inhabited by Tea Cake, Janie, and Joe Starks?

An answer to these questions lies in the way Bacon and Hurston represent the entrance to Bensalem and Eatonville, respectively, for the gateways to both idyllic places, oddly enough, prompt references to the same food. In Bacon's *New Atlantis,* the entrance to utopia is figured in the following terms:

[A] while after came the notary to us aboard our ship, holding in his hand a fruit of that country, like an orange, but of colour between orange-tawney and scarlet, which casts a most excellent odour. He used it, as it seemeth, for a preservative against infection. . . . [Later] there were brought in to us great store of those scarlet oranges for our sick, which, they said, were an assured remedy for sickness taken at sea.[10]

The citrus remedying the fever of these afflicted men reappears, in the very different world of Hurston's autobiography, as the key economic catalyst to Eatonville's development. As *Dust Tracks on a Road* (1942) observes:

The Negro . . . men went forth and made their support in cutting new ground, building, and planting orange groves. Things were moving so swiftly that there was plenty to do, with good pay. Other Negroes in Georgia and West Florida heard of the boom in South Florida from Crescent City to Cocoa and they came. No more back breaking over rows of cotton; no more fear of the fury of the Reconstruction. (8)

Thus, these excerpts reveal that one of the few aspects able to unite Bacon's Bensalem and Hurston's Eatingville is the orange. In both narratives, the orange is located at the entrance of the utopian landscape: it is handed to, and functions as a gateway for, the fortunate newcomers to Florida and Bensalem alike. The appearance of the orange within these otherwise divergent fictional episodes offers a raft of connotations useful to the narrative's unfolding.

In the case of *New Atlantis,* foremost among these useful connotations is the American association that the orange had acquired in European Renaissance cultures. This transatlantic association resulted from the fact that the orange was among the most successful of the many fruits and vegetables early European explorers brought to the newly discovered Americas. As John McPhee notes, the journey of citrus from "its origins near the South China Sea" to America was long and complicated and involved "four thousand miles of ocean current to the east coast of Africa, across the desert by caravan and into the Mediterranean basin, then over the Atlantic to the American continents."[11] Following the fruit's arrival in America, however, it adapted to the local ecology with unbelievable speed. No other tropical fruit converted so rapidly to American conditions. Brought to the Caribbean in the sixteenth century, it established itself within a few generations and even escaped the cultivated grove to grow wild alongside native pineapples, avocados, and guavas.[12] This proliferation swiftly captivated European colonial narrators. Already, in his "Discourse Concerning Western Planting" (1584), Richard Hakluyt was advocating a further planting of "oranges" and "lymons" in the Virginian "inland" as a strategy by which superior wealth and thus an imperialist advantage over Spain and Portugal could be attained (158). Though not pinpointing the Asian origins of the fruit, Hakluyt's depiction of the orange as a useful *import* to the Americas nevertheless acknowledged its general origins in an "older" world to the East.

Such colonial interventions prepared the ground for the later figuration, evident in *Robinson Crusoe* (1719) as well as in William Bartram's and Captain John Smith's travelogues, in which the American abundance of oranges and lemons, which actually resulted from imperialism, was painted as a virginal precursor of it. Whether fictional or factual in orientation, these English-language narratives of westward discovery sought to naturalize the orange, yellow, green, and pink orbs to America—to rank them alongside guava, coconut, and avocado—to claim citrus as a symbol of the native fecundity of the new imperial territories.

Robinson Crusoe thus carpets its shipwrecked protagonist's new home with an abundance of "orange, and lemon, and citron trees," the proclaimed "wild" status of which cannot be reconciled easily with the fact that the island has been briefly visited but never settled by Europeans.[13] Assimilation becomes total and ultimately transcends genealogy as Defoe's novel suppresses Richard Hakluyt's "Discourse" and its ambitious importation plans in order to resituate the fruit as undeniably, wholly American. Westward trade routes, which McPhee confirms first carried citrus to the Americas, are obscured as Defoe strips the orange of its past and grants it the full American "citizenship" of guava and avocado. Released from its inconvenient Asian genealogy, citrus is enlisted into a new body of imagery at once utopian and American. It epitomizes the benevolent fertility of the New World soil, which initially aids Crusoe's survival and eventually contributes to his utopian project. The facts of McPhee's history are obliterated as *Robinson Crusoe* catapults the orange into an entirely new realm rife with utopian connotations.

Seventy years following the publication of *Robinson Crusoe*, *Travels of William Bartram* (1791)—a narrative of journeys undertaken through Florida and the Carolinas—consolidates this suppositional nativeness of citrus. This becomes especially evident as Bartram describes British landowning practices in Florida:

> I have often been affected with extreme regret, at beholding the destruction and devastation which has been committed or indiscreetly exercised on those extensive fruitful Orange groves, on the banks of St. Juan, by the new planters under the British government, some hundred acres of which, at a single plantation, have been entirely destroyed, to make room for the Indigo, Cotton, Corn, Batatas, &c, or, as they say, to extirpate the musquitoes, alleging that groves near the dwellings are haunts and shelters for those persecuting insects. (213)

Even as he decries the desecration of the Florida orange plantations, Bartram suppresses the Asian provenance of the fruit, describing it only as "native" and thus implicitly as pre-Columbian. He refuses to acknowledge that these groves had been planted either by the ancestors of those now destroying them or by their Spanish imperialist rivals. Such an acknowledgment would undermine Bartram's revolutionary denunciation of European imperialism's wanton devastation of the perfected American biosphere. Bartram must portray the orange as a plant "native" to this original perfection if he is then to characterize its destruction as a symbol of the broader threat posed to nature by British imperialism's later thrust into the American interior. Only when the orange is clothed in this persistent yet falsified American provenance can its annihilation remain for Bartram a symbol of the merciless annihilation of the American wilderness from which the orange allegedly derives. By suggesting that the orange had long grown wild in American conditions, this false "native" provenance also denies the possibility that, beyond the gaze of European exploration, Seminoles may have nurtured the fruit after the manner of those Navajos who, Dee Brown observes, grew "especially proud of their peach orchards, carefully tended since the days of the Spaniards." [14]

Even when associating the orange with an anticipated ecological collapse—a presentiment markedly different from the untouched island biosphere of *Robinson Crusoe*—Bartram shares Defoe's tendency to invoke citrus as an embodiment of the virginal non-European properties of the new Americas. *Travels of William Bartram* differs from *Robinson Crusoe* only in that this virginity is no longer venerated so much as its defilement is decried. Bartram continues:

> Some plantations have not a single tree standing; and where any have been left, it is only a small coppice or clump, *nakedly exposed and destitute;* perhaps fifty or an hundred trees standing near the dwelling-house, having no lofty cool grove . . . to shade and protect them, exhibiting a mournful, sallow countenance; their *native perfectly formed* and glossy green foliage as if *violated, defaced, and torn to pieces.* (213, emphases added)

Though such language suggests an almost biblical Fall, the orange is here not the agent of this collapse but remains a victim of it. Unlike the apple, the orange in Bartram's account remains singularly prelapsarian, its perfection unspoiled by Christian humanity, which has apparently encountered it only after its development and formation beyond the horizon of the known world. Even on the verge of this new Eden's destruction, the orange retains its captivating luster: as American as it is utopian, it is presented by Bartram in diametrical opposition to the European imperialism responsible for its importation.

In Captain John Smith's *Generall Historie of Virginia, New-England, and the Summer Isles* (1624) and other earlier texts, a comparable obfuscation of the orange's transatlantic importation intermingles with an awareness of the fruit's usefulness as a remedy for scurvy.[15] In Smith's *Generall Historie* this awareness mixes with suppression of the fruit's Asian origins—a suppression now familiar to us through our readings of *Robinson Crusoe* and *Travels of William Bartram*. Defoe's and Bartram's layering of such genealogical suppression with Edenic virginity, for instance, recalls Smith's failure, when describing the orange trees of Bermuda, to mention their non-American origins even as he emphasizes their contribution to the islands' atmosphere of "serenity and beauty" (237–38, 340). Consequently, to the two signifiers that Defoe and Bartram attach to the orange—which tacitly refer, first, to the Garden of Eden and, second, to a manufactured American provenance—Smith's *Generall Historie* adds a new, therapeutic capacity that simply multiplies yet further the fruit's utopian potential within European literary traditions. Smith's *Generall Historie* elevates citrus into a natural savior for the Royal Navy—into a sign that, as a nourishment, cure, and geographical signifier rolled into a single orange sphere, encapsulated the welcome the America lands were extending to the English colonist. Edenic without being implicated in Eden's Fall, American without regard to their actual Asian provenance, oranges prompt in these texts a utopian inspiration. They appear as a sure sign of the mystical and wondrous experiences awaiting the fortunate entrant to America and utopia alike. They are installed as the key to a world that is not only far preferable to, but also that lies far beyond, England, where none but the bitterest oranges grow. What better proof of England's imperial destiny could there be than that in these Western lands there grew a fruit able to cure the very diseases contracted in the process of sailing there?

Let us compare this sense of imperial destiny to the following extract from Olaudah Equiano's *Interesting Narrative* (1789):

> [A] poor fisherman . . . had brought his little all for a venture, which consisted of six bits worth of limes and oranges in a bag; I had also my whole stock; which was about twelve bits' worth of the same kind of goods, separate in two bags; for we had heard these fruits sold well in that island. When we came there, in some little convenient time, he and I went ashore with our fruits to sell them; but we had scarcely landed, when we were met by two white men, who presently took our three bags from us. . . . We told them these three bags were all we were worth in the world; and that we brought them with us to sell when we came from Montserrat, and shewed them the vessel. But this was rather against us, as they now saw we were strangers as well as slaves. . . . Thus, in the very minute of gaining more by three times than I ever did by any venture in my life before, was I deprived of every farthing I was worth. An insupportable misfortune! (117)

The disaster of this mugging is overcome in part after Equiano, having traced the whereabouts of its perpetrators,

> besought them again and again for our fruits, till . . . [their companions] asked if we would be contented if they kept one bag, and gave us the other two. . . . We then proceeded to market to sell them; and Providence was more favourable to us than we could have expected, for we sold our fruits uncommonly well; I got for mine about thirty-seven bits. Such a surprising reverse of fortune in so short a space of time seemed *like a dream to me,* and proved no small encouragement for me to trust the Lord in any situation. (118, emphasis added)

Nowhere in his account does Equiano consider the utopian properties of oranges as revealed in *New Atlantis, Robinson Crusoe,* or Captain John Smith's *Generall Historie.* The account offers no description of the fruit whatsoever and, in its refusal to linger before the orange, mirrors the frantic desperation of the events that it describes. Equiano emphasizes these oranges' reified status as a desirable commodity able to fetch a price that might, in turn, allow him to "obtain my freedom" (119).

In a manner open to Marxist interpretation, Equiano, as a fledgling capitalist, encounters his property as a commodity from which all connections with both labor and the soil have been removed. He approaches it as mere converted capital, which he wishes to reconvert to money in order that he, another commodity, might "purchase" himself. What *Capital* calls the "fetishism of commodities"—a theory of capitalism's abstraction of goods from their point of production, which Marx elaborates with reference to the marketless world of *Robinson Crusoe*—implies that, for Equiano, these goods might as well consist of apples or bananas as of oranges (42). Yet such indifference only momentarily hides the fact that the fruit facilitating Equiano's entry into commerce is the same fruit whose Marxist designation as "just another commodity" would have been unimaginable to those who, like Francis Bacon, have constructed their utopian dreams around it. The utter lack of poetic imagery in Equiano's account, together with his urgent need for a commodity of any kind, lodges a startling and almost comic response to Bacon's and Defoe's valorization of the orange, which says much about the forced involvement of nonwhite peoples in the attempted construction of European social dreams in the Americas. The fetishism of the commodity here becomes not the self-perpetuating practice of those in control of a society's surplus value, as imagined in *Capital,* but the basis for a debunking of European utopian myths by those whose compelled labor produces the approximation of those myths in American reality.

Just as the question of whether an American is native or an immigrant has never been applied to African Americans, so, in Equiano's account, it is no longer a question of whether the orange is indigenous or imported to the New World. Rather, the question Equiano poses here is how can he, a slave trying to find the means by which to buy his freedom, approach the orange as anything other than food or money? How can he indulge in the utopian dreaming of a Francis Bacon? What forms will the utopias of the hungry, enslaved, and poor take when the freedom, foods, and wealth enjoyed by others comprise a fair approximation of paradise?

Yet it is equally clear that the orange emerges from this episode having regained some of the utopian capacity initially undermined by Equiano's commercially minded indifference toward his property. Initially propelling Equiano toward fetishism, emancipation, once obtained, prompts a retroactive reversal of the process and invests the fruits with a new utopian appeal the equal of that assigned to them by Bacon. At the end of this episode, which begins by dramatizing the way fetishism renders commodities anonymous, these oranges are associated with freedom itself. Oranges begin the episode as an interchangeable commodity and end it as the cause of a "reverse of fortune . . . [that] seemed like a dream to me"—a phrase that, by referring to only "thirty-seven bits," speaks volumes about the utopian luster commonplace objects can acquire to those dispossessed of them. Far from remaining the subject of capitalistic indifference, these fruits, by facilitating emancipation, find their original utopian allure reinvigorated. Although *The Interesting Narrative* does not surround oranges with Edenic imagery and forces them into a dehumanizing equation with freedom, oranges nevertheless ultimately find their position at the entrance to utopia to be as secure as it was in *New Atlantis*. Even in such a desperate episode as this, these oranges, as uncanny yet key agents of emancipation, acquire a new utopian capacity. They become the building blocks of what might be termed an achievable utopia: freedom itself.

The challenge this remarkable episode poses to preceding European utopian formations, together with the specific symbolic connection it makes between the orange and emancipation, are revisited in the oeuvre of Toni Morrison and particularly in *Tar Baby* (1981) and *Beloved* (1987). The first few pages of *Tar Baby* tell of how the as-yet-unnamed Son Green escapes imprisonment for an unspecified crime by climbing aboard a boat, *Seabird II,* in the Caribbean Sea. Son's runaway status, his entrance into a liminal space suspended between recapture and utopian freedom, strongly recall general figurations that have become familiar to us from the slave narrative tradition. Yet *The Interesting Narrative,* often acknowledged as this tradition's progenitor, in particular foreshadows Son's fugitive flight as Toni Morrison reiterates Equiano's emphasis not only on a surrounding capitalist system but also on the orange as a potential indicator of future freedom. Capitalism is summoned during the stowaway Son's explorations of *Seabird II;* as he smells fast food and admires the boat's classic furniture, it becomes clear that he has entered a propertied context as incompatible with his "underclass" background as the commercial market was to Equiano's slave identity. As Son pauses in the kitchen, scanning the shelves for something to eat, Equiano's three bags of citrus, which were "all we were worth in the world," morph into an equally commercialized "crate" containing "twelve miniature orange trees, all bearing fruit" (5). *The Interesting Narrative* and *Tar Baby* thus position citrus immediately before their protagonists' securing of freedom. We could dismiss this commonality as mere coincidence if the episode were not repeated by Beloved in Morrison's novel of that name. Following Beloved's arrival in Sethe's house, whereupon she falls ill and is forced to remain in bed, this mythic figure, whom Linda Krumholz characterizes as a "trickster," enters a similarly transfixed and liminal state prompted, it seems, by an encounter with orange.[16]

> It took three days for Beloved to notice the orange patches in the darkness of the quilt. Denver was pleased because it kept her patient awake longer. She seemed totally taken with those faded scraps of orange, even made the effort to lean on her elbow and stroke them. An effort that quickly exhausted her, so Denver rearranged the quilt so its cheeriest part was in the sick girl's sight line.[17]

In a domestic context and after her escape from an unspecified enslavement, Beloved undergoes an experience of orange no less transfixing than those of Son Green and Olaudah Equiano while on the Caribbean Sea. Encountering orange during an approach to freedom, these fugitives all inhabit narratives that characterize the fruit as a kind of edelweiss—as a plant, discoverable only after the hardest and most hazardous of journeys, that hopefully heralds the relative riches and freedoms of the future. Occasional European efforts to valorize the orange as both an American and an Edenic fruit are recast by *Beloved, The Interesting Narrative,* and *Tar Baby* into a fundamentally different context in which the imperialist subtext is overwhelmed by the new and achievable imperative of emancipation. Although these texts position the orange at the entrance to a utopian freedom, unlike in *New Atlantis,* for instance, this freedom is shaped not by its offering of unattainable wealth but by the contrast it presents to the captivity in which the utopian dreamer has hitherto been held. Though these texts transfer the orange from an Edenic environment into unsentimental domestic and commercial contexts, the fruit remains utopian because it now functions as a "cure" for captivity no less desirable than a cure for scurvy. Even when transported from their verdant tropical grove, these oranges remain idyllic, since they are now a harbinger not of imperialism but of a freedom long anticipated.

In the descriptions of Eatonville she wove into *Dust Tracks on a Road* and *Their Eyes Were Watching God,* Zora Neale Hurston effectively conflated the Edenic imagery of Bacon's and Bartram's descriptions with Equiano's and Morrison's more pragmatic association of the orange with emancipation. Hurston's representation of Eatonville at times concurs with Equiano's implication that the only two functions of the orange, to the hungry and poor, are as food and money. Such pragmatic interpretations emerge from a quotation already cited at greater length:

> The Negro . . . men went forth and made their support in cutting new ground, building, and planting orange groves. Things were moving so swiftly that there was plenty to do, with good pay. . . . No more back-breaking over rows of cotton; no more fear of the fury of the Reconstruction.

As in *The Interesting Narrative,* the industriousness of these self-improving actions is mirrored by the way this passage does not linger poetically before the orange but extols it only as a mere commodity whose prime function is fiscal. Oranges here cure the "scurvy" of poverty but little else: they offer those involved in their picking, processing, and packing nothing more transcendent or romantic than good pay. A few sentences later, however, we encounter the following scene:

> We lived on a big piece of ground with two big chinaberry trees shading the front gate and Cape jasmine bushes with hundreds of blooms on either side of the walks. I loved the fleshy, white, fragrant blooms as a child but did not make too much of them. They were too common in my neighborhood. When I got to New York and found out that the people called them gardenias, and that the flowers cost a dollar each, I was impressed. The home folks laughed when I went back down there and told them. Some of the folks did not want to believe me. A dollar for a Cape jasmine bloom! Folks up north there must be crazy.
>
> There were plenty of orange, grapefruit, tangerine, guavas and other fruits in our yard. We had a five-acre garden with things to eat growing in it, and so we were never hungry. We had chicken on the table often; home-cured meat,

and all the eggs we wanted. . . . Any left-over boiled eggs could always be used for missiles. There was plenty of fish in the lakes around town, and so we had all that we wanted. . . . We had oranges, tangerines and grapefruit to use as hand-grenades on the neighbors' children.[18]

Not only by the way such tropical foliage springs to life as though without effort on the part of Hurston's family, but also in the garden's positioning amid a world of "cypress swamps," the environment described here reanimates William Bartram's vision of an Edenic Florida. Within a single page of Hurston's autobiography, a world of industrial agriculture and capitalistic self-improvement passes to a burgeoning realm of mythic and tropical plenitude. A single page carries us from a South of economic opportunity to an imagined version of the region, to a utopia built on a wholesale reversal of the hunger with which it remained stubbornly associated. But both Hurston's economic history and her girlhood memories of an idyllic garden contrast markedly with the prevalence of malnutrition in the "real" South, as Gunnar Myrdal's exhaustive study, *American Dilemma* (1944), documented:

> Roughly 30 per cent of the "normal" Negro nonrelief families in the South did not consume any milk during a whole survey week in 1936. There was a similar proportion of Negro families reporting no consumption of eggs. Almost half the Negro farm and village families consumed no potatoes or sweet potatoes. Two thirds of the farm Negroes, one-half of the village Negroes and over one-fourth of the city Negroes failed to eat any fresh fruit for the week. . . . In every single case the Negroes were worse off [than neighboring whites]. (373)

Here Myrdal describes a scene that almost perfectly inverts the idyllic garden in which Hurston claims to have spent her childhood. All the foods that were so plentiful in Hurston's garden are negated, as though systematically, in his dismal picture. Eggs, which were so abundant in Eatonville they became ammunition for offensives against other children, here are unavailable, just as the fruit Hurston also threw at her neighbors completely disappears. These individual negations conspire to open a gap between Hurston's idealized South and its actuality—a gap no less wide than that between Bacon's Bensalem and Elizabethan England.

This gap results from more than mere self-censorship or Hurston's efforts to appease her patrons and publishers. After all, the wealth of foods encountered in Hurston's idyllic garden does not exaggerate the undeniably bountiful southern harvest as much as what Amartya Sen might term African Americans' entitlement to it. This exaggeration is so ambitious and contrasts so markedly with the malnutrition documented by Myrdal that it eventually becomes a representation of southern life as it should be rather than as it is. It becomes clear that Hurston's representation meets Terry Eagleton's definition of utopia, which discerns and "unlocks" the "dim outline of an alternative already implicit within" present conditions.

This particular "dim outline" is also discernible in *American Dilemma*. One can detect it in Myrdal's comments on malnutrition and from his acute appreciation that the impoverished families he studied contributed to a harvest of rare dependability and lived in a South where, as Hurston confirms, "orange, grapefruit, tangerine, guavas" grew more rapidly than even Hakluyt had foreseen. What distinguishes *Dust Tracks on a Road* and *Their Eyes Were Watching God* is that they shed light on this "outline," illuminate the fertility of the Southern soil, and thereby imply that hunger, within this bountiful terrain, must be avoidable. This subtle politicization of hunger then yields to an equally subtle connection between the fact that, as Hurston claims, she and her siblings "were never hungry" and the fact that local whites never disrupt or intrude upon her idyllic childhood garden. By these means, *Dust Tracks on a Road* and *Their Eyes Were Watching God* begin to associate nutritional satiety with racial freedom, to draw attention to the fact that Hurston's "eating town"—Eatonville—is populated entirely by African Americans. Hurston begins to suggest she has idealized Eatonville not only by importing foods into it but also by exporting white racism out of it.

Hurston takes this step because the only justification for the gap between her fiction and Myrdal's reality, the only way of making hunger absent from the former despite its overwhelming presence in the latter, is to expel the KKK, overseers, sawmill bosses, policemen, and other white authority figures. In Eatonville hunger becomes solvable at the exact moment when the ideology of racism is eradicated. By their common absence from the text and by their implicit connection, black hunger and white racism are characterized as surmountable obstacles to achieving Hurston's utopia.

Nowhere is Eatonville's abundance of food signaled more forcibly than on the few occasions when Zora Neale Hurston mentions hunger in connection with it. Such occasions are epitomized by a scene from *Their Eyes Were Watching God* whose prime function is to dramatize Joe Starks's egotism. Joe's "longing for peace but on his own terms" leads him to bait a shop customer, "Mrs. Tony Robbins." Robbins is a comical figure who continually yet falsely complains of hunger:

> "Ah'm hongry, Mist' Starks. 'Deed Ah is. Me and mah chillun is hongry. Tony don't fee-eed me!"
>
> This was what the porch had been waiting for. They burst into a laugh.
>
> "Mrs. Robbins, how can you make out you'se hongry when Tony comes in here every Satiday and buys groceries lak a man? Three weeks' shame on yuh!"
>
> "If he buy all dat you talkin' 'bout, Mist' Starks, God knows whut he do wid it. He sho don't bring it home, and me and mah po' chillun is *so* hungry! Mist' Starks, please gimme uh lil piece uh meat fur me and mah chillun."
>
> "Ah know you don't need it, but come on inside. You ain't goin' tuh lemme read till Ah give it to yuh." (113–14)

That Mrs. Robbins is here merely counterfeiting hunger is confirmed when, following her departure, the men on the porch ruminate on her and her husband's marriage:

> "In de fust place Ah never would spend on *no* woman whut Tony spend on *her*."
>
> Starks came back and took his seat. He had to stop and add the meat to Tony's account.
>
> "Well, Tony tell me tuh humor her along. He moved here from up de State hopin' tuh change her, but it ain't." (116)

The comic resolution of this scene hinges on a definition of the term *hunger* that has almost nothing in common with the one obtaining in *American Dilemma. Hunger* here, dislodged from its grave association with malnutrition or famine, seems synonymous with *appetite.* Judging from the incredulity of the men on the porch, Mrs. Robbins's professions of hunger no longer refer to dire bodily need so much as to a vaguer desire that, though physical and psychological, has lost its semblance of urgency. However, although Mrs. Robbins's hunger is in this way relegated to the passing and impulsive desire of the economically secure, her elaborate and (to the uninitiated) persuasive performance of want surely bears the imprint of genuine malnutrition. Mrs. Robbins might now only be hungry in the sense of wanting to snack between meals, yet the persuasiveness of her performance as an underfed person suggests she once experienced genuine malnutrition and now knows how to reproduce its characteristic gestures. The accomplishment of her confidence trick, the attempted mimicry of a "true" need meriting charity, suggest that, no matter how well fed Mrs. Robbins might be now, hunger has not always manifested itself so benignly. By turning hunger into a mere memory for Mrs. Robbins—who is, significantly, a new arrival to the area—Hurston subtly confirms that Eatonville is indeed unique, a utopia surrounded by hunger as Bensalem is surrounded by sea.

One might characterize Zora Neale Hurston's remarkable representation of Eatonville as a kind of gumbo because it mixes ingredients characteristic of European utopian narrative with a newly pragmatic sensibility derived from the writings of the African Diaspora. In Hurston's treatment of the orange, European utopianism and the appeal of emancipation intermingle, creating a new vision as achievable as it is Edenic. What this signal flavor of citrus, this intermingling of European and African American cultural tropes, demonstrates is that Equiano's simple dream of freedom can coexist with the dreaming of the unattainable. It demonstrates that, although Eatonville is an achievable utopia in the sense that a white authoritarian presence has been removed from it, such moderate ambition does not translate to the culture of the community. On the contrary, the removal of this authoritarianism from Eatonville and the town's subsequent achievement of socioeconomic targets by no means infects the field of culture with a corresponding leveling of ambition. Instead, it frees Hurston to deliver a more vivid and celebratory account of black communal life. Space that naturalistic representations of black southern life would have been obliged to devote to the inequities of Jim Crow is now left available for Hurston to do with as she pleases. Rather than refute the stereotyping of African Americans, she can capture the metaphoric dynamism of black southern dialect. Rather than confront the brutal sexual demands continually placed on the African American body, she can affirm female sexuality. And rather than concentrate on hunger as an integral experience of black southern life, Hurston can focus on moments of culinary transcendence, when such deprivation was fleetingly transcended and African American cooking elevated to the pageantry of the communal feast. Vanishing from Hurston's Eatonville alongside the racism now shown to be responsible for it, hunger no longer contaminates cooking with the association of nutrition's collapse. Rather, these utopian strategies enable Hurston to return us to a world Albert Murray, in a different context, calls a "paradise lost land of gumbo and barbecue." [19]

Public Speeches, Private Poisonings

Just as one of the fruits that made the biblical Eden idyllic also precipitated the Fall, so the same patriarchal zeal for leadership by which Joe Starks built up the town leads to its disintegration. In the early stages of *Their Eyes Were Watching God*, Janie's second husband is almost heroic. Energetic and passionate, he is at first as committed to and as convinced of the possibility of a collective racial uplift as Booker T. Washington. His claims to leadership—succinctly embodied in his recurring exclamation "I god!"—marshal Eatonville's skeptical inhabitants into building a town whose utopian aspects, though achievable, once seemed prohibited by the legacy of racial injustice. Locals who had "never seen no sich uh colored man befo' in all mah bawn days" forgo neither their reservations nor disbelief yet cautiously embrace Joe's ambitious, progressive project of turning Eatonville into an autonomous African American town (62). That this solitary man instigates Eatonville's uplift is confirmed as these citizens complete the town's regenerative construction work entirely at the office-bound Joe's behest, leaving them and even his wife, Janie, "astonished" (66). The building of new houses, the opening of the town store, the purchase of a street lamp—all these visible coordinates in Eatonville's seemingly inexorable upward trajectory are at this early stage attributed to Joe Starks's unique gusto.

Even as Janie retains a benumbed approval of her husband's orches-
tration of uplift, however, dissenting voices emerge, suggesting that Joe's
real motive is to become a patriarch akin to an antebellum slaveholder.
The exclamation "I god!"—always a sign of egoism—becomes yet more
dubious as the narrative gradually accompanies its utterance with suggestions that such self-proclaimed omniscience merely reenacts forms of
power redolent of slavery. Increasingly, Eatonville seems to be the municipal agency of an uplift not of its African American population but of
Joe Starks over this population. At its extreme, this altered view recasts
Joe as an antebellum plantation owner:

> The rest of the town looked like servant's quarters surrounding the "big house."
> And different from everybody else in the town he put off moving in until it had
> been painted, in and out. And look at the way he painted it—a gloaty, sparkly
> white. The kind of promenading white that the houses of Bishop Whipple,
> W. B. Jackson and the Vanderpool's wore. It made the village feel funny talking
> to him—just like he was anybody else. (75)

While this passage characterizes as mere servants the townspeople
whose houses huddle inconspicuously around Joe and Janie's significantly
white mansion, it also suggests they themselves would not be so discreet
and would articulate the unspoken metaphor of slavery haunting these
suggestive sentences. Certainly, the situation here consciously recalls "life
in the Big House," which, Eugene Genovese insists, matched "affection
and hatreds . . . extraordinary kindnesses and uncontrollable violence,"
incarnating "paternalism in its most heightened form."[20] Such historical
allusions reveal that the utopian appeal of *Their Eyes Were Watching
God* yields finally to a racial problematic; in this sense it is comparable
to Patricia Storace's description of Toni Morrison's *Paradise* (1998) as
a "novel about pioneers laying claim to a country, and, less explicitly,
about the ways in which possession of this country has been extended
and justified, . . . so that the story of its claiming almost irresistibly evokes
images of white founding fathers."[21] More frequently in *Their Eyes Were
Watching God,* race and class denunciation yield to a gender critique:
it is through the exposure of Joe's chauvinism that his individual Fall
is brought about. As we shall see, Joe's demands concerning what a

wife should be are both conservative and prescriptive. If Joe resembles Booker T. Washington because of the unstinting effort he pours into the uplift of Eatonville, he similarly dovetails with the Washingtonian perspective on domesticity. At the very least, the views Washington expounded in "A Sunday Evening Talk" (1910) find favor with Joe, who likewise demands that "a certain ceremony, a certain importance, be attached to partaking of the food." He, like Washington, demands that "food . . . not only [be] prepared in the most tempting way, but that it [be] served in the most attractive and beautiful way."[22] As we shall see, Janie achieves personal emancipation not only by publicly insulting her husband but also by privately rejecting such culinary demands.

This emphasis on Janie's public *and* private actions develops Henry Louis Gates Jr.'s and Barbara Johnson's readings of the novel. Gates and Johnson locate Joe's rejection exclusively in the moment Janie, sitting in on a signifying or Dozens contest on the Starkses' store porch, unexpectedly responds to one of her husband's many insults with a wittier and therefore more damaging insult of her own:

> "I god amighty! A woman stay round uh store till she get old as Methusalem and still can't cut a little thing like a plug of tobacco! Don't stand dere rollin' yo' pop eyes at me wid yo' rump hangin' nearly to yo' knees!"
>
> A big laugh started off in the store but people got to thinking and stopped. It was funny if you looked at it right quick, but it got pitiful if you thought about it awhile. It was like somebody snatched off part of a woman's clothes while she wasn't looking and the streets were crowded. Then too, Janie took the middle of the floor to talk right into Jody's face, and that was something that hadn't been done before. . . .
>
> "Naw, Ah ain't no young gal no mo' but den Ah ain't no old woman neither. Ah reckon Ah looks mah age too. But Ah'm uh woman every inch of me, and ah know it. Dat's uh whole lot more'n *you* kin say. You big-bellies round here and put out a lot of brag, but 'tain't nothin' to it but yo' big voice. Humph! Talkin' 'bout *me* lookin' old! When you pull down yo' britches, you look lak de change uh life." (121–23)

In *The Signifying Monkey* and *A World of Difference,* respectively, Gates and Johnson read Janie's startling allegation as a response not only to Joe's insult but also to his earlier statement that "mah wife don't know nothin' 'bout no speech-makin'. . . . She's uh woman and her place is in de home" (69). Both critics read this forceful scene as a cataclysmic detonation of Joe's attempts to "construct" Janie as he has constructed Eatonville—to force her into the Washingtonian mold of the passive, deferential wife. Both also emphasize, distinctly in *The Signifying Monkey* yet also evidently in Johnson's essay, the way Janie's accomplishment of a public voice translates into the accomplishment of a general and undiminished sense of selfhood. The prestige voice assumes in those talking "cookbooks" honoring the vernacular reemerges as Gates and Johnson parallel their emphasis on Janie's resistance to patriarchy with a further resistance, which the novel as a whole effects, to stereotyped representations of African American dialect.

In this way, Johnson and Gates identify Janie's insulting of Joe Starks as a radical and successfully stylized representation of black speech in which resistance to patriarchal expectation is enacted. Earlier associations of Joe with plantation ownership—which cover his marital home in white paint, as befits Genovese's envisioning of the antebellum Big House—subsequently supply a racial subtext to the gender affirmation of Janie's public denunciation of her husband. In Gates's and Johnson's reading, Janie's breathtaking insult constitutes the novel's critical rupture, which enables a declaration of independence at once feminist and African American. As Johnson summarizes the interpretation:

> [A]s store owner and mayor of the town, . . . [Joe Starks] proudly raises Janie to a pedestal of property and propriety. Because this involves her submission to his idea of what a mayor's wife should be, Janie soon finds her pedestal to be a straitjacket, particularly when it involves her exclusion—both as speaker and as listener—from the tale-telling sessions on the store porch and at the mock funeral of a mule. Little by little, Janie begins to talk back to Joe, finally insulting him so profoundly that, in a sense, he dies from it.[23]

Johnson supports these contentions with a long quotation from the novel that dramatizes the violent culmination of Joe Starks's attempts to force his wife into a preordained mold of domesticity.

"Dat's 'cause you need tellin'," he rejoined hotly. "It would be pitiful if Ah didn't. Somebody got to think for women and chillun and chickens and cows. I god, they sho don't think none theirselves."

"Ah knows uh few things, and womenfolks thinks sometimes too!"

"Aw naw they don't. They just think they's thinkin'. When Ah see one thing Ah understands ten. You see ten things and don't understand one."

Times and scenes like that put Janie to thinking about the inside state of her marriage. Time came when she fought back with her tongue as best she could, but it didn't do her any good. It just made Joe do more. He wanted her submission and he'd keep on fighting until he felt he had it.

So gradually, she pressed her teeth together and learned to hush. The spirit of the marriage left the bedroom and took to living in the parlor. It was there to shake hands whenever company came to visit, but it never went back inside the bedroom again. So she put something in there to represent the spirit like a Virgin Mary image in a church. The bed was no longer a daisy-field for her and Joe to play in. It was a place where she went and laid down when she was sleepy and tired.

She wasn't petal-open with him anymore. She was twenty-four and seven years married when she knew. She found that out one day when he slapped her face in the kitchen. It happened over one of those dinners that chasten all women sometimes. They plan and they fix and they do, and then some kitchen-dwelling fiend slips a scrochy, soggy, tasteless mess into their pots and pans. Janie was a good cook, and Joe looked forward to his dinner as a refuge from other things. So when the bread didn't rise, and the fish wasn't quite done at the bone, and the rice was scorched, he slapped Janie until she had a ringing sound in her ears and told her about her brains before he stalked on back to the store.

Janie stood where he left her for unmeasured time and thought. She stood there until something fell off the shelf inside her. Then she went inside there to see what it was. It was her image of Jody tumbled down and shattered. But looking at it she saw that it never was the flesh and blood figure of her dreams. Just something she had grabbed up to drape her dreams over. In a way she turned her back upon the image where it lay and looked further. She had no more blossomy openings dusting pollen over her man, neither any glistening young fruit where the petals used to be. She found that she had a host of thoughts she had never expressed to him, and numerous emotions she had never let Jody know about. Things packed up and put away in parts of her heart where he could never find them. She was saving up feelings for some man she had never seen. She had an inside and an outside now and suddenly she knew how not to mix them. (110–12)

Examining this long passage, Johnson does not mention the failed meal at its center and concentrates instead on the "relation" it sets up "between an inner 'image' and outward, domestic space." It is, Johnson suggests, "an externalization of Janie's feelings onto the outer surroundings in the form of a narrative of movement from private to public space." This "narrative of movement" formally mirrors what Johnson sees as Janie's growing awareness that her escape from domestic violence lies in the public sphere. This "movement" is toward a new, less inhibited persona and toward a more public and empowered role able to disturb Joe's Washingtonian association of the ideal wife with the ideal cook. It is "from this point on," Johnson suggests, "that Janie, paradoxically, begins to speak. . . . Henceforth, Janie will grow in power and resistance, while Joe deteriorates both in his body and in his public image."[24]

To Barbara Johnson's persuasive attempts to explain Janie's resistance to Joe in terms of public voice exclusively, I add the further reason of the failed meal that A World of Difference quotes but fails to mention. If anything, Janie's failure to produce an appetizing meal—a meal Joe can enjoy, with Washingtonian escapism, as a "refuge from other things"—bears greater responsibility for her husband's death than her unprecedented intervention in the store's signifying contest. The deterioration of Joe's body is more than a merely symbolic manifestation of Janie's triumph and insult. It also bears the hallmarks of a poisoning—of a physical reaction attributable to Janie's "scrochy, soggy, tasteless mess." Immediately following this meal, symptoms of the sickness that eventually leads to Joe Starks's death become manifest. His stomach becomes distended: Janie instantly notices that his "prosperous-looking belly that used to thrust out so pugnaciously and intimidate folks, sagged like a load suspended from his loins" (120). This symptom worsens with each day Joe's death draws nearer. Janie, noticing "how baggy Joe was getting all over," now regards his stomach as a "sack of flabby something [that] hung from his loins and rested on his thighs when he sat down" (125–26). That this distension is the principal cause of Joe's death is confirmed when the inflammation reaches an extreme in the final moments of Joe's life and his belly appears eaten away, emaciated, "like some helpless thing seeking shelter" (131).

Joe's physical reaction to this "scrochy, soggy, tasteless mess. . . . that chasten all women sometimes" thus suggests that, in addition to the verbal insult Johnson isolates, Janie has also found protection against future domestic violence in the form of a culinary "insult": poisoning. Significantly, the fact that this alternative solution does not require Janie to leave the home calls into question feminist theory's tendency to assume that gender equality belongs only in the public sphere and can be gained only when women exchange onerous domestic duties for jobs. Toni Morrison, among many others, has questioned whether the movement from domesticity to the public sphere premised by mainstream feminist theory is entirely applicable to those working class and African American women who were always forced into the job market and who found it as onerous as any domestic work. Yet, though it may be germane here to recall Hurston's years as a domestic laborer, *Their Eyes Were Watching God* seems to pose other questions about feminist theory. For one thing, Janie's discovery of a solution to domestic violence within the space of domesticity itself challenges the way feminism's public emphasis has assisted normative assumptions and made the departure of the beaten wife and not of the beating husband Western societies' favored solution to marital aggression. To the paradox Johnson identifies in Janie's discovery of both an inner personality and a public persona, we can thus add the further paradox that she achieves independence from Joe both through a public gesture characteristic of feminist liberation narrative and through a private poisoning atypical of it. She answers Joe's violence by staking her position outside the marital home and by returning violence in kind within it. Hazel Carby has noted that Janie reclaims power within the home so successfully that, when she comes to recount her life story, she can do so from the "porch because she *owns* it."[25] In the process, Janie's pivotal reclamation of both public and private space results in a mastery of her "inside" and "outside," thereby enacting Eagleton's characterization of "authentic utopian" thought's propensity to "break the system open . . . [along with] the very opposition between 'inside' and 'outside.' "[26]

Admittedly, Janie does not deliberately poison her husband. Unlike the day-to-day slave resisters Genovese describes, Janie claims to have no idea of the effect her cooking will have. Ostensibly, all she asks her husband to eat is an unappetizing meal. The resemblance between this "accidental" episode and deliberate poisonings elsewhere in Hurston's oeuvre is nevertheless compelling and suggests that, despite its surface appearance, the animus of Janie's mind has in this dramatic crisis transferred to her meal and made it toxic. This transference is suggested by the strong resemblance between Joe's symptoms and those endured by a violent neighbor whose punishment is recounted in the "Hoodoo" section of *Mules and Men*. In this ethnographic scene, a roots doctor places

> "uh gopher [tortoise] in her belly. You could see 'm movin' 'round in her. And once every day he'd turn hisself clear over and then you could hear her hollerin' for more'n a mile. Dat hard shell would be cuttin' her insides. Way after 'while she took down ill sick from it and died. Ah knowed de man dat done dat trick. Dat wuz done in uh dish of hoppin-john." (186)

Similarities between this scene and the poisoning of Joe in *Their Eyes Were Watching God* extend beyond the fact that this lethal dish of hopping John—defined by Hurston's footnotes as "peas and rice cooked together"—shares at least one ingredient with Janie's meal. In both episodes, we encounter a distension of the stomach that suggests an ingested yet living animal (a "belly" Janie now thinks of as a "helpless thing seeking shelter"). Intertextual affinities like these invite us to interpret Janie's dinner as a response to Joe's aggression, akin to the poisoned meal that is a response to neighborly transgression. In its disproportionately lethal effects, Janie's meal exhibits a concept of cooking that seems to take the conjure episodes of *Mules and Men* as an inspirational template, in much the same way that conjure, according to Houston Baker, serves as a model for Hurston's own writing. Just as Baker talks of the way *Their Eyes Were Watching God* enlists an "African-American cultural sign of conjure" in which "mythomania" and "classical cultural performance" unite, so one can say that Janie's cooking is founded on hoodoo's impenetrable inner logic and general cultural style. It may be too much to follow Baker—who describes *Mules and Men* and *Tell My Horse* not as books *about* conjure but as "conjure books of the first magnitude"—and describe Janie's ostensibly accidental poisoning as a form of "conjure" cooking.[27] Yet in its shocking provocation of violence, in its capacity to inject such plain ingredients as rice, fish, and bread with a deadly toxicity, the meal recalls how, in the "conjure books" cited by Baker, hoodoo generates poisons from such attractive ingredients as "filet gumbo with red-pepper" and "coconut."[28] Voodoo is also suggested in Joe's response to his stomach's inflammation, which is to turn to a "root-doctor" from "over around Altamonte Springs" and have her "cook for him." Since he had previously "been scornful of root-doctors and all their kind" (126), this response suggests that Joe suspects he has been the victim of conjure and is cognizant of the cultural wisdom, articulated in *Mules and Men,* that only conjure doctors can cure conjure because "[m]edical doctor[s] . . . can't do them kind of cases no good at all. Fact is it makes it worser."[29] Joe, "driven by a desperate hope to appear the old-time body in [his wife's] . . . sight," turns to conjure to restore his vanity and preserve his life and to find an antidote for what, to him, is the conjure worked on him by Janie's "scrochy" meal (126). Janie, meanwhile, remains the unwitting agency of the imminent physical disaster; a sign that her crime is indeed accidental is manifested in her wish for her husband to see a qualified "doctor, and a good one"(126).

Through these intertextual links, Hurston is clearly imagining that cooking is a much more potent and forcible cultural process than most preceding culinary texts allowed. Booker T. Washington's reformulation of a familiar Victorian stereotype wherein an idealized and silent wife and an idealized and silently efficient cook overlap disintegrates completely as Janie kills Joe with foods as well as with words. Emerging from *Their Eyes Were Watching God* is a new model of the female African American cook, one that no longer sees her as the mere facilitator of a therapeutic ceremonial space in which the industrious male might forget his tiredness and tribulations. Now this female cook has become the producer of a broader and far more potent array of physical and emotional effects: still able to convey love if so inclined, she now stands revealed as a potentially terrifying figure who possesses, among other things, the ability to kill.

Much of the force of the Garden of Eden myth's cautioning against temptation derives from the fact that, as a fantastical landscape, it is itself tempting. This irony—which qualifies the Garden of Eden as both *outopia* and *eutopia*—is what makes the fable so useful to such divergent texts as Nathaniel Hawthorne's *The Scarlet Letter* (1850) and Philip Roth's *American Pastoral* (1998). To the dispossessed, hungry, and cold, the Garden of Eden can induce neither a craving for more nor a desire for alternative modes of living but rather a sense of deep and well-founded satisfaction. Eden is a space in which the nudity of Adam and Eve connotes sexual availability, in which the absence of rival inhabitants guarantees peace, and in which the proliferation of wild fruits and other foods safeguards the health and vigor that adequate nourishment produces. That Eve is offered all this yet still seeks something else relativizes desire and envy; her dissatisfaction even in such a satisfying world illustrates the elusiveness of human contentment. A similar fate befalls Joe Starks in *Their Eyes Were Watching God*. A man whose hunger for change and uplift transforms Eatonville into a true "eating town"—a town from which malnutrition has been banished—is finally poisoned, like Eve, and forced by death to leave the site of his utopian dreaming. Lying on his deathbed, his emaciated belly resembling "some helpless thing seeking shelter," he himself seems transformed into food at which the town— *his* "Eatingville"—now gnaws away. He reminds Janie of a "hog dying down in the swamp" (131)—a hog that has escaped the roasting coals of the town's barbecues only to meet a more humiliating and protracted fate. Much as temptation becomes concentrated in an apple that Eve then ingests, so Joe Starks, as Eatonville's architect, seems swallowed up by the force he unleashes. And yet, if the fall of Eden comes about not because it is insufficiently satisfying but because of the human personality's incessantly relativizing attitude toward temptation, so Joe Starks's collapse is caused by his own vanity and not because the ideals behind the Eatonville project are necessarily flawed. *Their Eyes Were Watching God* remains committed to the self-evident fact that adequate nutrition and housing are, to those without them, aspirations worth striving for. The ceremonial feast that Joe Starks first weaves into the municipal fabric of the town remains intact and is repeated at his funeral. The death of Joe Starks does not entail a death of the utopian space his authoritarian leadership helped create. Rather, it marks the emergence of a new ambivalence regarding its more excessive patriarchal manifestations, an ambivalence tempered by a retention and reinvigoration of Eatonville's principal claim: the end of hunger. Nowhere, in short, are the utopian aspects of Eatonville clearer than in the downfall of its architect.

Barbecuing the Diaspora

Like the orange and other citrus fruits, the popularization of barbecue in America has long been the subject of competing and conflicting historical explanations. At first, during barbecue's assimilation into eighteenth-century colonial American culture, some Euro-American observers acknowledged its origins in the native Caribbean; for others it inspired visions of bloodthirsty savages. Some witnesses provided evenhanded accounts of the culinary practice. Robert Beverley's *History and Present State of Virginia* of 1705, for instance, referred simply to the "two ways of Broyling" practiced by the Powhatan Indians, noting that the latter of these involved the "laying" of meat "upon Sticks rais'd upon Forks at some distance above the live Coals, which heats more gently, and drys up the Gravy; this they, and we also from them, call Barbacueing" (178). During the same period, however, others provided far less temperate accounts of a "cannibalistic" barbecue, which painted the process as a means of making human rather than animal flesh edible. As early as 1661, Edmund Hickeringill embroidered his *Jamaica Viewed: With All the Ports, Harbours, and their Several Soundings, Towns, and Settlements* (1661) with verse alluding to how the "flesh" of the Caribs' enemies is "forthwith Barbacu'd and eat / By them, their Wives and Children as Choice Meat" (59). Similarly, in 1715 Cotton Mather begins a letter to the Edinburgh clergyman Robert Wodrow by reporting that, in the "colony of Carolina, to the southward of us, . . . the barbarities perpetrated by the Indians are too hideous to be restated" and ends his long restatement of "these diabolical operations" by describing the "barbikew-ing" of a white "gentleman" in some detail.[30]

However, as the popularity of barbecue among white Americans grew throughout the eighteenth century, its association both with cannibalism and with the native Caribbean receded. In broadly the same period that the Asian roots of oranges were smothered by texts keen to imbue citrus with an Occidental association, the Native American roots of barbecue were similarly silenced or hidden beneath newly manufactured narra-tives identifying a European provenance for the technique. As Jeffrey Steingarten notes, this Eurocentric project—which fabricated the etymol-ogy asserting that "the word 'barbecue' comes from the French *barbe à queue* [head to tail]," among other spurious derivations—is nowa-days largely discredited. Yet Eve Zibart, Muriel Stevens, and Terrell Ver-mont's recent observation that the Caribbean's "greatest contribution to the American diet—barbecue—isn't generally recognized as Caribbean at all" reveals that a certain degree of confusion and ignorance still reigns over the provenance of this now-global culinary style.[31] Even as such di-verse culinary texts as Norma Benghiat's *Traditional Jamaican Cookery* (1985) and José Rafael Lovera's *Historia de la Alimentación en Venezuela* (1988) acknowledge barbecue's native origins, others remain in need of the definition included in H. L. Mencken's eighty-year-old work, *The American Language* (1919):

> The noun *barbecue* came from a Haitian word, *barbacoa,* signifying a frame set up to lift a bed off the ground. But it got the meaning of a frame used for roasting meat soon after it appeared in Spanish, and the derivative word has had its present sense in American English since about 1660. (112)

I contend that Zora Neale Hurston's oeuvre harnesses this continuing confusion in order to enroll barbecue within a diasporic vision in which black Floridian and Maroon Jamaican culture become united. To some extent, this attempt to extol a hog roast exploited the fact that, when the dominant U.S. culture of the early twentieth century *did* associate bar-becue with a nonwhite group, this group tended to be black rather than Native American. An important cultural strain that straddled the distinc-tion between white racialism and Africanist fascination during this time situated barbecue as a signifier of the African American at play, feeding on preconceptions of black gourmandism and inspiring such lurid ragtime tunes as Vess Ossman's "The Darkey's Barbecue" (1896) and Will Marion Cook's "Darktown Barbecue" (1904). For all its bowdlerization of reality, however, this caricature at a basic level reflected the passion for barbecue prevalent among southern African Americans—a passion that resulted not only in Louis Armstrong's classic "Struttin' with Some Barbecue" (1955), but also, as Tracey Poe observes, in the opening of "sidewalk barbecue shacks" by recent migrant arrivals to the Chicago South Side, Harlem, and other northern ghettos.[32]

In the hands of Zora Neale Hurston, this cultural linking of barbecue with African America becomes material out of which to mold the diaspora. Even as the opening of barbecue "shacks" became a measure of the impact the Great Migration would have on U.S. metropolises, Hurston came to see that the implications of this cookery technique could exceed such domestic controversies and open new, international possibilities. What Hurston found in the practice of barbecue was a reflection of the environmental parallels between Florida and the Caribbean, which substantiated the affinity between these tropical landscapes by also linking the cultural practices of their black inhabitants. Hurston's realization of the symmetry between the black Floridian festival of the hog roast and the Maroon Jamaican festival of the jerked pig—both of which involved hours of smoking pork, the dissemination of stories, and the singing of songs—creates a radically new interpretation of barbecue, which installs this singularly popular culinary form as evidence of diasporic commonality.

Hurston announces the existence of this diasporic barbecue by emphasizing the similarities between hog roasts held throughout the American South and in the Caribbean. Even as the Eatonville hog roast of *Their Eyes Were Watching God* carefully negotiates the tensions between agrarianism and agricultural industrialization, it places this hog roast on a national and international plane by alluding to *Jonah's Gourd Vine* (1934) and *Tell My Horse*. *Their Eyes Were Watching God* initiates this outward movement, this shift from a regional to a national to an international plane: when Joe Starks announces the Eatonville hog roast, he explains that not only the townspeople but black citizens from throughout the area will be welcome to it. Joe says:

> "Y'all know we can't invite people to our town just dry long so, I god, naw. We got tuh feed 'em something, and 'tain't nothin' people laks better'n barbecue. Ah'll give one whole hawg mah ownself. Seem lak all de rest uh y'all put tuhgether oughta be able tuh scrape up two mo'. Tell yo' womenfolks tuh do 'round 'bout some pies and cakes and sweet p'tater pone." (71–72)

Joe's decision to extend this invitation to all and sundry results from a mixture of racial pride and personal egotism, from a desire not only to inspire but also to boast to those who live beyond Eatonville's town limits and have not yet learned the lessons of its utopian uplift. However, despite being shaped by his characteristic blend of chauvinism, vanity, and dictatorial aggression, the central motive behind Joe's announcement— that the town's acquisition of street lighting is a landmark worthy of a hog roast festival—remains favored by the narrative. Joe's egotism remains at this point viable, if only because the aggressive leadership that accompanies it is clearly what has enabled the town to complete its transformation from a collection of "shame-faced houses scattered in the sand and palmetto roots" (56). Because of this, any criticism of Joe at this point remains implicit. Neither the narrator nor Eatonville's other characters comment when, in an act combining autonomous action with a belated democratic gesture, Joe sends off to "Sears, Roebuck and Company for the street lamp" and tells "the town to meet the following Thursday night to vote on it" (71). Implicitly, however, this transaction awakens a certain skepticism. The intervention of a mail-order catalog at this key moment in Eatonville's uplift heralds the reappearance of the national context, suggesting that further civic improvements can only arise from increased participation in the surrounding economy. In this sense, *Their Eyes Were Watching God* resembles Richard Wright's "The Man Who Was Almost a Man" (1961), in which the protagonist Dave gains a new "sense of power" through a gun first glimpsed in the Sears Roebuck catalog. In both texts, white social control is strengthened by the fact that black empowerment—which in Dave's case merely extends to the ability to "[k]ill anybody, black or white"—depends on such commercial sources.[33] In both, the mere mention of Sears Roebuck reminds us that these insular narrative domains exist within a national super-structure, and that attempts to gain empowerment must be managed through these fiscal and social outlets. Capitalistic negotiations fore-close the fragile possibility of emancipation: Dave's utopian dream of "somewhere where he could be a man" is no sooner sensed than it is overwhelmed by the restrictions of economic circumstance.[34] Similarly, as Joe buys his mass-produced street lamp from a nationally distributed catalog, and as tinned produce and cans of Coke fill the shelves of his store, the civic progress he pioneered becomes firmly cast as capitalistic in nature.

However, if Eatonville's street lamp is associated with national capital-ism, then the hog roast that celebrates it is represented very differently. Joe does not donate tins of food or Coca-Cola to the proceedings but con-forms to a more traditional mode of communal food exchange by giving (rather than paying for) "one whole hawg mah ownself." The Eatonville townspeople are no more dependent on Sears Roebuck for their barbecue oven than Beverley's Powhatans had been centuries earlier. Rather than roasting hand-reared meat on a mass-produced oven, the townsmen, the "day before the lighting," had dug a "big hole in back of the store and filled it full of oak wood and burned it down to a glowing bed of coals" (72). One can say that these townspeople bury agrarianism even as they praise it; they practice their agrarian culture to mark a capitalist acquisi-tion implicated in this culture's decline.

Awareness of such tensions in *Their Eyes Were Watching God* is vital, for it enables us to avoid what Kadiatu Kanneh characterizes as those misinterpretations of Paul Gilroy's *Black Atlantic* (1993) that repudiate Eatonville as the embodiment of "a regional nostalgia for racial authentic-ity."[35] In light of Hurston's use of literary utopianism, we must recognize that her sentimentalization of "rural black folk" results less from a flaw in the novel than from a calculated attempt to pit the folkish agrarianism embodied in the hog roast against the commercial capitalism embodied in the street lamp. Hurston's description must be seen as a deliberately naive representation of barbecue, which anxiously negotiates the poten-tially disruptive impact of modernity:

The women got together the sweets and the men looked after the meats. . . . It took them the whole night to barbecue the three hogs. Hambo and Pearson had full charge while the others helped out with turning the meat now and then while Hambo swabbed it all over with the sauce. In between times they told stories, laughed and told more stories and sung songs. They cut all sorts of capers and whiffed the meat as it slowly came to perfection with the seasoning penetrating to the bone. (72)

Contradictions adumbrating this passage gain urgency as *Their Eyes Were Watching God* turns to the meal itself:

"Dis occasion is something for us all to remember tuh our dyin' day. De first street lamp in uh colored town. Lift yo' eyes and gaze on it. And when Ah touch de match tuh dat lamp-wick let de light penetrate inside of yuh, and let it shine, let it shine, let it shine. Brother Davis, lead us in a word uh prayer." . . .

As the word Amen was said, he touched the lighted match to the wick, and Mrs. Bogle's alto burst out. . . .

They, all of them, all of the people took it up and sung it over and over until it was wrung dry, and no further innovations of tone and tempo were conceivable. Then they hushed and ate barbecue. (73–74)

Here Hurston's playful transcription of African American dialect, her warmhearted burlesque of Joe's solemn paean to civic illumination, call attention to the obstacle preventing the completion of Eatonville's capitalist project: race. The pride saturating Joe's thanksgiving for the street lamp is implicitly yet starkly contradicted by the indifference with which those at Sears Roebuck would have distributed it. Similarly, the religious exaltation by Joe's flock of this replicable light, which is no more singular than a can of Coke, raises an array of paradoxes and seems to ask how black cultural forms associated with the Old South will survive the coming transition to capitalism. Although less elegiac regarding the fate of rural southern African Americans than Jean Toomer in *Cane* (1923), Hurston here seems to be whispering what Toomer says out loud: that the "spirit" of these Southern folk "was walking in to die on the modern desert."[36]

But even as she echoes Toomer's sense that industrialization and migration imperil the Africanist cultures of the South, Hurston rejects his fatalism along with *Cane*'s suggestion that the death of this cultural "spirit" is inevitable. Instead, Hurston's writings proactively seek ways of preserving the agrarian cultural practices exemplified in the Eatonville hog roast; they continually seek to place such events, not just in the past, but in a possible utopian future in which both cultural retention and economic progress can be accommodated. On one level, such cultural preservation is achieved through the act of writing—through Hurston's account of the hog roast itself, for instance, which supplies a sequence of details so precise they function as a potential recipe that future, metropolitan, African American audiences might follow. But Hurston also achieves this cultural preservation by drawing connections between "Eatingville" and other American islands in which African-influenced agrarian cultures survive, linking the consolidated town with Haiti, with Maroon Jamaica; it is from this strategy that her idea of diasporic affinity arises.

Diaspora arises in Hurston's oeuvre through her habitual use of revision, improvisation, and repetition. While this incessant intertextual play recalls Henry Louis Gates's conceptualization of "signifying," we must also emphasize that, whereas "signifying" imagines a series of conversations between African American writers, Hurston is instead involved in a kind of ceaseless monologue and signifies on no one as much as herself. As Alice Gambrell confirms, Zora Neale Hurston was indeed "a prodigious producer of textual variants." Citing Hurston's story of a rivalry between two conjure herbalists—versions of which she identifies in the anthropological works "Hoodoo in America" (1931) and *Mules and Men* (1935) as well in the autobiography *Dust Tracks on a Road* (1942)—Gambrell insists that such intertextual links must receive an

> analysis that is both conscious of Hurston's textual metamorphoses *and* of the historical determinants and political implications of those metamorphoses. . . . On one hand, then, self-revision reflects the sharply determined limits within which Hurston operated—it is a form of self-censorship and a sign of either voluntary acquiescence or victimization; on the other, however, and less pessimistically, it represents a constant inventiveness.[37]

Gambrell's analysis endorses my approach in this chapter, because it suggests that any interpretation of *Their Eyes Were Watching God* must consider publishing pressures and financial constraints without inflating these factors into an exclusive explanation for Hurston's decision to idealize Eatonville. In Gambrell's formulation, the "other" hand—the "inventive" hand—also inspires Hurston's production of those "versions" that, by placing a distinctive imprint on her publications, helped rein in an oeuvre scattered across ethnographic, literary, and journalistic genres.

But Hurston's production of these textual "versions" was not just a way of lending unity and coherence to her literary output. It also enabled her to complete the outward movement, the transition from a local to a national to an international plane, from which her conceptualization of diasporic commonality unfolds. One move in this transition, which switches Hurston's narrative concerns from a local to a national basis, is effected by *Their Eyes Were Watching God* itself, because its "street lamp" hog roast revisits and revises the Georgia barbecue of Hurston's debut novel, *Jonah's Gourd Vine*.

> When the cotton was all picked and the last load hauled to the gin, Alf Pearson gave the hands two hogs to barbecue.
>
> That was a night. Hogs roasting over the open pit of oak coals. Negroes from three other plantations. Some brought "likker." Some crocus sacks of yellow yam potatoes, and bushels of peanuts to roast, and the biggest syrup-kettle at Pearson's cane-mill was full of chicken perleau. Twenty hens and six water-buckets full of rice. Old Purlee Kimball was stirring it with a shovel. . . .
>
> The hogs, the chickens, the yams disappeared. The old folks played "Ole Horse" with the parched peanuts. The musicians drank and tuned up. Bully was calling figures.
>
> "Hey, you dere, us ain't no white folks! Put down dat fiddle! . . . Less clap!"
>
> So they danced. (58–59)

It is scarcely possible to read this scene without fast-forwarding to the "street lamp" hog roast that Hurston published only a few years later. Neither scene is told through the eyes of a participant in the meal: both are depicted through the distancing lens of a third-person narrator. Both describe the preparation of the barbecue at greater length than they do its consumption. Both frame the hog's consumption with a series of protracted shared experiences that engage not only with the sensory presence of the meat itself but also with the vital "garnish" of storytelling, music, and dance. Similarly, while the barbecue in *Jonah's Gourd Vine* is set in a very different context, on a plantation in which white control has been momentarily relinquished, this territorial difference works to sharpen the similarity between the actual barbecue ritual and that held in the pages of *Their Eyes Were Watching God*. It not only identifies a commonality linking the culture of African American sharecroppers in Georgia with that practiced in black Florida but also insists that this commonality will survive even when sucked into white structures of control.

With the forging of these connections, Hurston moves another step closer to acclaiming the African Diaspora. If Joe Starks's decision to invite all and sundry to the Eatonville hog roast effectively expanded the constituency of its African American culture beyond that town's limits, then the fact that this hog roast repeats actions Hurston had already set in Georgia broadens this constituency even further, elevating the Floridian ritual of barbecue from regional to national status.

The next step—to broaden the scope of barbecue yet further, to embrace the international idea of the diaspora—is, if anything, even more surefooted. The strong intertextual affinity between *Jonah's Gourd Vine*'s barbecue and Eatonville's "street lamp" hog roast is as nothing compared to the links between the latter and the "jerked-pig" scene of *Tell My Horse*. As we will see, through a process of self-quotation and self-misquotation, through her consistent textual association of *Their Eyes Were Watching God* and *Tell My Horse*—through her virtual plagiarizing of herself—Hurston's writings come to insist that black Floridians baste, smoke, turn, and eat pork in a manner almost perfectly analogous to that of Maroon Jamaicans. And it is through the forging of this textual kinship, through this explicit linking of jerk cookery with the domestic U.S. hog roast, that Hurston finally barbecues the diaspora, serving it up for her readers' consumption.

Tell My Horse's "jerked-pig" scene was the result of much patient preparation and research on Hurston's part. As Robert Hemenway notes, while in Jamaica Hurston "lived quietly" among the Maroons "residing in the forbidding Saint Catherine Mountains at Accompong," biding her time and winning their trust in order to form a new record of a culture that had long fascinated anthropologists and was later to enthrall Katherine Dunham. Eventually the patience and discretion Hurston displayed in this time paid off, and she was invited to join the men of the society on what Hemenway terms a "ritualistic hunt for a wild boar."[38] *Tell My Horse* begins its account of this experience by recounting the capture of the pig and concludes by describing its culinary treatment:

> [A]ll of the men began to cut dry wood for a big fire. When the fire began to be lively, they cut green bush of a certain kind. They put the pig into the fire on his side and covered him with green bush to sweat him so that they could scrape off the hair. . . . Everything was now done in high good humor. . . . The meat was then seasoned with salt, pepper and spices and put over the fire to cook. It was such a big hog that it took nearly all night to finish cooking. It required two men to turn it over when necessary. While it was being cooked and giving off delicious odors, the men talked and told stories and sang songs. One told the story of Paul Bogle, the Jamaican hero of the war of 1797 who made such a noble fight against the British. . . .
>
> Towards morning we ate our fill of jerked pork. It is more delicious than our barbecue. It is hard to imagine anything better than pork the way Maroons jerk it. . . . We came marching in singing the Karamente' songs. (36–37)

Here Hurston's closing observation that the Maroons' jerked pork is "more delicious than our barbecue" reveals a culinary difference that is emphatically contradicted by the preceding text, which, by quoting *Their Eyes Were Watching God* almost verbatim, instead suggests Caribbean jerk cookery and American barbecue are virtually identical. *Tell My Horse* and *Their Eyes Were Watching God* both portray the participants of the ceremonies in similar terms; both involve an all-male crowd, described by broad assertions as a single unit, which is said to "dig" this and to "do" that, to "cut dry wood" and to "cut all sorts of capers." Both also begin by describing a fire that is "a big fire [of] dry coals" in the former and a "glowing bed of live coals" in the latter. Both proceed to emphasize the time taken to cook the hog: "all night" in the former, the "whole night" in the latter. In both the meat is then turned by two men, who are identified as Hambo and Pearson in *Their Eyes Were Watching God,* but who remain nameless in *Tell My Horse.* A subsequent construction in the former—"while it was being cooked . . . the men talked and told stories and sang songs"—directly echoes a description in the latter—"in between times they told stories, laughed, and told more stories and sung songs." Quoting each other nearly word for word, describing a veritable concatenation in the firing, basting, and eating of the hog, these scenes mirror each other, creating a reflection that spans the sea separating Jamaica from Florida. In this way, Hurston's oeuvre completes its transition from a regional to a national to an international plane, weaving a transcontinental web whose threads closely follow the contours of the diaspora itself. Regional and national boundaries are obliterated as the barbecue scenes of *Tell My Horse, Jonah's Gourd Vine,* and *Their Eyes Were Watching God* reunite a people whom slavery had strewn across the Black Atlantic, showing that their cultures share a common root. Self-revision, Hurston's ceaseless production of "versions," thus sustains a rich response to barbecue, which transforms this culinary process into the very substance of diaspora itself.

Hurston's insightful revelation that black Floridians and Maroon Jamaicans were "barbecuing" the diaspora numbers among the greatest achievements of her oeuvre. Even as Arthur Schomburg launched a proposal for an exhaustive survey of African and African American culinary history—a proposal that, Doris Witt suggests, "continues to be underutilized," despite the appearance of Harris's *Iron Pots and Wooden Spoons* (1989)—Hurston was clearly forging a new way of negotiating the diasporic links that would inevitably emerge from such an undertaking.[39] Her innovation enabled the postwar publication of works such as Vertamae Smart-Grosvenor's *Vibration Cooking* (1970), Harris's *A Kwanzaa Keepsake* (1995), and Ntozake Shange's *If I Can Cook / You Know God Can* (1998), which recall her geographical reach and celebrate the diaspora as an oppositional agency from which the black individual can draw strength. It also offers a more muscular alternative to Toomer's plaintive vision of black agrarian culture's demise, shoring up this culture by showing its links with other cultures in the Americas. And it testifies to the dazzling existence of black cultural retention in those unpromising corners of the continent where slavery had been most lethal, uncovering from this terrain new narratives of cultural preservation, resistance, and triumph.

If Hurston's acclamation of a diasporic barbecue is one of the most innovative aspects of her work, however, it is also among the most problematic. We cannot fail to notice that this enlisting of barbecue into the African Diaspora comes at the expense of its roots in native Caribbean culture, which Hurston seems to suppress as thoroughly as those Euro-American etymologists who attributed the term to the French *barbe à queue*. Although Hurston never plunges to this depth and never attributes barbecue to a falsified African provenance, both *Jonah's Gourd Vine* and *Their Eyes Were Watching God* surround their depictions of this culinary ritual with other practices widely seen to be of African extraction. One need only consider the scene from *Jonah's Gourd Vine* in which Bully reminds his fellows that they "ain't no white folks" before bidding them dance to the "instrument that they had brought to Africa in their skins—the drum" (58–59). A chief purpose of *Tell My Horse*, meanwhile, is to locate Haitian and Jamaican cultural practices that can be traced back to West Africa, yet this sensitivity to the question of provenance does not extend to the native Caribbean, whose presence, at least in the "jerked-pig" scene cited earlier, is reduced to the place name Accompong.

We can interpret Hurston's failure to declare barbecue's native origins by placing it in the context of our earlier discussion of the orange. As this discussion demonstrated, all foods can become unanchored from their sources, can be claimed by new groups and subjected to new explanations, new narratives, new myths. Thus the appropriation of barbecue by members of the African Diaspora, as witnessed in the oeuvre of Zora Neale Hurston, merely repeats countless appropriations of countless other foods that perpetually escape their original contexts. If we are to reduce foods to their origins, this logic suggests, then we must not only insist that barbecue is of native Caribbean provenance but also that pasta is of Asian provenance, that its current importance to Italian and Italian-American formations of identity is predicated on a falsification of culinary history, and so on. Barbecue, in this view, can become a part of the African Diaspora as soon as members of this diaspora cook it and regard it—as Hurston's characters undoubtedly do—as important to their group history.

A great deal can be said for this position. Yet, given her ethnographic interest in issues of cultural provenance—and given the popularity during the interwar years of H. L. Mencken's *American Language,* with its acknowledgment of barbecue's Caribbean origins—it remains difficult not to interpret *Tell My Horse*'s failure to declare barbecue's true roots as deliberate obfuscation. It remains difficult to escape the conclusion that, in the composition of this and other texts, Hurston sacrificed native provenance, and the more complex histories of interracial exchange that it opened up, in order to preserve what she saw as the authenticity of the diaspora. For Hurston, it seems, the transition from a local to a national to an international plane had to be consummated by a further and final step: the diaspora had to become triangular, had to cross not only the Caribbean Sea but also the Atlantic Ocean; if certain facts did not support this movement back to Africa, then they could be disregarded. A certain racial essentialization, in which cultural commonality and a shared ancestral memory overlap, motivates Hurston's representation of barbecue, leading her to prioritize particularity and unity over what Paul Gilroy characterizes as the diaspora's capacity to use creatively all "the syncretic complexities of language, culture, and everyday modern life in the torrid areas where racial slavery was practiced."[40]

Put another way, Hurston effectively chose one source of pride over another. If pride can be taken in the incomparable courage of those first African Americans who resisted the Middle Passage by retaining elements of the cultures they had been forced to abandon, then pride also can derive from the fact that many of these slaves, soon after their arrival on plantations, grew interested in the culinary culture of another nonwhite group terrorized by European racial ideology. African individuals who rejected the European classification of people by race instigated alliances with Native Americans of similar disposition and contrived, from these inherently antiracist coalitions, to disseminate a culinary form that has proven more durable and influential, in global terms, than anything then being cooked in traditional white American kitchens. Only by acknowledging these myriad and unrecorded interracial alliances—only by realizing that they, too, constitute a source of pride—can we begin to understand fully the diaspora that Hurston helped to articulate, and to see it less as an inversion of or counterpoise to the European legacy of race than as a means of finally liberating ourselves from it.

Only then can we begin to see that the consistencies evident in Black Atlantic cultures derive neither from coincidence nor necessarily from Africa. Such a diasporic model, which focuses on the influences of American social and ecological environments, helps to explain why citrus fruit appears not only throughout Hurston's oeuvre but also in *Beloved, Tar Baby,* and *The Interesting Narrative.* It explains why diverse novels such as the Martiniquan Patrick Chamoiseau's *Texaco* (1992) and Jean Toomer's *Cane* describe similar landscapes of intensive sugar production, and why almost all the family of that most influential Black Atlantic thinker, C. L. R. James, found work in Trinidad's sugar processing plants.[41] As Hurston's anticipation of this diasporic geography confirms, throughout the Americas, wherever sugar and orange plantations are to be found, so, in general, are African Americans. With few exceptions, such as the "breadbasket" of the American Midwest, regions of the continent historically committed to the intensive production of specific cash crops were also the prime destinations for African slaves. A map locating the major sites of cotton, tobacco, citrus, and sugar production throughout north America is also, by and large, a map showing the regions where slave regimes remained at their most vigorous and African American populations, at least before urbanization, at their densest. In the process of documenting the consistencies between the material cultures that slaves encountered throughout the continent, Hurston uncovers, but then submerges beneath her valorization of African retention, a new explanation for international diasporic commonalities. She ushers us toward a view that she herself rejected, a view able to see that similarities between the black cultures of, say, North Carolina and Brazil result not merely from ancestral memory, but from a shared experience of forced labor amid a new, American ecology rich with new foods and new culinary methods. As the sign of cultural kinship between marooned black communities scattered throughout the Americas, Hurston's self-revision of her barbecue scene persuasively insists on a diasporic connection already anticipated in the affinity between her representation of citrus and those of Toni Morrison and Olaudah Equiano. Our task now is to forge new theories of the diaspora, to place new emphasis on the occurrence of fusion and interracial exchange, in order to reread Hurston's groundbreaking portrayal of "Eatingville," an island that exists not only amid hunger but also within an archipelago of other autonomous islands.

The Uses
of American
Hunger

ZORA NEALE HURSTON was not the only twentieth-century African American writer whose oeuvre was fragmented by publishing demands. Richard Wright's work suffered a similar fate and was disrupted by myriad editorial interventions, amendments, and rejections. Of these interventions, those surrounding Wright's autobiography, which is the focus of this chapter, remain especially difficult to unravel. As Arnold Rampersad notes, Wright at first titled his autobiography *Black Confession* but quickly changed his mind and renamed it *American Hunger*. Having settled on this title, Wright divided his narrative into two lengthy sections, titled "Southern Night" and "The Horror and the Glory," which dealt respectively with his childhood in the Deep South and his migration to Chicago in early adulthood. In January 1944, Harper and Brothers accepted Wright's autobiography under the new title and in this bisected format. Wright's unabridged autobiography only gained publication in 1991, however, because in 1944 Harper and Brothers repeated a marketing ploy that had served *Native Son* well in 1940: they forwarded the manuscript to the Book of the Month Club. The response of the club was illuminating and perhaps betrayed a desire to repeat the sales but not the controversy surrounding Wright's first novel. The literary organization imposed two conditions on its distribution of the autobiography, which led to a published version radically different from Wright's original intentions. First, the club demanded the removal of the autobiography's second section, "The Horror and the Glory," which described events following Wright's arrival in Chicago. Among other things, this removal silenced the comparisons Wright's full manuscript draws between the racial ideologies held by southern whites and by certain white Communists, employers, and colleagues he encountered in the North. At the time, as Rampersad points out, Wright suspected that "pressure from Communists had led the book club to ask him to drop" the concluding section of his autobiography.[1] This suspicion was founded in Wright's awareness of the influence the party retained among contemporary, metropolitan intellectual circles. I am, however, skeptical that such influence extended to as capitalistic an institution as the Book of the Month Club, which Joan Shelley Rubin has characterized as a "child of advertising" with a "consumer mentality" steeped in "the intrinsic values of the liberal arts."[2] When we consider the Book of the Month Club's reduction of Wright's manuscript alongside its second intervention, an alternative to Wright's political explanation for these changes emerges. This second request, for Wright to reword his *American Hunger* title, complemented the first in that it, too, limited the implications of this incendiary autobiography to regional rather than national dimensions. Eliminating its northern section and asking Wright to formulate a new title, *Black Boy,* the Book of the Month Club effectively localized the autobiography's narrative and racialized its name, slanting it toward the "South, where the race question is forever on the mat," in H. L. Mencken's phrase. Regardless of the rationale behind them, these interventions ultimately rendered Wright's autobiography less discomfiting and thus more marketable to anyone wishing to follow Mencken's view of race relations as a "national problem" only in the sense that white northerners "bear a part of the burden" for white southerners' mistakes.[3] Anxieties surrounding the North's role in the promulgation of a racism many still chose to associate exclusively with a seemingly distant Jim Crow were soothed by the renaming and abbreviation of Wright's autobiography.

This chapter designates as *American Hunger* an autobiography that has previously been known either as *Black Boy* or by the accommodating compromise of *Black Boy (American Hunger)*. This designation is intended as a minor contribution to the restoration of Wright's original autobiography, a process that began with the publication of its unused portion by Harper and Row in 1977 and culminated in the complete Library America edition of 1991. My primary motivation for this decision is the fact that, as Rampersad confirms, *American Hunger* was the title Wright "originally applied to the work as a whole."[4] The dual interventions of the Book of the Month Club not only narrowed the national dimensions of Wright's narrative but also implicitly reduced the hunger announced by its original title to a leitmotif of the text. Via its titular abridgement, hunger lost its textual significance, becoming interpretable strictly as a reference to nutritional want rather than as a broader thematic umbrella under which such want could be grouped with—and thus related to—desires for education, enlightenment, and political reform. By returning to the original title, *American Hunger,* this chapter reasserts the centrality such want occupies within Wright's autobiography. It recognizes and acts upon the retrospective compensation that, during interviews to promote *Black Boy,* Wright seemed to pay to his formerly eponymous keyword. Many of these promotional interviews betray a desire to compensate for the disappearance of hunger from the autobiography's title. In an interview conducted mere weeks before *Black Boy*'s publication in 1945, Wright asserted that "colored people are thinking about meat and food now and meat and food after their jobs close."[5] In an interview following the book's publication, Wright insisted that the "judgment" the autobiography delivers is that "the environment the South creates is too small to nourish human beings, especially Negro human beings."[6] This characteristic progression from literal to "human" nourishment, no less than Wright's repeated return to the concern of hunger, suggests that to refer to the autobiography as *American Hunger* is to contribute to a restatement of its thematic priorities, which Wright himself initiated on *Black Boy*'s publication.

But it also reminds us that the title *American Hunger* ascends and then descends—that it pits a familiar patriotism against the political reformism that the presence of malnutrition often provokes. In the manner of Gunnar Myrdal's contemporaneous *American Dilemma* (1944), the title *American Hunger* juxtaposes a form of nationhood intrinsically linked to egalitarianism and the pursuit of happiness with a disruptive and unsettling reminder that, for many, such revolutionary pledges remain unfulfilled. *American Hunger,* by placing malnutrition in such close quarters with an adjective that notoriously inflates national into continental boundaries, combines an image of shrinkage with an almost imperial image of expansion and, in the process, pinpoints the narrative's concerns with material, social, and cultural inequalities. Elements in Wright's original title thus prepare readers for a narrative of protest—for a denunciation of hunger, in all its interrelated cultural, nutritional, and political manifestations.

Yet Wright's autobiography does more than protest hunger. It also *resists* it. Paradoxically, it protests "this hunger of mine" at the same time as it prizes a "hunger for life."[7] That is, the autobiography simultaneously treats malnutrition as a social fact to be denounced and as a galvanizing experience that profitably commits those who endure it to the path of political activism. *American Hunger* freights its denunciation of nutritional want with a valorization of such hunger's propensity to motivate politically the formerly docile. The three parts of this chapter chart this autobiographical progression from protest to resistance, cataloging and interrogating the debilitations as well as the ultimate advantages bound up in Wright's conceptualization of want. It seeks to establish this conceptualization as neither a leitmotif nor a passing concern of the text, but as the pivot on which it turns, as the overarching sensation under which myriad other desires are accommodated. Ultimately, then, this chapter seeks to establish Wright's conceptualization of hunger as the source for other desires, not only for food but also for philosophy, not only for reformism but also for the self-education by which he completed an autobiography henceforth designated *American Hunger.*

Protest

While many scholarly texts published between the wars condemn hunger as one among many aspects of poverty, Richard Wright's oeuvre often consolidates such condemnation by engaging with the actual impact nutritional hunger has upon the body. A tendency to assume that hunger is undesirable without explaining why emerges in the way many of Wright's academic contemporaries refer extensively to malnutrition in their text but not in the indexes of their books. Although the title of Cayton and Drake's survey of segregation and ghettoization in interwar Chicago, *Black Metropolis* (1939), lays claim to scholarly comprehensiveness, its index contains no references to nutritional matters. Indeed, the presence in *Black Metropolis*'s text of "sausage cakes," "bread," "stewed prunes," and other dishes, as noted by Tracey N. Poe, makes the absence in its index of Cooking, Diet, Food, or Nutrition even more startling and interpretable as a refusal to recognize the scholarly importance of such issues. [8] One could make similar remarks about E. Franklin Frazier's *The Negro Family in the United States* (1939) (673–86). By contrast, Wright's oeuvre abounds with representations of meals and of cooking, with inquiries into hunger, and with episodes fraught with dilemmas between physical safety and nutritional satiety. If novels had indexes, Wright's would be stuffed full of page references to nutrition. This is exemplified not only in *American Hunger* but also in *Native Son* (1940), which Wright characterized as an attempt to distill "the emotional and cultural hunger" of American slum experience into the single, nihilistic personality of Bigger Thomas. [9] It is conceivable that *Black Metropolis*, although published scarcely a year earlier than *Native Son,* influenced this rigorous profiling of nutritional and psychological want. At the very least, in his 1945 introduction to the work, Wright acknowledged the links between the texts, paying tribute to Cayton and Drake for picturing "the environment out of which the Bigger Thomases of our nation come." [10] Yet, as the indexical absences of *Black*

Metropolis reveal, the methodological representation of this environment by these social scientists includes far fewer references to food and hunger than does the austere fictionalization it received in *Native Son*. Even when *Black Metropolis* refers to the diet of a population it otherwise exhaustively surveys, the function of the reference remains chiefly metaphoric, as in the following recollection of the onset of the Depression:

> [Before 1929, Chicago's white] papers talked of unending prosperity and were advertising a second World's Fair to celebrate a Century of Progress. But Negroes were a barometer sensitive to the approaching storm. They had reason to fear, while most of the Midwest Metropolis seemed to suspect nothing, that the Fat Years were about to end.
>
> Chicago's banking structure broke at its weakest link—in the Black Belt. In July of 1930, Binga's bank closed its doors, while mobs cried in the streets for their savings. Within a month every bank in Black Metropolis was closed. As white housewives balanced the budget, their Negro servants were often the first casualties. When factories cut production, unskilled Negro labor was usually the first to go. . . . The Depression had come to Midwest Metropolis and Black Metropolis reflected the general disaster. The Lean Years were at hand. (84)

Here Cayton and Drake's decision to cast the transition from boom to bust as one from fat to lean years, even though the latter presents it in nutritional terms, ultimately points mainly to unemployment and only secondarily to the impact it might have on diet. By contrast, *Native Son* is filled with images of dietary want and with the impact hunger has on the mind of Bigger Thomas. Characteristic of *Native Son*'s food imagery is the scene wherein Bigger Thomas, having half-accidentally murdered his white employers' daughter, finds his equally amateurish attempts to extract a ransom obstructed by food's visual promise of imminent physical satisfaction:

> [Bigger Thomas] had strained himself from a too long lack of sleep and food; and the excitement was sapping his energy. He should go to the kitchen and ask for his dinner. Surely, he should not starve like this. . . . On a table were spread several white napkins under which was something that looked like plates of food. . . . There were sliced bread and steak and fried potatoes and gravy and

string beans and spinach and a huge piece of chocolate cake. . . . He rested his black fingers on the edge of the white table and a silent laugh burst from his parted lips as he saw himself for a split second in a lurid objective light: he had killed a rich white girl and had burned her body after cutting her head off . . . and yet he stood here afraid to touch food on the table, food which undoubtedly was his own. (175)

By viscerally intensifying Bigger's conflicting impulses for satiety and for flight, the sensory presence of this tantalizing meal establishes concerns about the disciplinary usefulness of food to which Wright, unlike many contemporary social scientists, consistently returns. The following discussion investigates the ways in which the representations of hunger supplied by Wright's narratives, and in particular by *American Hunger,* intersect with and disrupt those of contemporary methodological analyses of poverty. Notwithstanding the gaps in *Black Metropolis*'s index, this analysis involves more than simply contrasting the formidable presence hunger achieves in Wright's oeuvre with its disappearance from much contemporary scholarship. It also requires us to engage those statements on nutrition issued by contemporary scholars and to clarify the aspects distinguishing them from the imagery Wright employed.

Principal among these differences is the challenge Wright's literary narratives pose to the tendency among many contemporary social scientists to characterize hunger as a byproduct of poverty. Evidence of this causative perspective arises from *Black Metropolis* itself. As the excerpt from that work attests, Cayton and Drake's survey parlayed contemporary assumptions that hunger was symptomatic, was a branch sprouted from the malignant root of economic inequality. Characterizing the fractious transition from boom to bust as one from "Fat" to "Lean Times," Cayton and Drake vividly establish an economic cause—unemployment—which then has a direct effect on the waistbands of those turned away from Chicago's warehouses, packing houses, and factories. Nor does this sequential link proceed from a single economic cause to a single nutritional effect: "Lean Times" clearly refers synecdochically to an economic climate in which African Americans found not just food but everything scarce. While Cayton and Drake's metaphor prioritizes nutritional concerns, it also encompasses many other shortfalls, many other "branches," all of which, as elements within a generalized dispossession, point to the one malignant root of economic poverty. Like so many rashes, spells of dizziness, and bouts of nausea, shortfalls in insurance, healthcare, housing and, explicitly, food function symptomatically as diagnosable signs of a single malaise: poverty.

Despite sharing with *Black Metropolis* a title that announces its scholarly ambition, Gunnar Myrdal's *American Dilemma* refers to nutrition in its index and discusses problems arising from malnutrition in its text. However, while Myrdal's inquiry acknowledges that noneconomic factors can differentiate nutritional intake even when "income is kept constant," it more frequently reiterates the symptomatic conceptualization of hunger underlying Cayton and Drake's analysis. *American Dilemma* characterizes hunger as one among many symptoms of poverty, not just by conceding that "deficiencies in diet . . . [are] highly dependent on income," but by bracketing its discussion of such diet alongside subheadings like "The Family Budget" and "Housing Conditions" in a chapter on money (372–73).

No evidence suggests that Wright considered the causational approach to hunger typified by *Black Metropolis* and *American Dilemma* to be anything other than useful, not to mention necessary. Accordingly, this discussion is not intended as an attack on those postwar social scientists who endorse the causational view embodied, for instance, in the subtitle of Isobel Cole-Hamilton and Tim Lang's *Tightening Belts: A Report on the Impact of Poverty on Food* (1986). It is obvious that, in highly industrialized economies like that of interwar Chicago, hunger all but invariably results from an economic setback. Manifestly, those who sought the alleviation of relief stations and were thus forced into what *American Hunger* terms "a public confession of . . . hunger" had only been brought to such a low following a collapse in income (353).

Justifiable and necessary though these symptomatic conceptualizations are, it is significant that they are rarely reiterated in Wright's oeuvre. What one often encounters instead is a figurative approach that isolates hunger from other symptoms of poverty and, having established it as a "disease" in its own right, engages it as a political condition. Interestingly, this approach can be detected in the aforementioned introduction to *Black Metropolis,* which begins with Wright's memory of how, after his flight from the South to Chicago, he "lived half hungry and afraid" (xvii). This prefatory focus on a word to which the text of *Black Metropolis* only intermittently refers is made explicit as Wright continues:

> Current American thought . . . has quite forgot the reality of the passion and hunger of millions of exploited workers and dissatisfied minorities. . . . Let us disentangle in our minds Hitler's deeds from what Hitler exploited. His deeds were crimes; but the hunger he exploited in the hearts of Europe's millions was a valid hunger and is still there. Indeed, the war has but deepened that hunger, made it more acute. (xxiii–xxv)

Anxieties surrounding totalitarianism, the feeling, expressed by C. L. R. James, that the "German intellectual" before 1933 had been "at much the same stage that the American intellectual is today," here collide with another of Wright's preoccupations—hunger—to propose a new and startling corollary to the black urban experience that Cayton and Drake documented.[11] Wright's references to hunger here remain characteristically ambiguous—it is difficult to establish whether this "valid hunger" is metaphorical or literal, whether it expresses the Nazi ambition of Lebensraum or refers to the actual starvation Germany experienced immediately after World War I. Yet this ambiguity is deliberate. Wright's work continually enlists such ambiguity in its representation of want, not to disrupt the empirical investigations of colleagues in the social sciences, but to advance a new conceptualization equipped to acknowledge the ambiguity existing in the experience of hunger itself. Wright's view of hunger dissolves the clear denominative boundaries separating "actual" hunger such as that afflicting Germany after Versailles from the "metaphoric" hunger motivating Lebensraum; his view reveals that, psychologically, the two are far more mutual and mutable than is often acknowledged in social science practice. Part of this broader, more complicated conceptualization of hunger in all forms emerges from Wright's introduction to *Black Metropolis.* If we place Wright's words in a temporal rather than a textual relationship with Cayton and Drake's work, they become interpretable less as an introduction to the sociological investigation than as a postscript by which Wright voices his responses to it. It is then tempting to speculate that, given Cayton and Drake's failure to incorporate an extended and analytic discussion of nutrition into their text, Wright is actually implicating *Black Metropolis* in his criticism of the significant silences "current American thought" displays on the "passion and hunger" of the "exploited." Whether this is true or not, it is significant that Wright subsequently renews his concentration on hunger, isolates it from other social "symptoms," and almost treats it as *Black Metropolis* treats poverty: as an organizational umbrella under which material shortfalls can be grouped. Similarly, although Wright's "valid hunger" phrase recalls Cayton and Drake's metaphoric use of "Lean Times," his countervailing refusal to anchor this hunger to a specific economic referent releases it from any rigidly causative conceptualization in which it would synecdochically invoke distinct symptomatic shortfalls in housing, insurance, or healthcare. Nor does Wright here conceive hunger as merely a metaphor for political desire: by affirming its reality, validity, venality, and inexorability, he presents a broader, more fluid condition able to accommodate nutritional desires together with those political passions with which they are now blurred. In the process, this new fluidity and breadth remind us that, psychologically, the desire for economic reform and the desire for food might actually resist the compartmentalization that the causative, symptomatic approach of certain social scientists' premises. It reminds us that neither the hungry nor the revolutionary might as efficiently distinguish the perception of political oppression from the experience of malnutrition—that, within such "exploited" personalities, reformism and hunger may overlap and, as mutable desires, coalesce to become as inseparable as yeast and flour in dough.

In his "Black Studies and the Contemporary Student" (1969), C. L. R. James recounted a dinner in France that Richard Wright, who "fancied himself as a bit of a cook," prepared "in some Southern way." Before this African American meal commenced, James received a guided tour of his host's temporary European home. Pausing before some bookshelves, Wright declared to his fellow writer: "Look here, Nello, you see those books there? They are by Kierkegaard. . . . I want to tell you something.

Everything that he writes about in these books, I knew before I had them." Having reported the remark, James insists that Wright intended it, not egotistically, but to attribute intellectual foresight to African Americans in general. Understanding Wright in social terms, James concludes: "What he was telling me was that he was a black man in the United States and that gave him an insight into what today is the universal opinion and attitude of the modern personality." [12] Interpreting the anecdote in *Black Atlantic* (1993), Paul Gilroy confirms this view, noting that "Wright's apparently intuitive foreknowledge of the issues raised by Kierkegaard was not intuitive at all. It was an elementary product of his historical experiences as a black growing up in the United States between the wars." [13]

In some ways, *Black Metropolis*'s introduction itself demonstrates the "insight" into modernity Wright's comments on Kierkegaard assign to much African American cultural production. Similar to James's and Gilroy's suggestion that American racial hierarchies foreshadowed elements Kierkegaard explored, this introduction's representation of a hunger bound by these hierarchies foreshadows directions in Western intellectualism after the war. In particular, by resisting Cayton and Drake's causative approach, Wright's introduction to *Black Metropolis* constructs a rich and sustainable affinity with Raymond Williams's research in the 1970s. His tacit subversion of foregoing efforts to separate the desire for food from the desire for political change exemplify Williams's insistence in *Marxism and Literature* (1977) that "[p]ractical consciousness is almost always different from official consciousness" (130). Rejecting the "handling of fixed forms and units" that *Marxism and Literature* assigns to "official" thinking, Wright embraces political and nutritional desires as mutable facets within an overarching hunger, thus anticipating Williams's emphasis on "what is actively being lived, and not only [on] what it is thought is being lived" (130–31).

American Hunger substantiates these interconnections. Describing the days immediately following his flight to Chicago, Wright recalls that he "hungered for a grasp of the framework of contemporary living, for a knowledge of the forms of life about me, for eyes to see the bony structures of personality" (334). Such terms virtually paraphrase those by which *Marxism and Literature* sets out what Edward Said terms the "seminal phrase 'structures of feeling.' " [14] Almost uncannily they call to mind Williams's advocacy of a new intellectual engagement with "meanings and values as they are actually lived and felt" (130–32). Nor are *Marxism and Literature*'s "structures of feeling" and *American Hunger*'s "structures of personality" only comparable semantically but also because both recommend lived experience as the ideal guide for future intellectual engagements. Nor is it accidental that Wright's autobiography articulates its version of this call using the language of hunger. Even before its 1991 restoration, Wright's original title, *American Hunger*, burnished his "official" autobiography palimpsestically, reemerging in smuggled references to his concern with "the plight of the Negro in America" as a whole rather than in part (321). Despite the renaming of the autobiography, the trope of hunger remains central to the narrative. Throughout the book, Wright imbues the condition of hunger with a certain determinism: his very "consciousness" is "riveted upon obtaining a loaf of bread" (274); he asserts that "I lived on what I did not eat" (161); he describes hunger as "my daily companion" (307). Constantly positioning hunger as an omnipresent experience, the autobiography shapes from it a lens through which the living, moving world is filtered—a lens that exerts such influence on Wright's perception as to qualify under Williams's "structure of feeling" designation.

In turn, the differences between the representation of hunger by certain social scientists and by Wright crystallize. On one hand, scholarly texts published by Democrats, liberals, or socialists in the Depression and New Deal eras often imply that American capitalism, which produces many intolerable conditions for its victims, is in urgent need of reform. Wright, however, collapses the economic fulcrum within this construction, concentrating its terms, to establish an equivalency between the desire for bread and the desire for political change. Hunger, in Wright's oeuvre, *is* reformism: it *is* radicalism; if exploited with Machiavellian intelligence, it can even become the totalitarianism that, in its fascist and Stalinist forms, preoccupies much of his autobiography.

One might say that this treatment of hunger, far from realizing a "structure of feeling," merely manifests a rhetorical conceit designed to blur meaningful distinctions between income and nutrition in order to capture a particular political temperament. Such an interpretation is bolstered by the fact that Wright's trade was in the imaginative use of language, whereas Cayton and Drake's lay in its uses as an analytic tool. Wright's autobiography, however, offers evidence that his representation of hunger results from more than mere aesthetic considerations, for it dramatizes the uses underfeeding offers to social authorities wanting to force the potentially troublesome into acquiescence. This dramatization of hunger as a disciplinary tool first emerges in the autobiography's opening pages, which recount childhood experiences when Wright knew that he was hungry but did not yet know that he was poor. Wright uses childhood naivete in these pages to reverse the cause-and-effect sequence that informs much contemporary scholarly writing on hunger. This reversal establishes hunger instead as a foundation on which a postponed yet inevitable realization of poverty can be constructed. This, in turn, allows *American Hunger* to position nutritional want, not as an "incidental" symptom of poverty, but as a condition, as a disease in its own right that exerts pressures and sets limits to maintain social acquiescence.

During these childhood years, Wright admits, "I was not aware of what hunger really meant" (16)—was not yet cognizant either of its potential for enforcing subordination or of its profundity as a perspective filter for an emergent "structure of feeling." Yet although hunger resists explanation, and although it remains a "cloudy notion," the young Wright nevertheless recognizes it as a guide to his initial encounters with white-dominated social authorities and institutions (10). The privileges of white Americans, which Wright later denounces in extensively analytical terms, are first forced into his consciousness because of their unexplained access to an unimaginable supply of food. Mystification mixes with an inarticulate sense of injustice as Wright recalls that, if his mother's white employers "left anything, my brother and I would eat well; but if they did not, we would have our usual bread and tea. Watching the white people eat would make my empty stomach churn and I would grow vaguely angry" (22). Even Wright's attitude to the black church is shaped by anger born of this vague and as yet unstructured hunger. Preachers—whom *American Hunger* later denounces in an extensive and sophisticated diatribe—are not at first condemned due to problems of faith or dogma, but because these representatives on earth are gourmands:

> In the center of the table was a huge platter of golden-brown fried chicken. I compared the bowl of soup that sat before me with the crispy chicken and decided in favor of the chicken. . . .
>
>   "Eat your soup," my mother said.
>
>   "I don't want any," I said. . . .
>
>   The preacher had finished his soup and had asked that the platter of chicken be passed to him. It galled me. He smiled, cocked his head this way and that, picking out choice pieces. I forced a spoonful of soup down my throat and looked to see if my speed matched that of the preacher. It did not. . . .
>
>   As piece after piece of chicken was taken, I was unable to eat my soup at all. I grew hot with anger. The preacher was laughing and joking and the grownups were hanging on his words. My growing hate of the preacher finally became more important than God or religion and I could no longer contain myself. I . . . screamed, running blindly from the room.
>
>   "That preacher's going to eat *all* the chicken!" I bawled. (30–31)

Thus, years before he adopted Marxism and decades before he embraced existentialism, Wright was converted to the atheism that customarily accompanies these philosophical ideologies by hunger and hunger alone. The complex and extensive analyses by which Wright elsewhere condemns white southerners and black preachers are prefigured in this sequence of his autobiography by the accusation that neither group intervened to assuage his hunger.

Following this scene, *American Hunger* details those years of late childhood when the mental and physical deterioration of Wright's mother stripped his family life of the small semblance of security it once possessed. Chronicling his relatives' failed attempts to keep him within the family circle, Wright turns to the representation of what he calls a Methodist "orphan home" in Memphis. The fact that Wright, unlike Oliver Twist and Jane Eyre, knows his parents survive but still must be designated an orphan in order to qualify for state guardianship prime the narrative for a representation saturated in earlier portrayals of institutional life.

The orphan home was a two-story frame building set amid trees in a wide, green field. . . .

The house was crowded with children and there was always a storm of noise. The daily routine was blurred to me and I never quite grasped it. The most abiding feeling I had each day was hunger and fear. The meals were skimpy and there were only two of them. Just before we went to bed each night we were given a slice of bread smeared with molasses. The children were silent, hostile, vindictive, continuously complaining of hunger. There was an over-all atmosphere of nervousness and intrigue, of children telling tales upon others, of children being deprived of food to punish them. . . .

Each morning after we had eaten a breakfast that seemed like no breakfast at all, an older child would lead a herd of us to the vast lawn and we would get to our knees and wrench the grass loose from the dirt with our fingers. . . . Many mornings I was too weak from hunger to pull out the grass; I would grow dizzy and my mind would become blank. (33–34)

In its Puritanical atmosphere, which actively intensifies and exploits the guilt orphans are expected to feel about their orphanhood, *American Hunger*'s Memphis institution recalls Lowood House in Charlotte Brontë's *Jane Eyre* (1847) as well as the "branch-workhouse" that introduces Charles Dickens's *Oliver Twist* (1837–39).[15] Implicitly, by alluding to British representations issued from the early phase of what Michel Foucault termed the Great Confinement, *American Hunger*'s orphanage scene effects a necessary racial complication that emphasizes the disproportionate presence African Americans assume within this imprisoning movement's later cycles in the United States. This scene effectively links the class dynamics of the utilitarian workhouse with the class and race dynamics of the state penitentiary because it is set in the pre–World War I period, which Rayford Logan identified as "the nadir of the Negro's status in American society."[16] In *The Betrayal of the Negro* (1954), Logan notes that this period witnessed state disfranchisement of African Americans, both constitutionally and by stealth; an escalation in lynchings; record KKK membership; and the consolidation both of segregation and of racial stereotyping. In short, *The Betrayal of the Negro* summons the society of Wright's youth, which was dedicated to preserving, often by violent means, the essentialist hierarchies it had inherited from slavery.

Of these tools of control, the distribution of food occupies the foreground of Wright's orphanage scene. Wright and his fellow inmates "continuously complain of hunger": the "most abiding feeling I had each day was hunger"; hunger so debilitates Wright, he cannot wrench grass from the ground. Obviously, any attempt to attribute this hunger to a disciplinary tool must first negotiate the possibility that it merely arises from a financial shortage—that it is merely a symptom of institutional poverty. It is, however, significant that such financial restrictions remain unmentioned in *American Hunger* as they are in *Oliver Twist,* which describes the utilitarian regime by which orphans "got thin" as being "rather expensive, . . . [owing to the] necessity of taking in the clothes of all the paupers" (55).

Wright's refusal to explain institutional hunger financially, because it implies that malnutrition is intentional rather than symptomatic, also buttresses the ideological foundations upon which Zora Neale Hurston builds her Eatonville utopia in *Their Eyes Were Watching God.* That is to say, the absence of financial considerations in *American Hunger* confirms Hurston's implication that, given the Edenic abundance of the American harvest, African American malnutrition is neither incidental nor inevitable but an intentional result of racial inequality. What *Their Eyes Were Watching God* achieves via the positive representations of Eatonville—an African American community from which an intertwined white racism and black hunger have been expelled—*American Hunger* thus confirms by protesting an orphanage wherein malnutrition is shown to be no less solvable and unnecessary.

In the course of this denunciatory exposure, *American Hunger*'s accumulating references not only isolate and engage with hunger as a condition in its own right. They also show this isolation to result from something other than a merely aesthetic motivation. They reveal the autobiography's isolation of hunger to be a verisimilar representation of an isolation first initiated by an orphanage regime eager to enlist such want in its imposition of acquiescence. They suggest, in other words, that this prioritization of hunger over poverty results, not from a rhetorical conceit, but from Wright's realist ambition to capture the principal position nutrition occupied in his early experiences.

Let us return to the key phrase "Great Confinement" and to Foucault's empathetic commitment to those subjected to the "institutions of repression, rejection, exclusion, marginalization . . . that permit the fabrication of the disciplinary individual."[17] In another manifestation of the insight James and Gilroy interpret from Wright's remarks on Kierkegaard, *American Hunger*'s orphanage scene anticipates Foucault's concerns with the limitations institutionalization places on individual free will. *American Hunger*—which elsewhere identifies Wright's "need" to "use words to create religious types, criminal types, the warped, the lost, the baffled" (334)—engages with the archive of "marginalization" that Foucault explores in *Discipline and Punish* (1975). Moreover, this interest in the treatment of the socially marginal by the socially authoritative extends, in *American Hunger* and *Discipline and Punish* alike, to the institutional segregation of inmates both into cells and into fixed timetables. What *American Hunger* signals through repetitious phrasing—hunger abides "each day," molasses is served "each night," and grass is uprooted "each morning"—is a "daily routine" that, in *Discipline and Punish*'s terms, regulates "the relations of time, bodies and forces" (157). One insight of *Discipline and Punish* is that such temporal and spatial segregation increases institutional authorities' ability to withhold and to grant, to mete out punishments and to dole out rewards, to turn "need" into "a political instrument meticulously prepared, calculated and used" (26). Punishment, Foucault suggests, thus becomes "only one element of a double-system: gratification-punishment." This "double-system" secures acquiescence by defining "behaviour and performance on the basis of the two opposed values of good and evil." Foucault's identification of this institutional "circulation" both of "debits" and of "awards" reminds us that inmates' desires can be manipulated as profitably as their fears—that beatings, deprivations, isolation, and humiliations can all produce acquiescence, but so can bribery (180–81).

Because it determines who will be fed and who will not, however, the distribution of food that the Memphis orphanage enforces is also a distribution of hunger. It, too, is a "circulation" that, by simultaneously parading food's presence as an "award" and threatening food's absence as a "debit," meets both polarities delineated by Foucault's "double-system" of "gratification-punishment." Further, this "circulation" is intensified because the "debit" of hunger, which can be defined as a desire that solicits its own cessation, inordinately increases the appeal of food's "award." Children are punished by a distribution of hunger—they are "deprived of food to punish them"—yet they are also bribed into submission by the mutual counterweight of hunger's promised termination, which perhaps tempts inmates into "telling tales upon others." Functioning complementarily as threat and as promise, the oppositional yet interdependent distributions of hunger and food thus enable the institution to resolve in its favor disputes, and rebellions, securing a regimented, disciplined tranquillity.

Given that food and hunger thus unite into this institutionally useful double system of "punishment-gratification," it is unsurprising that Wright should charge the orphanage authorities with attempting to maximize their inmates' feelings of appetite. Certainly, it seems significant that, like Oliver Twist, Richard Wright is *underfed* rather than *unfed*. Wright *is* given food—he is not simply being starved to death. But it is possible that the orphanage regime actually maximizes Wright's appetite via the very paltriness of the food it promises, via the very inadequacy of the meals it awards. Literary and academic evidence suggests that the rationing of Wright's orphanage intensifies appetite more effectively than any other dietary regime. Oliver Twist, after all, grows "voracious and wild with hunger" because he is being subjected to the "tortures of slow starvation" rather than to starvation outright (56). In his investigation of the short-term effects of hunger, the biopsychologist Andrew John Hill suggests:

> It is generally recognised that for those people who totally abstain from eating, the feeling of hunger disappears in a matter of days. . . . On the other hand, hunger is a constant presence when people are only semi-starved. . . . The desire . . . to redress the energy deficit spills over into daily life and for some people becomes the central feature of their interest. It is apparent that satiety is a state never achieved in these circumstances.[18]

Hill's remarks suggest that "a breakfast that felt like no breakfast at all" optimizes Wright's psychological desire for food far more efficiently than would a breakfast that *was* "no breakfast at all." Because this morning meal seems to vaporize before Wright's eyes, postponing indefinitely the satiety it visually promises, it simultaneously revitalizes this promise, reinvigorating the potent memory of adequate nutrition.

Nor does Wright's dismay at these institutional meals result only from their paucity but also from the character of the social ceremony framing them. Between the meals that *American Hunger* depicts both inside and outside the Memphis orphanage, there exists a fragile unity, a concatenation in the deployment of ritualistic detail and the use of peripheral material. These meals incorporate the same saying of grace, the same tables, chairs, cutlery, and crockery; they draw the same veil of silence across the table at the moment of the food's arrival. "Granny said that talking while eating was sinful," Wright observes of one such family meal. "God might make the food choke you" (165–66). The duplication of this fearful silence, the saying of grace, and the echoes of the institutional "dishes rattling"—these microscopic effects conspire to cast the shadow of a Sunday or holiday family dinner across the institutional table (36). The intruding shadow is a point of comparison: it reminds inmates of what they are missing, of the memory of prandial satisfaction, of an idealization of the family table as the font of both food and nurturing love. Yet one can also see it as a kind of mirror, because it generates an illusion of substance that is shattered the moment its viewers reach out to touch it. This moment, when the knife strikes the plate, imbues these meals with their strange, paradoxical duality, wherein they remain what they nominally are—breakfast—at the same time as they achieve their own negation as "no breakfast at all."

Consequently, useful though brief spells of starvation may be, it is *underfeeding*—the slow drip of routine rationing—that most successfully keeps inmates' hunger alive and with it food's venal potential. As a material within a "circulation" of nutrition, foods are thus, as Foucault suggests, "meticulously prepared" and "calculated" to produce a diet precisely sufficient to prevent outright starvation, yet precisely insufficient to assuage malnutrition. These evaporating meals, ostensibly fulfilling yet actually reneging on the promise of satiety, promote the hunger that they allegedly abolish, prompting Wright, like Twist, to ask for more.

Since underfeeding rather than outright starvation guarantees hunger's omnipresence as an "abiding feeling," molasses, as the only food specified in the orphanage scene, can be seen as a kind of prison guard that locks Wright inside his "cell" of nutritional desire. Molasses is certainly well equipped for this role, for three interrelated reasons. First, like the equally calorific white sugar from which it is separated during sugar-cane processing, molasses produces an intense rush of energy that rapidly induces a craving for more. Molasses concentrates the mind on hunger, especially so in those children who, like Wright, depend on it as their only source of the nutrition they need for bodily growth.

Even more significant, however, molasses is bound up with the economic histories of U.S. and Caribbean slavery—is as deeply steeped in these histories as cotton and tobacco. Both the gathering of cane from the fields and its pulping in the sugar refineries were duties historically delegated to slaves and later to descendants of slaves such as C. L. R. James's "pan-boiler" grandfather; both were crippling, arduous forms of work.[19] Indeed, if Ntozake Shange has persuasively characterized cane picking as "torturous labor" that callused the hands and ruined the spine, then W. L. Mathieson's 1926 history, *British Slavery and Its Abolition*, equally convincingly characterizes sugar refinement as "the most onerous of West Indian industries."[20] In sugar refineries during slavery and the sharecropping era, pulped cane was treated in the boiling house and then transferred to the cooling room, or purgery, where it would be held "in hogsheads . . . over a cistern into which the molasses dripped."[21] From this slow separation, two useful commodities resulted: refined crystallized sugar and blackstrap molasses. The first of these was white, expensive, and destined for Europe and North America, while the second was dark, viscous, cheap, and destined for less prestigious markets. Although some of the molasses was distributed to rum plants, most was typically reserved and introduced into domestic circulation on the plantation itself. Apparent in the development of this binary distribution was what we might term an essentialization of the sweetener, which valued the whiteness and expense of refined sugar as signs of its innate superiority, and the darkness and cheapness of molasses as testimony to its equally intrinsic inferiority. Rumors about the distribution of adulterated molasses, of molasses that had been bleached by "the addition of lime, chalk, gypsum, plaster of paris, or any white material" to look like refined sugar, abounded in Britain and the United States during slavery and the sharecropping era; these periodic bursts of hysteria confirmed the contemporary white belief that the darkness or lightness of sweeteners betokened their respective positions on a fixed hierarchy of color.[22] Yet this fixed hierarchy also clearly mirrored a hierarchy of race; molasses, its cheapness attributed to innate inferiority rather than to entrenched cultural connotations, was fed to slaves in order to persuade them, too, that their social inferiority was neither designated nor imposed but natural. Booker T. Washington's *Up from Slavery* (1901) recounts how he looked forward to the distribution of molasses "once a week from the 'big house' "; Washington confirms that this food was involved in a racialized culinary relationship by noting that only "the whites had been accustomed to use" sugar.[23] Moreover, the racialized relationship between white sugar and brown molasses that *Up from Slavery* confirms is far from unique. Divisions imposed by sugar refinement resemble, for instance, the divisions that pork butchery more forcefully imposes on pig carcasses, as it produces binary relationships between pork chops and chitterlings, between bacon and pig feet, which can be classified according to a price hierarchy similar to the one that relegates molasses beneath sugar. Nor should the fact that sugar refinement is often reduced to a chemical process and pork butchery to a biological one mislead us into thinking there is something natural or innate about these price hierarchies. While we may share cultural preferences for sugar or bacon, we must always view these preferences as socially constructed forms of evaluation. Washington's assertion that molasses was "much more enjoyable to me than [was] a fourteen-course dinner," like Bessie Smith's demand for a "pig foot and a bottle of beer," must thus be seen as radical disruptions of demarcating binary relationships—should be seen, in Ntozake Shange's phrase, less as "arbitrary predilections of the 'nigra' [than as] . . . symbolic defiance."[24]

Nonetheless, *American Hunger*'s orphanage scene by no means reassesses molasses in the radical manner of *Up from Slavery*. If Washington's assertion questions why molasses should be thought inferior, Wright's orphanage scene questions why he should be fed something thought inferior. This distinction brings us to the third factor that qualifies molasses for its corporal role in *American Hunger*'s orphanage scene, a factor that lies in its traditional use as animal feed. The historical use of molasses in animal husbandry is reflected in the Victorian guide for British children, *Sugar; How it Grows, and How it is Made* (1844), which intersperses its illustrations of happy, healthy colonial laborers with observations that, for example, in the Caribbean, "tender fresh canes are also used after being crushed in the mills, as food for the horses and cattle."[25] These uses continued after the Second World War, as confirmed by the memory of "silage ricks fed with molasses" that introduces Raymond Williams's *The Country and the City* (1973) and by the food scientists Neil Pennington and Charles Baker's classification of "blackstrap" molasses as "cattle feed."[26] Not only *was* molasses frequently distributed to the poorer populations of the southern states: it *is* frequently distributed to cattle throughout the West. This practice in itself invites us to interpret the molasses that so thinly coats Wright's evening bread as the digestible agent, not only of inferiority, but of what Paul Gilroy terms "infrahumanity."[27] It suggests that the racialized relationship between molasses and sugar that *Up from Slavery* sketches, by subordinating blackness to whiteness, actually inflates this latter polarity into a new and exclusive equivalence with humanity able to animalize insidiously its darker binary opposite. *American Hunger*'s juxtaposition of molasses and the animalization encapsulated in its references to "herding" also recall the characterization in William Faulkner's "The Bear" (1942) of the white, poor, and vulgar Boon, whose red face, as he bestially consumes "popcorn-and-molasses," looks "more and more like he should never have brought it out of the woods."[28] Such animalizing capacities of molasses mean that, by nominating the food as the corporal custodian of hunger, Wright's institutional authorities can unsettle their inmates' self-image as humans and, in the process, prime them for the bovine activities at the end of *American Hunger*'s orphanage scene. In this concluding image Wright describes how he and his fellow orphans are forced out onto "the vast lawn" and then to "get to our knees and [to] wrench the grass loose from the dirt with our fingers. . . . I would grow dizzy and my mind would become blank." Wright and his fellow orphans involuntarily embody a compromised and contorted infrahumanity presaged in their consumption of cattle feed. This startling image, which implies that the molasses being processed in Wright's stomach will soon be joined by clumps of indigestible grass, vividly recalls Dee Brown's report of the behavior of white trader Andrew Myrick, who, when confronted with the hunger of the Sioux, paraphrased Marie Antoinette's alleged remark and said: "Let them eat grass."[29] For Wright and his fellow "orphans"—who are forced to join a "herd," to sink to their "knees," and to make their minds bestially "blank"—are similarly expected to submit to caricature, to assume, metaphorically, a quadruped shape. As Wright's autobiographical account recalls Myrick's invocation of buffalo, so its characters' enlistment into a dehumanizing performance also echoes the animalizing imagery that punctuates *Narrative of the Life of Frederick Douglass* (1845) and its descriptions of slave auctions, slaves' "feeding," and punishments. In Wright's Memphis orphanage obtains a racialized definition of humanity that remains comparable to the slave auction described by Douglass, wherein "old and young, married and single, were ranked with horses, sheep, and swine. There were horses and men, cattle and women, pigs and children, all holding the same rank in the scale of being, and were all subjected to the same narrow examination" (27). Such dehumanization reaches an extreme as Douglass recalls the manner in which slave children were fed:

> Our food was coarse corn meal boiled. This was called *mush*. It was put into a large wooden tray or trough, and set down upon the ground. The children were then called, like so many pigs, and like so many pigs they would come and devour the mush; some with oyster-shells, others with pieces of shingle, some with naked hands, and none with spoons. He that ate fastest got most; he that was strongest secured the best place; and few left the trough satisfied. (16)

American Hunger's orphanage scene must be cast against this dismal historical background. By creating another institutionalized environment in which slave children, having "been worked," were forced to do without human comforts like chairs and cutlery in order to gain sustenance, Douglass vividly prefigures the outrageous animalization implied in the grass-cutting duties enforced by Wright's Memphis orphanage. Just as Henry Louis Gates argues that the dehumanizing imagery of Douglass's autobiography highlights the brutality of slaveholding ideology, thus negating "those very values on which it is built," so the animalization of *American Hunger*'s institution counterproductively corrodes the human validity of those who cling to racial thinking.[30] In both texts, animalization ultimately animalizes those who attempt to implement it. It questions the personalities of those who claim to belong to a supreme race. It makes pigs and cows seem preferable to those human beings who seek to reduce other humans to their barbaric level. Finally, it reanimates the intertwined etymologies of "cattle" and "chattel," drawing these words back to their common root, equating, at last, the orphan institution with the "peculiar institution" of slavery.

These slices of "bread smeared with molasses," then, not only consolidate the authority of the orphanage because of their calorific quality and inadequate quantity. They also mirror racial binary relationships influencing the social hierarchies prevailing in the external world of the United States as a whole. As a foodstuff involved in a binary relationship with a designated "superior," molasses introduces Wright to the broader, racialized role in which Jim Crow has already cast him. Fetishizing and branding inferior the brown food that he consumes, the Memphis orphanage forces Wright to face the mirror and fetishize his skin—to see himself in essentialist terms, as a boy whose blackness is to whiteness as molasses is to sugar. Constructing race through the consumption of a dark substance posited against a white opposite deemed superior, these molasses sandwiches thus contribute to what Doris Witt terms African American cookery's capacity to function as a "site of interracial struggle over the regulation of . . . blackness." In its relationship with normative and nominally refined white sugar, molasses bears comparison with that "social order [in which] hog bowels are overdetermined to be both fetishized and abjected." Routinely fed to animals, molasses thus numbers alongside chitterlings as an item that "transgresses the boundaries between food and excrement . . . through which privileged identities such as whiteness, masculinity and heterosexuality are maintained."[31]

Via its orphanage scene, then, Wright's autobiography demonstrates that hunger can be imposed as a way of subordinating African Americans to a racial hierarchy that designates them inferior. It shows that hunger is more than a mere symptom that arises, as though incidentally, from poverty. It is instead a tool of the economy of propaganda and psychological manipulation dedicated to preserving the racial foundations upon which national American culture is built.

As I have suggested, the significance of Wright's elevation of hunger into a "structure of feeling" is not that it discredits but that it complements the causative approach adopted by the social sciences with its emphasis on lived experience. Differences between Wright's approach and that of contemporary social scientists amount less to an ideological distinction than to subtler variations in rhetorical emphasis. Wright interrogates hunger as a vital sensory experience, dissecting the impact it has on individual free will, the pressures it can exert, the limits it can impose. This rigorous and analytical protest against hunger, by vividly dramatizing the psychological and physical debilitations resulting from malnutrition, assists contemporary social scientists' economic analyses because it explains exactly why the hunger they assume to be undesirable *is* undesirable. Thus, ostensible discrepancies between the social science approach and that adopted in Wright's oeuvre lead to an ultimate agreement on the urgent need for hunger's cessation. Wright simply reaches this ideological destination via a radical route, via an iconoclastic view that sees poverty as symptomatic of that "structure of feeling" that the social sciences term the "disease" of hunger.

From Protest to Resistance

By segregating inmates, by threatening food's absence and promising food's presence, and by supplying an inadequate diet of molasses and other nutritionally insufficient foods, *American Hunger*'s orphanage regime imposes a contract that punishes insubordination with hunger, awards acquiescence with food, and regulates behavior in general through a distribution of nutrition. Subsequent episodes in Wright's autobiography extend this disciplinary food contract beyond the walls of the Memphis orphanage. They establish hunger as what Wright's *Twelve Million*

Black Voices (1944) terms the automatic "punishment if we violate the laws" throughout the United States (64).

Presenting the food contract with national dimensions in the process necessitates a readmission of those economic aspects about which the orphanage scene remains silent. Wright reconsiders financial factors omitted in this scene as he describes his entry into a society in which wages complicate and mediate the direct equation that the orphanage constructed between behavior and nutrition. Even as he acknowledges these factors, however, Wright continues to resist conceptualizing hunger as symptomatic of poverty. Despite Wright's disenchantment with Communism, *American Hunger* retains the fundamentally Marxist view that the capitalist economy in general merely manifests and exacerbates preexisting social stratification and that money in particular merely functions as exchangeable value. Reiterating *Capital*'s position that, even when currency takes the form of gold, "commodities" remain the truly "precious metals," Wright engages with income only insofar as it can provide him with the means of subsistence, with what Marx terms "natural wants, such as food." [32] Unaffected by the fetishism of commodities, by the translation of objects into sellable and purchasable commodities, which enabled Olaudah Equiano to reestablish his freedom, Wright limits the terms of his economic involvement to those of food. "Frantically . . . [converting] all of [his] spare money into food," Wright conceives his wages as a mere means to an end and, by extension, as a mere intermediary of a food contract whose primary equation between behavior and nutrition is now modified but remains essentially intact (327). Realizing currency's value only in terms of its ability to answer his physical needs, Wright observes: "I felt that pork chops were a fundamental item in life, but I preferred that someone else chart their rise and fall in price" (423). The combined nutritional prioritization and economic effacement of this characteristic statement reveal that Wright remains bound in a food contract that, although complicated by the intervention of the economy, repeats disciplinary strategies first encountered in the money-free world of the institution.

What these consistencies between the institutional and the national imply is that life has been debased on either side of the orphanage walls—

that the ambitions of African Americans have everywhere been forcibly reduced to the vulgar materialism of "the culture that condemns" them (321). *American Hunger* protests a situation wherein African Americans who submit or pretend to submit to an infrahuman servility, like those orphans who figuratively kept their noses clean by literally thrusting them into the "lawn outside," secure neither financial security nor cultural uplift but the vulgar reward of food. Throughout the United States, *American Hunger* suggests, the credits and debits of a national food contract degrade conformity and misbehavior alike to a level where civilization and education are relegated beneath a nutritional distribution calculated to treat humans and machines similarly. Thus, *Twelve Million Black Voices* insists that, much as Marx's proletarian laborer was given food "as to a mere means of production," white landowners and overseers considered "black bodies" to be "good tools that had to be kept efficient for toil."[33]

That the Memphis institution is a kind of disciplinary gateway that introduces neglected children into an ultimately national food contract is highlighted by *American Hunger*'s account of Wright's failed escape:

> The dinner bell rang and I did not go to the table, but hid in a corner of the hallway. When I heard the dishes rattling at the table, I opened the door and ran down the walk to the street. Dusk was falling. Doubt made me stop. Ought I go back? No; hunger was back there, and fear. . . . Where was I going? I did not know. The farther I walked the more frantic I became. In a confused and vague way I knew that I was doing more running *away* from than running *toward* something. I stopped. The streets seemed dangerous. . . .
>
> I stood in the middle of the sidewalk and cried. A "white" policeman came to me and I wondered if he was going to beat me. He asked me what was the matter and I told him that I was trying to find my mother. His "white" face created a new fear in me. (36–37)

These sentences specifically style Wright's attempted flight as one "*away* from" from the orphanage's "dinner bell," the chiming of which resounds in Wright's mind no matter how far he removes himself from its source. *American Hunger* thus substantiates its anticipatory interconnections with Foucault's critique of institutionalization further, centering on what *Discipline and Punish* terms that "precise system of command" by which "the activity of the disciplined individual must be punctuated and sustained by injunctions whose efficacy rests on brevity and clarity." As a signal that neither explains nor adjusts its external circumstances, the monosyllabic bell of *American Hunger*'s orphanage kitchen acts in a manner identical to Foucault's "system of command," which "triggers off the required behaviour and that is enough."[34] The effects of this bell are twofold and hasten the orphanage's animalization of its inmates while at the same time reminding them of this institution's disciplinary debt to slavery. Even as it enforces the debasement incarnated in the institution's distribution of fodder in the form of molasses, this bell also echoes Frederick Douglass's memory, recalled in his *Narrative of the Life,* of the "horn" that "was blown . . . [to recall slaves] from the field to the house for breakfast."[35] And, of course, the "correct response" stimulated by this "dinner bell" and "horn"—to prompt orphans and slaves, respectively, to herd together for food—then constructs a third echo, with Pavlov's bell, which corroborates yet further the allegation of animalization. In fact, the Pavlovian echo of this dinner bell specifies the allegation, revealing that the orphanage authorities intend to adjust their inmates to the characteristic behavior not of *all* animals but of tamable animals like cows and dogs. As Paul Gilroy reminds us, a "dog is not a fox, a lion, a rabbit, or a signifyin' monkey"—nor, it might be added, is a cow.[36] Unlike Brer Rabbit, a food forager extraordinaire whose thefts are discussed in the next chapter, neither dogs nor cows hunt independently; they are, instead, fed from bowls and troughs. Both are as dependent upon the sustenance of their human owners as the inmates of *American Hunger*'s orphanage are upon rations. Both are servants to human needs. Tamed, obedient, industrious, and cheap, these useful animals act as a guide to the infrahuman automation wherein, *Twelve Million Black Voices* suggests, "black bodies" become "tools."

On one level, then, this Pavlovian dinner bell completes the self-negation of food that *American Hunger* has already signaled through its references to a "breakfast that felt like no breakfast at all." By tolling for a meal Wright equates with "hunger" and "fear," it confirms that both malnutrition and malnutrition's solution here coalesce into a system of "gratification-punishment" far more involved and complex than the discrete "good" and "bad" polarities that *Discipline and Punish* imagined. On another level, however, the fluid duality of this Pavlovian bell uncannily yet fittingly equips the escaped Wright's hearing with an optimized canine range that forces him to hear it tolling for hunger even after it is out of human earshot. In the process, this particularly malicious "call of the kitchen" (to borrow Era Bell Thompson's phrase) reveals that, for Wright, it is far easier to escape the physical boundaries of the orphanage than the hunger it has manufactured within him.[37] The hunger emanating from this institutional regime remains a call to which, long after it has disappeared from view, Wright must in some way respond. Like a cellmate to whom he has been handcuffed, hunger is an unwanted accomplice to the breakout, which finally leads into the disciplinary embrace of a policeman whose "white" race is revealed, courtesy of the enclosing quotation marks, as no less negotiable than Wright's alleged infrahumanity.

If hunger's collaboration in Wright's breakout and recapture establish the national dimensions of the food contract, these dimensions are confirmed by textual interconnections that *American Hunger* later constructs between the orphanage and Wright's attempts to gain service work. One such interconnection emerges from a scene depicting Wright's first white employer:

I was sweating. I swept the front walk and ran to the store to shop. When I returned the woman said:

"Your breakfast is in the kitchen."

"Thank you, ma'am."

I saw a plate of thick, black molasses and a hunk of white bread on the table. Would I get no more than this? They had had eggs, bacon, coffee. . . . I picked up the bread and tried to break it; it was stale and hard. Well, I would drink the molasses. I lifted the plate and brought it to my lips and saw floating on the surface of the black liquid green and white bits of mold. Goddamn. . . . I can't eat this, I told myself. . . . The woman came into the kitchen as I was putting on my coat.

"You didn't eat," she said. . . .

"Well, I just wasn't hungry this morning, ma'am," I lied. . . .

"You don't like molasses and bread," she said dramatically. . . . "I don't know what's happening to you niggers nowadays," she sighed, wagging her head. She looked closely at the molasses. (172–73)

Most of the interconnections between this scene and *American Hunger*'s representation of the Memphis orphanage flow from the reappearance, here, of molasses and bread. By itself, the reappearance of this singularly unappetizing meal connects the world of the labor market to the world of the orphanage, revealing that paid work, for Wright, amounts to little more than a means of maintaining a subsistence level first endured in state care. These interconnections are elaborated by the figurations with which *American Hunger* surrounds its representation of this nauseatingly viscous, neither solid nor liquid meal. They are sustained, for instance, because the designated destination of this molasses—the mouth of an African American servant—confirms its status within dominant white culture as inferior food suitable only as highly calorific "fuel" for laborers or animals. *Up from Slavery*'s binary relationship between sugar and molasses is, meanwhile, enlisted here within a broader yet equally racialized opposition, as, for reasons we have already noted, molasses actively increases a hunger that is then manipulated by Wright's sensory perception of designated "white" foods like "eggs, bacon, coffee." That this and the orphanage's distribution of molasses to African Americans both aim to consolidate social hierarchies is further substantiated by the fact that the white woman's response to Wright's rejection of the food is also an apprehension of racial rebellion. "I don't know what's happening to you niggers nowadays," she states, her invective revealing that her provision of molasses, like that within the orphanage, springs less from patronal concern than from a desire to lock Wright into a preordained social role of tamable infrahumanity.

Even as this scene furnishes the food contract with national dimensions, however, it reveals flaws within this expanded disciplinary system, flaws that enable Wright to initiate the resistance we examine in the remainder of this chapter. The scene reveals that this disciplinary system has failed to abolish the possibility of rebellion—that it has neglected to prepare for the resurgence of humanity, for those disruptive personalities willing to reject molasses along with the inferiority it implies. Possibly, this neglect explains why Wright's spurning of molasses provokes the same dismay as Oliver Twist's request for second helpings—explains why "I don't know what's happening to you niggers nowadays" echoes the threatening prophesy of Dickens's workhouse authorities: "That boy will come to be hung" (58).

Molasses's status as a highly calorific foodstuff that optimizes appetite means that, although Wright's unsettling request is for less rather than more, it remains interpretable as a defiance of imposed hunger and is therefore comparable to Twist's workhouse rebellion. Although superficially opposites, Wright's request for less and Twist's request for more are comparable insofar as both reject the prescription of diet by external authorities and cast this rejection as a reassertion of individuality. Dickens scathingly describes his workhouse regime as a "system of farming" (49)—a phrase that, by anticipating the bovine imagery of *American Hunger*'s orphanage scene, confirms that Twist's and Wright's rebellion resist broadly similar efforts to manufacture in humans the docile virtues of tamable animals.

Crucially, though, the resistance this scene lodges against the animalization of a national food contract is not limited to the actions it describes but proceeds from its very status as a scene, from its very existence as an artifact that describes events in writing. *American Hunger* consistently pits the animalizing uses that hunger extends to disciplinary authorities against the countervailing, humanizing uses that literacy extends to the disciplinary subject. It consistently draws from and reinvigorates into a twentieth-century context the advantages that literacy held to those slaves for whom, as Henry Louis Gates observes, it often constituted "an irreversible step away from the cotton field toward a freedom larger even than physical manumission."[38] Of these manumitting advantages, particularly relevant to Wright's scene of dietary rebellion is the opportunity such self-education opens up for retrospective, polemical revenge. Control over the weaponry of words, as represented in *American Hunger,* arms Richard Wright and enables him to prevail over battles he had lost when illiterate. Remembered episodes of racist insults and violence, in their transmission to an audience of millions through a newly empowering literacy, are fought anew, the victorious aggressors of an earlier time now, within the context of the book, overshadowed by the retrospective authorial victory of their erstwhile loser. Cultural associations equating literacy with humanity in this way enable Wright to reconfigure his rejection of molasses into a scene whose cast contains an indisputable villain. Literary style and access to publication permanently contextualize this rejection within an antiracist purview, creating a narrative world in which a white woman who describes African Americans as "niggers" automatically describes herself as something mentally inferior, brutalized, and abject. By suggesting that those who seek to animalize others effectively inflict animalization upon themselves, *American Hunger*'s corrective rhetoric enables the adult Wright to join arms with his younger servile self against the food contract. That reclamation of humanity, that antiracist resurgence of undiminished selfhood, which the young Wright initiates via his spurning of molasses, is ultimately upheld by the adult Wright's use of literacy's capacity to, as it were, write wrongs. Self-education as such emerges in Wright's autobiography as the means by which to escape the lasting call of the Pavlovian hell, to defy the infrahumanity implied in the consumption of molasses—to protest and resist, in short, what now stands as a truly national, truly *American Hunger*.

Resistance

In common with *American Hunger* itself, the narrative Wright's biographers present of their subject's life often position self-education as a fulcrum on which his elevation in status turned, transforming a bellboy into a spokesman, a mere statistic into a thorn in the side of the American government. Keneth Kinnamon, for instance, suggests that self-education effected an "imaginative and emotional liberation" and was thus instrumental to what his biography terms *The Emergence of Richard Wright* (1972) (36). At the same time, *American Hunger*'s description of the transformation that Wright's exposure to Mencken's incendiary, militarizing polemic provoked is very different from that experienced by Cross Damon, who, in *The Outsider* (1953), must obliterate all documentation of his former life in order to recast himself as a new man. Literacy, in its application in *American Hunger*, orchestrates no such Gatsbyesque razing of the past but deliberately calls it to mind, voluntarily summoning dehumanizing hungers to denounce such political conditions. Yet, literacy's capacities to resist such dehumanizing hungers also explain why Wright's efforts to obtain it are so consistently blocked. Although free, Wright enjoyed neither an adequate education nor the partial privileges of the "talented tenth" and was instead schooled by a Jim Crow system that, he observed in 1945, spent "$40 a year on the education of a white child, $5 a year on a black child."[39] *American Hunger* confirms such inequalities, insisting that, a century after its postbellum decriminalization, African American literacy remained no less subject than foods to the controls of a white supremacist oligarchy that rightly recognized the implications such knowledge held for black political consciousness. Machinations Wright famously completed to steal into a Memphis library that "Negroes were not allowed to patronize" (288) confirm that, in this disciplinary society, literacy is a prestigious signifier of the demarcations of political power:

> That afternoon I addressed myself to forging a note. Now, what were the names of books written by H. L. Mencken? I did not know any of them. I finally wrote what I thought would be a foolproof note: *Dear Madam: Will you please let this nigger boy*—I used the word "nigger" to make the librarian feel that I could not possibly be the author of the note—*have some books by H. L. Mencken?* I forged the white man's name.
>
> I entered the library as I had always done when on errands for whites, but I felt that I would somehow slip up and betray myself. I doffed my hat, stood a respectful distance from the desk, looked as unbookish as possible, and waited for the white patrons to be taken care of. When the desk was clear of people, I still waited. The white librarian looked at me.
>
> "What do you want, boy?"
>
> As though I did not possess the power of speech, I stepped forward and simply handed her the forged note, not parting my lips. (291)

The success of this forgery leads to a subsequent scene of literary liberation:

> That night in my rented room, while letting the hot water run over my can of pork and beans in the sink, I opened *A Book of Prefaces* and began to read.

I was jarred and shocked by the style, the clear, clean, sweeping sentences. Why did he write like that? And how did one write like that? I pictured the man as a raging demon, slashing with his pen, consumed with hate, denouncing everything American, extolling everything European or German, laughing at the weaknesses of people, mocking God, authority. . . . Yes, this man was fighting, fighting with words. He was using words as a weapon, using them as one would use a club. Could words be weapons? Well, yes, for here they were. Then, maybe, perhaps, I could use them as a weapon? (293)

To be successful, a forgery must complete three interrelated subterfuges. Visually it must reproduce the idiosyncrasies of its subject's handwriting style. Linguistically it must impersonate the distinctive semantics of this subject's prose. And logistically it must manufacture an impression of the circumstances of dispatch quite distinct from those that have actually transported the message from sender to receiver. Wright's forgery accomplishes each of these three subterfuges. Wright outmaneuvers the white librarian not just because of his forgery's imitation of "white" handwriting and prose, but also because of the no less deceitful circumstances in which he delivers it. In this progression from composition to performance, Wright graduates from an authorial mimicry of a white bourgeois literary style to a theatrical mimicry of an "unbookish" meekness that, though stereotypically suited to the color of his skin, is no less incompatible with his private literary ambitions and talents. The sheer speed of this transformation from an authoritative white to a submissive black persona enables Wright's forgery to succeed, which is to say that it enables his authorship to remain invisible. And yet such authorial invisibility should be seen not as Wright's relinquishment of authority in relation to his text, but, on the contrary, as a sign of his mastery over it. Wright's declaration that he "*addressed [himself]* to forging a note" reveals the tautology operating behind this forgery's manufacture, wherein its author must write *to himself*—must achieve supremacy over the text, installing himself as its principal writer *and* reader—in order to absent himself creatively from it. Nor must Wright, to achieve such supremacy, simply erase, paradoxically, all trace of his own voice from the text. It also requires him to erase all clues as to his authorial motives—to excise any profit he, as the forgery's camouflaged author, stands to gain from the request that it makes. Possibly this camouflaging of authorial motive explains why Wright's desire for words, which the autobiography figures elsewhere as another form of American hunger, also obliges him to erase all signs of literal appetite from his performance, forcing him to lock his mouth and remain silent, "not parting my lips." For this mimicry of the facial gestures by which hunger is characteristically suppressed suggests that Wright is here subconsciously reverting from impersonating black servility back to that forged authorial persona, whose whiteness, in the terms of *American Hunger*'s disciplinary food contract, guarantees access both to foods and to libraries. It is as though hunger could here disqualify the aspiring autodidact as automatically as blackness itself: as though Wright, who cannot mask his color, might at least attempt to act away the hunger whose identification would expose him as an unwelcome and politically troublesome reader in the library.

Yet, while this episode can be read as an intense competition between the white controllers of literature and the blacks whom they exclude, this competition also reveals a certain consensus between these warring parties, since it is contested over a knowledge both recognize as a source of intellectual enfranchisement. The librarian, whose duties include the maintenance of an apartheid of education, must blockade the apparently meek black boy precisely because she agrees with him that his successful penetration of literature would confirm an African American humanity, which, in turn, would defeat the animalizing hungers of Jim Crow. At no point during Wright's self-education is the prestige that such white custodians reserve for the literature they safeguard challenged or eroded. Rather, the nutritional value of words remains undiminished, and Wright, having raided these enemy grounds, merely uses the weaponry of Mencken et al. to subject the hungers imposed by Jim Crow to an unorthodox, guerrilla-like resistance. While this episode stands alone because it tells of a victory won at the time instead of retrospectively, it shares with the autobiography's other, belated revenges a conceptualization of writing as defiant enlightenment—as a nourishment for a hunger through which Wright has hitherto experienced the world.

Contrast this episode with a more notorious forgery, composed during the lengthy interval between Wright's claimed infiltration of the Memphis library and his autobiographical representation of this event at the close of World War II. Significantly, the fictionalized author is Bigger Thomas, the forgery an attempt to secure dollar bills rather than the intangible profits of a rhetorical education.

> He put on the gloves and took up the pencil in a trembling hand and held it poised over the paper. He should disguise his handwriting. He changed the pencil from his right to his left hand. He would not write it; he would print it. He swallowed with dry throat. Now, what would be the best kind of note? He thought, I want you to put ten thousand. . . . Naw, that would not do. Not "I." It would be better to say "we." *We got your daughter,* he printed slowly in big round letters. That was better. . . . There was in his stomach a slow, cold, vast rising movement, as though he held within the embrace of his bowels the swing of planets through space. He was giddy. He caught hold of himself, focused his attention to write again. Now, about the money. How much? Yes; make it ten thousand. *Get ten thousand in 5 and 10 bills and put it in a shoe box.* . . . That's good. He had read that somewhere . . . *and tomorrow night ride your car up and down Michigan Avenue from 35th Street to 40th Street.* That would make it hard for anybody to tell just where Bessie would be hiding. He wrote: *Blink your headlights some. When you see a light in a window blink three times throw the box in the snow and drive off. Do what this letter say.* Now, he would sign it. But how? It should be signed in some way that would throw them off the trail. Oh, yes! Sign it "Red." He printed, *Red.*[40]

Read alongside the similar scene from *American Hunger,* this moment from *Native Son* confirms that both forgeries are inspired by a hunger in which, as a broad structure of feeling, desires for self-education and desires for food coalesce. Modern readers, given what they know about Bigger Thomas, might find his textual deception more problematic than Wright's attempted penetration of the Memphis library, and not least because this latter action so presciently anticipates 1960s struggles over the racialized designation of public space. Such readers might consider it significant that, whereas Wright's forgery transgresses a segregation law now abolished, Bigger's ransom demand remains a federal offense. But conceptualizations distinguishing the autodidactic motivations of *American Hunger*'s library note from the material ambitions of Bigger Thomas must contend with the fact that both aim to defy hunger. Wright's forgery is inspired by a desire to assert humanity—by a desire to resist the animalization bound up in a food contract to which he has previously been subjected. Want also forces Bigger's ransom demand in *Native Son* into existence, as is confirmed when the note's composition is interrupted by the "slow, cold, vast rising movement" of hunger. That Wright was not content to infect Bigger with an "emotional and cultural hunger," but also conferred literal, physical malnutrition on him is demonstrated by the dizziness that interrupts the forgery's composition and by the circumstances under which its logistical subterfuge is then consummated. Creeping into the Daltons' palatial home, Bigger finds his efforts to dispatch the ransom demand and escape detection disturbed by a "strange sensation" that "enveloped him." Bigger's "knees wobbled" as he entered the house, only to be confronted by the sight of "sliced bread and steak and fried potatoes and gravy and string beans and spinach and a huge piece of chocolate cake." Hence, in a matter of pages, *Native Son* moves from Bigger's composition of his ransom demand to a representation of his anxious contemplation, filtered by hunger, of an unimaginably generous meal. What this narrative shift confirms is that the primary desire motivating Bigger's forged demand for money is also what prompts Wright to steal into the library. The characters of Wright and Bigger—one inspiring sympathy, the other discomfort; one a focus for antiracist morality, the other for the nihilism of ghettoization—act in tandem against an omnipresent American hunger.

What, in fact, distinguishes these scenes is their respective success. Wright's forgery is unequivocally victorious: he withdraws Mencken's *Book of Prefaces* from the library, in the process initiating an autodidactic resistance that proves central to his emergence at the autobiography's close as a voice of political dissent. On the other hand, Bigger Thomas ends *Native Son* facing the electric chair: *his* forgery sows the seed, not of triumph, but of defeat. This significant contrast becomes clearer when considered in the light of Barbara Johnson's recent essay collection *The*

Feminist Difference (1998), which mainly deals with *Native Son*. Reflecting both on Bigger's pseudonymous signature and on Wright's own erstwhile Communist allegiances, Johnson remarks that, like "Richard Wright himself in 1940, Bigger is compelled to sign his writing 'Red.' Yet the note is signed 'Black' as well: '*Do what this letter say.*' Hidden behind the letter's detour through communism is the unmistakable trace of its black authorship" (61–73). By implication, such remarks confirm that Wright's own performances as author and actor in *American Hunger*'s forgery meet with unqualified success. By contrast, they also identify the seed of failure of *Native Son*'s forgery as lying, not merely in Bigger's infantile use of ambidexterity and gloves, but in his linguistic failure to displace the destabilizing presence of "native" African American demotic.

Even without the aid of *The Feminist Difference*, the forgeries of *American Hunger* and *Native Son* call to mind the tensions between assimilation and autonomy that nuance much African American cultural production. For instance, the fact that, to achieve any kind of nourishment, both Bigger and Wright must forge "white" writing suggestively parallels the way in which the first slave cooks, faced with the demands of colonial plantation owners, effectively "forged" the dishes of a foreign culinary tradition. Read in this light, the invective volunteered by *American Hunger*'s hidden self-address—"*Will you please let this nigger boy*"—intersects with the inclusion of such foundational English dishes as rhubarb pie and Yorkshire pudding in *What Mrs. Fisher Knows* (1881). In Abby Fisher's instruction to "rub the butter and lard into the flour," we again encounter an image of black hands working to produce a cultural form—in this case, shortening pastry—more often associated with an English provenance and with a contemporary white American constituency (24). Shortening pastry and writing *nigger,* respectively, the fingers of Fisher and Wright reproduce signifiers that so manifestly belong to a perceived white cultural vocabulary that their use now consummates the overall forgery, decisively hiding from slaveholders and librarians alike the indigestible fact of African American cultural creativity.

Since notions of forgeries hinge on a binary relation between "alien" and "natural" cultural paradigms, potentially drawing us into the volatile territory of racial essentialism, we should reiterate here an aspect of *What*

Mrs. Fisher Knows stressed in the introduction. That is, among the recipes offered by Abby Fisher, stereotypically English dishes like roast beef or rhubarb pie coexist both with what are now seen as soul food standards like fried chicken and with such ingeniously misspelled native and Creole titles as "Circuit Hash" (succotash) and "Jumberlie" (jambalaya). On one level, the foregoing observations are not affected by this nascent culinary multiculturalism. Abby Fisher's specifically English dishes are so devoid of any discernible American, let alone African American influence, that they can be viewed in isolation as the vestigial legacy of a colonial period when plantation cooks were obliged to "forge" European foods. On another level, however, and now *with* the assistance of *The Feminist Difference,* we can broaden this analogy to accommodate multicultural, polyglot recipes in *What Mrs. Fisher Knows.* Johnson's insight that Bigger's ransom demand exceeds "its contextual function" enables us to imagine a literary biography, punctuated by the forgery's recurrence as event and as episode, wherein Wright masters white cultural style in Memphis and then, during *Native Son*'s composition, deliberately disrupts such mimicry by unsettlingly resorting to the black vernacular. This progression from the accomplished veil of "*nigger*" to the intended black signifier of "*do what this letter say*" recalls the way slave cooks, having gained proficiency in European cuisine, experimented with it, leaving, as Karen Hess puts it, "their thumbprint on every dish" they ostensibly imitated.[41] Complicating English dishes with ingredients or techniques either retained from Africa or originated in America, those slave cooks, of whom Abby Fisher is one of our nearest available historical representatives, gradually inscribed on the colonial foundation of southern cuisine new cultural influences from which plantation cookery and eventually soul food emerged. Fisher's recipe for sweet potato pie— like hoppin' John and grits, among the dishes we most closely associate with southern cooking—supplies a clear example of this intergenerational business of culinary experimentation. Baking the same shortening pastry she uses for rhubarb pie, Abby Fisher layers this English foundation with a signal ingredient that figures prominently in African American cookery. Sweet potatoes also are frequently confused with yams, which not only feature prominently in West African cuisine traditions, as Jessica B. Harris notes, but also prompt the famous cry of Ralph Ellison's invisible man: "I yam what I am!"[42] Sweet potato pie thus emerges from *What Mrs. Fisher Knows* as an exemplary culinary fusion that blends two venerable African and European ingredients to produce a new dish entirely original to America. As such, we can venture that Bigger's *"do what this letter say"* functions much as these sweet potatoes function—that it decisively intervenes, as an irrepressible sign of African American cultural creativity that rests in the European "pastry case" of Marxism and standard American English. Thus, if it is true that "hidden behind . . . [Bigger's ransom demand's] detour through communism is the unmistakable trace of its black authorship," as Barbara Johnson suggests, then sweet potato pie's "detour through" English pastry cooking surely displaces similar clues as to the dish's suppressed yet discernible African American provenance. Just as "the possibility—and the invisibility—of a whole vernacular literature" lies behind *"do what this letter say,"* so behind sweet potato pie's signal ingredient must lie the possibility—and the invisibility—of an entire African American cookery tradition.

American Hunger casts little direct light on these interconnections between cooking and writing; any evidence to support C. L. R. James's observations regarding Wright's prowess as a cook is starkly absent from his autobiography. This reflects a broader displacement, effected in Wright's oeuvre as a whole, wherein the concomitant valorization of writing and prioritization of hunger effectively cuts out the middle (wo)man: the cook. This displacement is evidenced in several episodes from *American Hunger*. For example, in the Sunday dinner and orphanage meals analyzed earlier, foods often appear to arrive ready-made at the table with no acknowledgment of the processes that produced them. Episodes in which culinary processes *are* declared, meanwhile, replace such invisibility with a reductive representation that limits cookery to an inartistic, merely scientific functionalism. What Wright claims to be the first sentence he ever wrote—"The soft melting hunk of butter trickled in gold down the stringy grooves of the split yam"—is also among the few sentences of his autobiography that sites food unequivocally as a source of sensory pleasure. More representative of *American Hunger*'s attitude to food are those passages describing the menial positions Wright held before *Native Son*'s success, such as the moment when he finds himself alone in a white employer's kitchen and, exploiting this brief and precarious solitude, "hurriedly scramble[s] three or four eggs at a time and gobble[s] them down in huge mouthfuls" (176). Although Wright in this scene radically disrupts food binary relations that the virtual force-feeding of molasses previously imposed on him, enabling him to ingest expensive foods nominally reserved for white consumers, time pressures also mean that he here dispenses with any notion that cooking may comprise a creative or artistic form of cultural production. This abnegation of the artistry of a process culturally associated with women culminates in a scene in a Chicago restaurant, in which the appalled Wright witnesses a European immigrant cook periodically "clear her throat with a grunt, . . . cough, and spit into the boiling soup" (323). Wondering "if a Negro who did not smile and grin was as morally loathsome to whites as a cook who spat into the food," Wright presents this desecration of food less as a potential proletarian rebellion than as a desecration of the imaginative or creative capacities of cooking (326). *American Hunger* also denies the artistry of cooking in less dramatic ways—in the way certain scenes limit food to a kind of textual decoration that adorns but in no way determines the action. This technique is epitomized by the earlier episode in which Wright, having consummated his library forgery, returns home to discover what exactly in Menckenian polemic obliged white southern authorities to deny African Americans access to it. This scene so strenuously focuses on Wright's illegal encounter with Mencken's words that readers could be forgiven for not noticing that this act of reading is accompanied by a concurrent act of cooking. Letting "the hot water run over my can of pork and beans in the sink"—the stark contrast between this definitively inartistic act of cooking and Wright's exalted absorption in Mencken's humanizing polemic consummates his oeuvre's repeated neglect of the potential craft involved in food's cultural production.

On one level, one can cite this reductive approach in support of the anxieties many critics continue to feel regarding Wright's general treatment of gender. Insofar as *American Hunger*'s discussion of enlightening literature concentrates on such canonical figures as Dostoevsky and Mencken, writing is gendered as a male pursuit and thus opposed to those modes of cooking historically delegated to women. The question of how Wright genders cooking and writing—Barbara Johnson's questioning of where, "in Richard Wright, does the black woman stand with respect to the black man's *writing?*"—can perhaps be answered simply: in the kitchen. *American Hunger*'s description of Wright's first attempt at writing concludes with a scene in which Wright enters the house of a neighbor, interrupts "her as she was washing dishes and, swearing her to secrecy, . . . read[s] the composition aloud. . . . God only knows what she thought" (141–42). Close juxtapositions between a writing figured as male and domestic activities figured as both female and functional potentially contribute to the charges of sexism more often sustained with reference to repeated portrayals of misogynist violence in Wright's oeuvre. In *The Feminist Difference*, however, Johnson resists this view; the more complicated interpretation she supplies accepts that the maleness of literature and the functionalism of cooking, as represented by Wright's oeuvre, merely reflect the legacy of patriarchy and the prevalence of menial labor among African Americans, respectively. Johnson suggests that encounters between male writers and female cooks instead function as negotiations of the power and insight of black women to which, as an unresolved anxiety, Wright's oeuvre repeatedly returns. Wright's fiction often situates African American women in kitchens, Johnson suggests, because that is where they were often situated in Wright's life, as in society in general. Crucially, however, Wright's narratives often complicate such gender demarcation by making "the figure of the black woman as *reader* in his work . . . fundamental" (73). This complication of Wright's admiration for the figures within a male-dominated literary canon, no less than the fact that he actually "fancied himself as a bit of a cook," suggest we must look elsewhere for an explanation for the relative lack of representation cooking receives in *American Hunger*.

This complicating factor also reveals that *American Hunger* presents a profound and unsettling contradiction, whereby Wright's original title foregrounds a narrative that focuses on hunger but at the same time consigns hunger's solution—food—to the background. Given Wright's expansion of hunger into a broader condition that only self-education can satiate, his simultaneous cooking of "pork and beans" and reading of *A*

Book of Prefaces creates an absurd and illogical situation wherein words counteract an appetite increased by the consumption of such debased foods. The coalescence of multiple psychological and physical desires within this overarching conceptualization of want produces a warped situation in which what Wright phrased as a "hunger to know" loses its metaphoric aspect.[43] It is as though the memory of semistarvation remained so vivid in Wright's mind as to contaminate food itself—as though, in contrast to biopsychologist Andrew Hill's remarks, *any* kind of dietary regimen, *any* kind of nutrition here becomes implicated in the hunger only self-education can resolve. Just as he resists the causative approaches of social scientists, Wright accordingly involves hunger so profoundly in his analyses of disciplinary mechanisms that ultimately food itself can no longer solve it, can no longer challenge writing's supreme capacity to resist Western racial ideology.

The
Blossoming
of Brier

THE WRITINGS of Richard Wright and Zora Neale Hurston both reflect the racial segregation of America.[1] In *American Hunger*, Wright's boyhood experiences occur in a world split into two islands. One island is white, the other black; one is where he labors, and the other is where he sleeps; and Wright's nightly crossing from the former to the latter is marked by nothing more than a disappearance of foods and a reappearance of hunger. This binary cleaving of America also inspires *Their Eyes Were Watching God*, because Hurston's utopian fiction is shaped by a desire to import the economic benefits of white America into the island of Eatonville, and to see what then happens to its distinctive agrarian culture.

In the "Tar Baby" folktale, the supernatural battleground for Brer Rabbit and Brer Fox's fight for food is similarly split into two distinct yet adjacent islands.[2] The orderly rows of peanuts or corn or cabbage, depending on which transcript you read, that grow on Brer Fox's land recreate it as an island of agricultural plenitude and thus as the diametric opposite of the brier occupied by his "wild" adversary, Brer Rabbit. But much as Wright creeps into a white kitchen to steal and then "hurriedly scramble three or four eggs at a time," so Brer Rabbit breaches the border separating these Manichean islands, to exploit the similarly generous larder constituted in Brer Fox's neat fields.[3] Brer Fox interprets these nocturnal incursions as a threat to the unequal land distribution from which, as the sole food producer among the folktale's creatures, he so visibly benefits. He fashions a mannequin from some viscous substance and christens it Tar Baby. Drawing on a heterosexuality that Brer Rabbit's masculinization presupposes, Brer Fox then identifies this mannequin as a "she," confirming that, unlike a scarecrow, the function of this particular sentry of food is to attract rather than to repel. Lured by this curiously inanimate, female figure, Brer Rabbit embraces its gluey surface and is infuriated to what Ralph Ellison's *Juneteenth* (1999), in another context, calls "that quick, heated fury which springs up in one when dealing with the unexpected recalcitrance of some inanimate object" (8). Immobilized, his feet and hands manacled by the sticky substance, Brer Rabbit stands imprisoned, his fur slowly tarred by black skin, which exposes him as the thief of Brer Fox's food. When Brer Fox finally confronts him, Brer Rabbit realizes that linguistic deception is his only means of escape. Saying no punishment could be worse than being sent to the brier patch, Brer Rabbit manipulates Brer Fox's preconceptions about this abject territory, persuading his captor that even death is preferable to its unimaginable terrors. Thus the end of "Tar Baby" finds Brer Rabbit back home as a result of Brer Fox's failure of imagination: Brer Fox could not believe that the brier patch might be habitable.

The present chapter proceeds from a sense that this folktale endures: that the lessons it teaches us, its vivid distillation of nutritional inequality, continue to be alluded to by a host of African American writers. As we will see, Ralph Ellison, Albert Murray, Ntozake Shange, and Carole Weatherford, among others, discover in the folktale a parable of hunger that retains enormous relevance to modern American society. It should be remembered that the United States not only embraces much amazing opulence but is also home, as a study of 1985 indicated, to twelve million hungry children and eight million hungry adults.[4] Anyone tempted to interpret the recent successes of individual African American musicians, politicians, and entrepreneurs as signs of racial progress would do well to consider that African American children in the United States remain more likely to be born at a dangerously low weight than children in Senegal, Lesotho, and the Ivory Coast. Similarly, anyone doubtful that common ground could exist between the underdeveloped Third World and the black citizens of overdeveloped America must consider that, as Liz Young notes, infant mortality rates "in poor inner city areas of the U.S.A. are comparable with those found in Bangladesh."[5] As reliable indicators of continuing malnutrition, the low weights and frequent deaths of African American infants clearly reveal that, as a story that sides with the underfed against the overfed, "Tar Baby" still has much to say to the modern United States.

Given the continuing relevance of "Tar Baby," we must begin this section by overhauling the folktale's turbulent publishing history, which has led some to attribute it solely to Joel Chandler Harris. If (as my introduction suggests) *What Mrs. Fisher Knows* belongs to a genre of works conceived by illiterate African Americans but transcribed by literate white Americans, then this problematic archive is also home to "Tar Baby," if only because Harris's version remains the folktale's most famous incarnation. A need to reinvigorate the folktale's roots in slavery, to disentangle the knotty strands of its complex history, motivates the first part of this chapter, which also questions the casual assumption that this work of children's literature cannot also be political or contain stark racial implications.

Foremost among African American literary responses to "Tar Baby" is Toni Morrison's 1981 novel of that name, which also shares its sense of a sundered world, of a nourished world and a hungry world existing side by side. The wild woods, careful rows of cultivated foods, and cracks in the fences through which Brer Rabbit shuttles morph, in the Caribbean household where much of *Tar Baby* is set, into servants' quarters, master bedrooms, and corridors connecting these black and white islands. Built on the island of Dominique, the house in Morrison's novel is the retirement home of the white American Valerian Street, a Philadelphia confectionery magnate who has never quite left Pennsylvania behind, and who dedicates his dotage to classical music, to "white" foods, to growing temperate plants in tropical conditions, and to recreating, in general, a Eurocentric culture from which all local black influences are ruthlessly exorcised. As this chapter's second part suggests, however, *Tar Baby*, by following Valerian's black servants into their quarters and so into their private lives, reveals that this enclave of white culture is no less dependent on nonwhite labor than were those Indian outposts of the British Empire where the colonizers read *The Times* and took afternoon tea. Funded by the sugar industry and built by migrant Haitian builders who have "no union," Valerian's day-to-day Eurocentrism is effectively enabled by black "wallahs"—by a staff of African American and Caribbean servants.[6] By exposing Valerian's dependence on black labor and by implicitly referring to the similar situation in Stanley Kramer's *Guess Who's Coming to Dinner* (1967)—a film also set in a palatial "white" house built on land once inhabited by black Americans—Morrison not only draws on the spatially intimate inequality dramatized in "Tar Baby" but also opens it up to a new reading. Her depiction of a white house built on Caribbean soil reminds us that—since brier refers not just to blackberry bushes but more generally to weeds, to wild terrain of any kind—Brer Fox's fields can also be seen as the product of land appropriation, of a privatization of common land that has reduced Brer Rabbit's home to the merest "patch." And this rereading casts new light over the thefts of Brer Rabbit, suggesting that these acts merely correct past injustice, merely return foods to their rightful owners, from fields to brier, from white to black islands, and from the over- to the undernourished.

As I contend in the concluding part of this chapter, *Tar Baby* ultimately exceeds even this rereading of its folkloric source, exploring not only interracial theft but also questions of culinary resourcefulness. Undernourished African Americans can achieve satiation, *Tar Baby* suggests, not just by stealing "white" foods but also by transforming "white" waste, by foraging for wild berries, and by growing their own fruits and vegetables. Morrison's sensitivity to the key importance that these resourceful strategies have played in the survival of African Americans surfaces in *Sula* (1973) and *Beloved* (1987), as well as in the kitchen garden of *Paradise* (1998); it is nowhere more evident, however, than in *Tar Baby*'s account of how Son forages in the jungles encircling Valerian's estate, and of how Ondine creates meals using only foods that her employer Valerian and his wife, Margaret, have spurned. Finally, then, the stark adjacency of nutritional inequality in *Tar Baby* narrows the islands of black hunger and white plenty from which both *Their Eyes Were Watching God* and *American Hunger* arise, intensifying the suggestion that African American malnutrition can be remedied by a more equitable distribution of food. But *Tar Baby* insists on a further point. It suggests that, because white Americans have historically proven reluctant to undertake such a redistribution of food, African Americans have developed new ways of overcoming hunger—of turning molasses from animal feed into human food, offal into delicacies—of encouraging the brier that surrounds them to blossom and bear fruit.

The Literary History of "Tar Baby"

As the earlier reference to Ellison's *Juneteenth* indicates, the African American literary canon frequently revisits an archetypal episode in which assailants are paralyzed in the throes of attack by the unforeseen stickiness of their victims. While hiding "in the weeds" of Central Park, the protagonist of Alice Walker's *The Third Life of Grange Copeland* (1985) shocks a white woman who falls and then reaches out her "small white hand . . . [that] let go when she felt it was *his* hand" (145–52). In Richard Wright's *The Outsider* (1953), Cross Damon sees his lover "as an image of woman as body of woman" and fights his "urge to bind her to him," thus imbuing her with a volatile and disembodied sexuality somehow redolent of the uncanny charisma of Tar Baby (66). Ellison himself alludes to the folktale not only in *Juneteenth* but also in *Invisible Man* (1952), which begins with an attack on a white man in which the narrator "seized his coat and lapels and, . . . butting him as I had seen the West Indians do, . . . kicked him repeatedly" (7–8). In their sudden violence, in *The Third Life of Grange Copeland*'s preoccupation with the "weeds" of Central Park, and in their obsession with limbic contact, these violent, sexualized episodes disclose a clear debt to the frozen moment when Brer Rabbit's arms and legs become glued to his passive adversary.

Elements of the folktale arise not only in these twentieth-century works of fiction but also in Olaudah Equiano's *Interesting Narrative* (1789). A scene in Equiano's work is set on the same Isle of Wight that, in Jane Austen's *Mansfield Park* (1814), becomes the focus of Fanny Price's ignorance of the world. In Austen's novel, Fanny Price is castigated for thinking "of nothing but the Isle of Wight" and for calling it *"the Island, as if there were no other island in the world"* (17). In the light of Edward Said's suggestion in *Culture and Imperialism* that *Mansfield Park* is actually "more implicated in the rationale for imperialist expansion" than it can appear, Austen's reference to the Isle of "Wight" arguably reveals an awareness of its racial homophone (100). At the very least, such racial permutations make it seem significant that Equiano should choose the same island as the setting for an encounter that, by concluding with an embrace, evokes the encounter between Brer Rabbit and Tar Baby:

> [O]ur ship . . . [was] stationed at Cowes, in the Isle of Wight. . . . While I was here, I met with a trifling incident which surprised me agreeably. I was one day in a field belonging to a gentleman who had a black boy about my own size; this boy having observed me from his master's house, was transported at the sight of one of his own countrymen, and ran to meet me with the utmost haste. I not knowing what he was about, turned a little out of his way at first, but to no purpose; he soon came close to me, and caught hold of me in his arms as if I had been his brother, though we had never seen each other before. (85)

Similarities between this episode and "Tar Baby" raise the possibility that elements of the famous folktale predate even the Joel Chandler Harris version with which it remains closely associated. These similarities are possible because scholars currently believe that the folktale originated in West African cultures, a provenance corroborated by narratives Melville and Frances Herskovitz transcribed on a 1931 tour of a Dahomean region where Harris's *Uncle Remus: His Songs and Sayings* (1881) had not circulated. Stories cataloged in *Dahomean Narrative* (1958) include "Tar Drum," a fable in which the trickster figure Yo finds his nightly forays into Dada Segbo's compound confounded by a drum covered with "a sticky thing." Distracted from his efforts to gain food, Yo seems as transfixed by this drum as Brer Rabbit is by Tar Baby: he approached it "and struck it with his hand. And his hand stuck. He said, 'Let go.' The drum would not let go. . . . Yo said, 'I am angry!' . . . He kicked it with his foot. His foot stuck. He struck with his other foot, and both feet stuck. He struck it with his head, his head stuck" (326–29). Although this exact story would have been unknown in the Igbo valley of Essaku, where Equiano grew up, the influence of an underlying version of the tale becomes apparent in the parallels *The Interesting Narrative*'s Isle of Wight anecdote sustains both with it and, more obviously, with "Tar Baby" as we have come to know it. Here Equiano pictures himself standing in a cultivated "field" whose association with whiteness is signaled by its ownership by "a gentleman" and then confirmed via a punning on the Isle of "White" that anticipates *Mansfield Park*'s knowing deployment of the homophone.[7] This field "belonging to a gentleman," then, also figures Equiano as alien: his trespass on it, like that of Brer Rabbit, is exposed by a black figure who, catching "hold of me in his arms," intertwines his limbs in a locking embrace. In the process Equiano substitutes the violence and sexual aggression emphasized by Walker, Wright, and Ellison with an emotionally turbulent scenario that, by dramatizing the empathy between those forced into minority status, calls attention to the mysterious allure that first draws Brer Rabbit and Tar Baby together. Walker's, Wright's, and Ellison's transplantation of the agrarian context of "Tar Baby" into the brutalized territories of an urban demimonde is in this way challenged by its molding in Equiano's hands into a parable of the kinship felt between those forced into minority status.

Despite their differences, however, the allusions all these episodes make to the folktale subvert certain prevailing assumptions about Brer Rabbit and Brer Fox's contest for food. To note that Equiano's Isle of Wight anecdote bears comparison with "Tar Baby" is to establish the folktale as Henry Louis Gates Jr. has sought to establish the Esu-Elgebra stories: as a myth, born in Africa and nurtured in slavery, that shapes the African American literary tradition. Equally, to observe that Walker's and Ellison's scenes of interracial violence reformulate key elements of the story is to suggest that the speaking animals Brer Rabbit and Brer Fox are not only personified but also racialized. Both these suggestions demand that we dismantle those longstanding cultural assumptions that have subordinated the folktale to the authorship of Joel Chandler Harris and characterized it as a naive story entirely innocent of racial subtext.

Literary articles and newspaper reviews published at the height of Joel Chandler Harris's popularity during the 1880s and 1890s were as unclear about the provenance of "Tar Baby" and other folktales as earlier colonial literature had been about the origins of citrus fruit. Even as Harris himself insisted that "the animal stories told by the Negroes in our Southern States . . . were brought by them from Africa," some of these articles submitted English folklore, the writings of Thomas More, and the Indian subcontinent as alternative explanations.[8] Meanwhile, commentaries less concerned with questions of provenance tended to emphasize what was generally accepted to be the beguiling "childishness" of the stories while at the same time praising Harris, the creator of their fictional narrator, Uncle Remus, to the hilt. A *New York Times* review of 1892 suggested that within these stories "the machinery is so simple. An honest colored man, who loves the family he was born in, and a little white boy, his darling, and that is all." Yet, the reviewer continues, the stories of this loyal "colored man" are mere "lesser details" compared to the "literary art of the author, the creator," Harris himself.[9] In this way, the *New York Times* repeated a pattern laid out by Mark Twain, who, eleven years earlier, had dismissed Harris's reluctance to accept credit for the tales. This dismissal stemmed partly from Twain's impatience with the modesty of Harris, the "shyest full-grown man" he had ever met. But it also encouraged the tendency to see Remus as the work of a writer who was far more sophisticated than the tales he happened to tell, which, with their elaborate cast of supernatural animals, appeared to betray the legacy of a primitive if charming polytheism. "In reality," Twain wrote to Harris, "the stories are only alligator pears—one merely eats them for the sake of the salad-dressing."[10]

Disagreements regarding the provenance and mediation of the published version of "Tar Baby" produced a discourse in which those elements that appeared to necessitate artistic expertise were attributed to Harris, while those connoting noble simplicity were read as the textual remnants of his African American sources. Twentieth-century academics have been quick to point out that, if anything, the reverse was the case. In an introduction to a 1986 Penguin reissue of *Uncle Remus: His Songs and Sayings*, Robert Hemenway affirms the African provenance of the folktales and notes that "Brer Rabbit expresses archetypes of . . . liberation embedded deep in Afro-American history" (30). However, Hemenway's observation that Harris, rather than an African American source, engineered the retreat these stories effect "from an adult, public world of difficult decisions" still stands in contrast to Craig Werner's remark that, even now, "almost no one recognizes . . . [the] harshly realistic . . . separatist implications" of "Tar Baby."[11] The recent consensus regarding the African and African American roots of the folktale markedly contradicts an ongoing scholarly failure to assimilate Hemenway's complementary assertion that their mediation by Harris served not so much to render their innocence as to *render them* innocent. It is as though the Victorian prioritization of Uncle Remus over the stories he tells has been inverted, as modern critics now suspect that the soothing naiveté embodied in this suspiciously faithful figure infects "Tar Baby," discouraging the interrogation of its racial permutations. Only Lawrence W. Levine, Houston A. Baker, and a handful of other critics have been willing to divorce the folktale from its depoliticizing Remus context and to see it, as Hemenway urges, as part of "a revolutionary consciousness which says that one need not accept the world as it is."[12]

This curious situation, in which many scholars attribute the authorship of "Tar Baby" to African American oral storytellers yet continue to characterize its content as childish and, by extension, as racially innocent, emerges in such postwar texts as Richard Dorson's *American Negro Folktales* (1967). Dorson's anthropological survey, like J. Mason Brewer's *American Negro Folklore* (1968), acknowledges that slaves identified with Brer Rabbit.[13] Dorson nonetheless remains reluctant to conclude that "Tar Baby" might allegorize race in the manner of Hurston's folktale

"Kill the White Folks" or those concerning the actual slave John.[14] Dorson seems unable to disengage Brer Rabbit from his neutralizing association with Remus. Unlike Hurston, who ranked Brer Rabbit among those trickster figures who are "continuations of . . . John," Dorson ignores the possibility that this trickster's adventures might revolve around unmentioned yet decisive racial codes.[15] Instead, these animal stories remain for Dorson a naive archive he can contrast with later cultural forms—jazz, the blues, and "urban" folktales in which "the note of social protest has come to sound more overtly."[16] Dorson characterizes manifestations of Brer Rabbit in twentieth-century African American cultures not as instances of continuity, but as satires in which modern storytellers ironically juxtapose past innocence with the ingrained cynicism of the urbane present. Discussing *Deep Down in the Jungle* (1964), Dorson attends far more to Roger Abrahams's awareness of folkloric changes caused by urbanization and ghettoization than to his attendant identification of maintained traditions. Thus, Dorson interprets Abrahams's comment that Brer Rabbit "becomes the hard man" on the Philadelphia streets to mean he becomes unrecognizably transformed into a "fast-talking, sporty hipster."[17]

Melville Herskovitz often betrays a comparable contradiction. Although he affirms the African provenance of the animal folktales and acknowledges that slaves identified with Brer Rabbit, he continues to characterize tales involving this trickster as innocent of racial subtext. While Dorson consigns "Tar Baby" to agrarian cultures effectively terminated by the Great Migration, Herskovitz approaches the exploits of Brer Rabbit as an innocuous and deracialized stratum of folklore on which the more politicized strata of recent years has settled. When discussing folktales collected before the Great War, Herskovitz comments that "animal tales predominate, *with the result that* Negro lore was, and still is, largely looked upon as the epitome of primitive naiveté."[18] Similarly, when referring to Georgian folktales that describe the Tar Baby's "black lips [as] ever parted in an ugly grin," Herskovitz fails to note that a similarly crude distortion was commonly enacted in the caricatures by which white American culture pictured the story's black originators. The possibility that this distortion reformulates racist caricature never arises in *The Myth of the Negro Past* (1941), which opts instead to read the lips from which the Tar

Baby's "supernatural powers" spring as an individual "abnormality."[19] Whereas Negroid caricature conventionally directs attention toward this facial feature, Herskovitz views these "lips" as the aberrant characteristic of an implicitly deracialized individual. This peculiar conclusion drama tizes the contradictions permeating both his and Dorson's approach to "Tar Baby." On one hand, they and other twentieth-century scholars are quick to interrogate Joel Chandler Harris's mediation of what came to be known as the Uncle Remus stories. They have successfully registered the decisive authorial interventions that the dissembling modesty of Harris's prefaces disguise. With equal success, they have rebutted those who, like Twain, ignored Harris's own protestations and attributed the ingenuity behind the stories to him rather than to an African American constituency. On the other hand, Herskovitz's reduction of Tar Baby's clearly caricatured racial identity to individual abnormality reveals that he and other folklorists and anthropologists remain to some extent trapped in a Victorian purview, which categorized the folktale as childish and thus automatically deracialized.

By contrast, Arthur Frost, Frederick Church, James Moser, and other illustrators of Joel Chandler Harris's work suffered no such uncertainty. Whereas Harris's version of "Tar Baby" mentions the blackness of this central figure only in passing references to "turkentine" and "tar," Frost's accompanying illustrations and the sketch Church and Moser provided for *Legends of the Old Plantation* (1881) explicitly retrace contours drawn in contemporary Negroid caricature.[20] Drawing on this caricatural paradigm, these illustrations accentuated the whiteness of the Tar Baby's eyes, for example, thus anticipating the stereotypically petrified black servants who were to fill cinema screens a few decades later. The drawings of Frost and Church and Moser give Tar Baby a prominent mouth, as though anticipating the "thicker tongue [and] less flexible lips" that the aforementioned *New York Times* review attributes to Harris's African American sources.[21] In the process, these caricatures expose as untenable Harris's attempt to smother the starkly racial world out of which Uncle Remus narrates under the deracialized world that his narrating opens up. The blankness in which Harris's text envelopes Tar Baby is destabilized, disrupted, and finally announced as blackness in the illustrations that accompany it. Nor should these illustrations' flirtation with obscene racist caricature blind us to the key point that the racialization they, unlike Harris's writing, acknowledge originally was attributed to Tar Baby by "her" African American creators. Works on which Harris and his illustrators collaborated, like the close juxtaposition of contradictory positions that they construct, articulate an unresolved dialogue on caricature and deracialization, which anticipates tensions enacted in less brutal fashion by the anthropological prose of Herskovitz and Dorson.

The denigration of Tar Baby by A. B. Frost and Church and Moser, their decision to picture this archetypal figure in a caricature more often applied to its black originators, sheds light on the continuing scholarly reluctance to classify the folktale as anything other than a naive and essentially childish narrative. Craig Werner's observation that "each element [of the tale] . . . remains open to a multitude of interpretations" is proven not only by Harris and his illustrators' tense collaborations but also by scholars' continuing inability to disentangle the dilemmas between deracialization and caricature outlined by their uneasy coalition.[22] All these artistic and scholarly negotiations reveal "Tar Baby" to be well named and to share with its eponymous material a certain sensual ambiguity, which sustains disparate interpretative possibilities. Neither solid nor liquid, tar is both black and viscous; it is difficult to capture; it can be molded to fit any given shape, any given interpretation. Equally, Hemenway's remark that "the allegorical identification between Brer Rabbit and black people is extremely complicated" receives ample literary support from recent reformulations of Tar Baby by Carole Weatherford, Albert Murray, Ntozake Shange, and others. For instance, Carole Weatherford's poem "Tar Baby on the Soapbox" dramatically inverts the Cimmerian blackness of nineteenth-century caricatures into an equally pronounced and fabricated whiteness, which qualifies this impassive figure to appear in a washing-powder advertisement where it can "mouth white lies."[23] Morrison's *Sula,* meanwhile, includes among its cast Tar Baby, an appropriately "beautiful" yet inappropriately lightened man who "Eva said . . . was all white."[24] These radical reinterpretations, by lightening Tar Baby into a white as extreme as the blackness of its nineteenth-century stereotype, thus exemplify Mary Douglas's description of the viscous as "a state halfway between solid and liquid" that gives "an ambiguous sense impression."[25]

Yet these reinterpretations also demonstrate that Toni Morrison's publication of *Tar Baby* in 1981 marked a pivotal moment that decisively refuted preceding attempts to characterize the folktale as either apolitical or childish. Continuing tensions between these literary reformulations and anthropological analyses reveal that upon publication of *Tar Baby*, Morrison entered an unresolved debate whose participants were by no means unanimously predisposed to accept her insistence, lodged throughout her novel, that her folkloric source allegorized interracial encounters and exchange.

Tar Baby manifests this insistence, imposing on the folktale from which it takes its name a racialized reading, both explicitly and implicitly. Explicitly, *Tar Baby* effects this racialization by providing opportunities for characters to retell the folktale and, in the process, layer it with nuances and emphases displaced by negotiations left unresolved in Harris's "official" transcript. In the following narration of the folktale in Morrison's novel, for instance, Jadine's lover, Son Green, transforms Brer Fox into a "farmer" whose race is explicitly stated. Son tells Jadine:

> She looked at him and when he saw the sheen gone from her minky eyes and her wonderful mouth fat with disgust, he tore open his shirt, saying, "I got a story for you."
>
> "Get out of my face."
>
> "You'll like it. It's short and to the point."
>
> "Don't touch me. Don't you touch me."
>
> "Once upon a time there was a farmer—a white farmer . . ."
>
> "Quit! Leave me *alone!*"
>
> "And he had this bullshit bullshit bullshit farm. And a rabbit. A rabbit came along and ate a couple of his . . . ow . . . cabbages. . . . Just a few cabbages, you know what I mean? . . . So he got this great idea about how to get him. How to, to trap . . . this rabbit. And you know what he did? He made him a tar baby. He made it, you hear me? He made it!" (273)

Given that Son is a black fugitive who repeatedly articulates pride in his identity, it is tempting to interpret this retelling as an act of racial reclamation, in which a self-proclaimed heir of the story's oral originators redeems their cherished template from its corruption and commercialization by Harris. Such an interpretation is complicated by the fact that this retelling not only racializes but also modernizes the folktale, tailoring it for a newly urban, newly cosmopolitan audience. The grievance here is directed neither at slavery nor at Harris's alleged plagiaristic exploitation of the black folkloric tradition. Instead, it focuses attention on continuing injustice: it draws on Son's seeming awareness of racial inequality and then equates national and global racism with the injustices produced by the spatially intimate segregation operating inside Valerian Street's grand estate. In this new scenario, the viscous "sheen" of Jadine's eyes and her "wonderful mouth," from which issue paradoxically attractive injunctions against touch, identify her as the latter-day agent, the latter-day Tar Baby, of an ongoing spatial apartheid that may be compared with slavery but nevertheless belongs very much in the present. By implication, the identifications of Jadine as Tar Baby and of Brer Fox as white also combine to associate Son with Brer Rabbit. This latter identification occurs implicitly, revealing that Morrison here radically inverts the assumptive literary tendency, identified in *Playing in the Dark,* that normalizes white identity into a presupposed character trait signaled when, and indeed because, "nobody says so."[26] Whereas nineteenth-century illustrations of Tar Baby fetishize her blackness by stereotyping her facial features and inking in her body, Son here turns the whiteness of his reinvented Brer Fox into a feature demanding description, eliciting blackness, by contrast, via absence.

Implicitly, *Tar Baby* consolidates this explicit racialization of the story through a series of references to viscous substances and through a series of metaphors equating these substances with skin. Summoning the interpretative instabilities and possibilities Douglas identifies in the viscous, *Tar Baby*'s references to saliva, molasses, sealskin, and quicksand call to life an array of racial permutations that the novel pursues, negotiates, and underscores. Pigmentation and other classifying bases of racial differentiation are destabilized as they become connected with neither solid nor liquid substances, the indeterminate consistencies of which ultimately render the idea of race itself unstable. Many episodes throughout *Tar Baby* could be cited in this context, yet the imagery of the following beach scene, which juxtaposes the neither solid nor liquid state of quicksand against the neither black nor white but "yelluh" skin of Jadine, invests these disruptive alliances with special urgency.

> The circle of trees looked like a standing rib of pork. . . . It was amazing; the place looked like something by Bruce White or Fazetta—an elegant comic book illustration. . . . [Jadine] walked toward it and sank up to her knees. . . . She struggled to lift her feet and sank an inch or two farther down into the moss-covered jelly. The pad with Son's face badly sketched looked up at her. . . . Movement was not possible. At least not sudden movement. . . .
>
> [W]hen Son came sweating up the hill she was crying a little and cleaning her feet and legs with leaves. The white skirt showed a deep dark and sticky hem and hung over the door of the jeep. . . .
>
> "What the hell happened to you?" . . .
>
> She didn't look up, just wiped her eyes and said, "I took a walk over there and fell in."
>
> "Over where?"
>
> "There. Behind those trees."
>
> "Fell in what?"
>
> "I don't know. Mud I guess, but it felt like jelly while I was in it. But it doesn't come off like jelly. It's drying and sticking."
>
> Son kneeled down and stroked her skin. The black stuff was shiny in places and where it was dry it was like mucilage. (183–85)

By establishing Jadine as the victim of a viscous substance, this traumatic encounter with quicksand effectively undermines Son's attempt to identify himself with Brer Rabbit and his "model" lover with Tar Baby. The role reversal also undermines those critical interpretations that characterize the cast of Morrison's novel as a straightforward mirror image of the cast of her folkloric source. It reveals that Susan Willis's definition of Jadine as "a contemporary 'tar baby,' a black woman in cultural limbo" must always be considered in tandem with those oppositional scenes, such as the one just cited, where she, like Brer Rabbit, becomes the subject rather than the object of a viscous substance's attentions.[27] Morrison achieves this reversal, this attempt to write against as well as

with "Tar Baby," through at least three different allusions. She extends
the shadow of her folkloric source across the scene, first, by ensuring that
Jadine initially yields to the quicksand as voluntarily as Brer Rabbit embraces Tar Baby. Lured by its uncanny resemblance to an "elegant comic
book illustration," Jadine willingly enters the enchanted forest clearing
and, once there, becomes imprisoned like Brer Rabbit in the "permanent
embrace" of a tree's inanimate limbs (184). Morrison's folkloric source
also emerges as she translates the contrast between Tar Baby's impassiv-
ity and Brer Rabbit's animation into a battle wherein Jadine, frantically
"fighting to get away," struggles against a quicksand ossified by its assimilation of a static "pad with Son's face badly sketched" on it. The third
authorial method by which Morrison acknowledges the influence of the
"Tar Baby" folktale derives from her use of color. Colorings recalling
Morrison's folkloric source surface most conspicuously in descriptions of
the quicksand, which is not only as "black" as tar but, as a simultaneously
"shiny" and "dry" substance, shares its ambiguous viscosity. The absorption of Son's "badly sketched" portrait into this quicksand then lards the
color binary relation between it and Jadine's "white" skirt with an addi-
tional gender relation, which reinvigorates the heterosexual coupling presupposed in the reciprocal feminization of Tar Baby and masculinization
of Brer Rabbit. In this way Morrison's third and final allusion, by tacitly
adumbrating Jadine's struggle with a sexual subtext, assists her authorial
effort to establish the folktale as a pivotal influence on the scene.

This suggestive play on color binary relations reveals that Morrison
is seeking to establish a new view of "Tar Baby" itself, to persuade audiences that it, too, narrates interracial encounters and exchange. This
point becomes yet clearer because the scene is written not only against the
novel's eponymous source but also against a raft of cultural and literary
sources, foremost among them Nella Larsen's *Quicksand* (1928). Nor
is it that Jadine's quicksand simply recalls *Quicksand* because Larsen's
work is often seen as pioneering the postwar flowering of black women's
writing with which Morrison's oeuvre is closely associated. *Quicksand*
also provides a vital reference point because its protagonist, Helga Crane,
shares with Jadine an ambiguously "mixed" racial identity, which *Tar
Baby* encapsulates via the chef Thérèse's references to the latter's "yelluh"

skin. A novel Barbara Johnson characterizes as a "story of the neither/nor self," *Quicksand* is revisited by *Tar Baby*'s depiction of Jadine and is then literalized by her confrontation with the neither solid nor liquid substance Larsen's title invokes.[28] In the process, Morrison forces both the folktale and Larsen's novel into a triangular frame of intertextual reference wherein the latter's explicitly racial concerns illuminate not only those of *Tar Baby* itself but, by extension, anxieties aired in code within the animalized world of Brer Rabbit. Implied references to *Quicksand* reveal that the struggles fought not only by Jadine but also by her occasional literary antecedent Brer Rabbit unfold along inescapably racialized parameters. What Doris Witt terms "soul food's complicity with certain pivotal, powerful, and enduring stereotypes of blackness" is here consolidated by the quicksand's association with the tree that resembles "a standing rib of pork," a standby of southern barbecue calorific enough to threaten Jadine's modeling career.[29] Together, these associations insist that the quicksand and the tar with which these characters wrestle must be recognized neither as deracialized substances that happen to be black nor as mere embodiments of blackness itself, but as portentous signs of a racial essentialism intent on fixing this blackness in eternal opposition to whiteness. References to Larsen's racial concerns in this way nourish two distinct ambitions, exposing not only *Tar Baby* but, retrospectively, its folkloric namesake as narratives whose startling associations of viscosity with blackness render the idea of race as unstable, fluid, and "sticky" as molasses, quicksand, and tar.

The delight of Hollywood's special effects technicians, viscous substances have been reconstructed pixel by pixel and their computerized simulations placed center stage in productions like *The Abyss* (1989), *Alien Resurrection* (1992), and *Terminator 2* (1991). In what is now a familiar scene, human heroes race from assassins whose superhuman flexibility enables them to convert every chromosome to viscosity and so flow like treacle through keyholes, under doors, and down telephone lines. In Hollywood productions, viscosity erodes boundaries, collapses doors and gateways, and guarantees that dreaded, violent encounters will occur no matter the lengths mere mortals take to avoid them. *Tar Baby*'s multiple references to viscosity facilitate a similar focus on encounters between opposed cultural worlds. Quicksand, sealskin, molasses, and saliva exist in a fictional context that, by pressing segregation codes into the spatial intimacy of a single household, undermines and even ridicules those characters who wish to retreat into their respective milieus. Willed ghettoization, the desire to seal oneself off in a hermetic racial enclave, becomes an impossible maneuver as Son and Jadine increasingly bridge both the white world of Valerian Street and the black world of his staff, rendering the corridors between these spaces permeable. Thus, as the next part of this chapter illustrates, Toni Morrison's references to "Tar Baby" do more than retrospectively establish this folktale as a fable that allegorizes and comments on modes of interracial encounters. They also establish her novel as another text concerned with interracial exchange, as another text focusing on the capacity of the viscous, or of those with neither-nor racial status, to form a bridge between artificially divided worlds.

Guess Who's Coming to Dinner

Parallels between "Tar Baby" and *Tar Baby* are reinforced as the latter text splits its Caribbean milieu into two. The architect of this split is Valerian Street, who, because he "loved the island, but not his neighbors," imposes a distinction between his retirement home and its beautiful yet inhospitable surroundings:

> It was a wonderful house. Wide, breezy and full of light. . . . One or two had reservations—wondered whether all that interior sunlight wasn't a little too robust and hadn't the owner gone rather overboard with the recent addition of a greenhouse? Valerian Street was mindful of their criticism, but completely indifferent to it. . . . The new greenhouse made it possible to reproduce the hydrangea. . . . The rest of what he loved he brought with him: some records, garden shears, a sixty-four-bulb chandelier . . . and the Principal Beauty of Maine. . . . And whatever he did think about, he thought it privately in his greenhouse. . . . At first he'd experimented with Chopin and some of the Russians, but the Magnum Rex peonies, overwhelmed by all that passion, whined and curled their lips. He settled finally on Bach for germination, Haydn and Liszt for strong sprouting. (9–12)

Attempting to expel psychologically the island's native inhabitants, Valerian's fabrication of a hermetic white enclave is nourished by a familiar binary opposition between Northern civilization and the uncultivated "brier" of the Caribbean. The sheer effort involved in maintaining this binary relation despite the ample evidence of island society finds absurd expression in Valerian's commissioning of a greenhouse that simulates temperate conditions in a tropical climate rather than vice versa. Like an iceberg in a jungle clearing, this greenhouse sits amidst a local biosphere whose superior fertility it denies, a folly of Valerian's melancholic Eurocentrism. Ants, marching in from the surrounding brier, are at first dispatched from the greenhouse by spray and then, after Son's ironic suggestion, by mirrors that, from inside, transform its glass panes into walls (148). Musical pieces to which Valerian treats his hydrangeas and peonies draw exclusively from a classical canon from which he has ruthlessly weeded out any later jazz-influenced European or American works.

Valerian's attempts to deny the land on which he stands expose his greenhouse as a territorial "palimpsest"—what the *Oxford English Dictionary* terms a "parchment . . . written upon twice, the original writing having been erased or rubbed out to make place for the second."[30] Hydrangeas and peonies write on Valerian's recondite site a Eurocentric script calculated to obliterate native roots and close off the rhizomorphous possibilities of interracial fertilization. Yet in a manner similar to Stuart Hall's observation that colonial labor is ingrained "in the sinews of the famous British 'sweet tooth,' " *Tar Baby* juxtaposes the expulsion of nonwhite cultural materials from Valerian's greenhouse against the fact that it, like his fortune, is built on the cocoa and sugar industries. Juxtapositions like these complicate Valerian's Eurocentrism by pointing out that, as a confectionery magnate, his individual version of Hall's "economic blood-stream" has received a particularly generous transfusion from postcolonial cocoa and cane farmers.[31] They expose Valerian's "temperate" greenhouse to be, not only a part of his Eurocentric project, but an extravagance made possible by the labor of those whom this Eurocentrism displaces. Valerian's simultaneous dependence on and denial of Caribbean society as such unmasks a vexed dynamic that recalls both Richard Godden's illuminating readings of Faulkner's novels and Walter Johnson's recent characterization of the antebellum South. As Johnson observes, the "Old South was made by slaves. . . . Yet through the incredible generative power of slaveholding ideology, the slave-made landscape of the antebellum South was translated into a series of statements about slaveholders." Just as "all of the things that made the South the South were accomplished through the direct physical agency of slaves," so Valerian's greenhouse actually depends on the culture it obfuscates, becoming a territorial palimpsest that must draw sustenance from its buried script.[32]

Nor is this palimpsest manufactured only by the greenhouse, which is instead an external manifestation of a Eurocentric suppression played out in the internal regions of Valerian's gut. Almost all the foods that Valerian and his wife swallow are imported from the United States, which is to say that almost all of them could be grown in his uniquely cooling greenhouse but nowhere else on the island. Excluding local produce from his stomach as rigorously as he bans musical "passion" from his greenhouse, Valerian shuns chili, salt fish, avocado, and fresh pineapple in favor of such expensive imports as croissants and, ironically, *tinned* pineapple (21). Valerian's exclusion of local produce from his diet culminates in the plans he and his wife, Margaret, concoct for an "American" and "traditional Christmas dinner." These plans require the household to redouble the imports it consumes, to prepare a feast composed entirely of European and Euro-American foods, the massive expense of which recalls the Roman emperor Valerian and the famously lavish feasts held during his reign. While the feasts of the late Roman Empire boasted ostriches, peacock brains, and flamingo tongues, Valerian Street merely imports foods he has eaten back home, yet he still shares with his imperial namesake a willingness to spend vast amounts of money to get particular ingredients and to eat them while remaining monumentally indifferent to the hunger of his neighbors.

Valerian and his wife, Margaret, achieve such gourmandism as they discuss what meat should form the Christmas dinner's centerpiece. Valerian suggests that the family enjoy a "goose," but Margaret, underwhelmed by this Dickensian suggestion, offers an alternative to it no less steeped in Euro-American tradition:

"Geese?" She stared at Valerian for suddenly she could not imagine it. . . . Turkey she saw, but geese. . . . "We have to have turkey for Christmas. This is a family Christmas, an old-fashioned family Christmas, and Michael has to have turkey."

"If Tiny Tim could eat goose, Margaret, Michael can eat goose."

"Turkey!" she said "Roast turkey with the legs sticking up and a shiny brown top." She was moving her hands to show them how it looked. "Little white socks on the feet."

"I'll mention it to Ondine, ma'am."

"You will not mention it! You will tell her!"

"Yes ma'am."

"And apple pies."

"Apple, ma'am?"

"Apple. And pumpkin."

"We are in the Caribbean, Margaret."

"No! I said no! If we can't have turkey and apple pie for Christmas then maybe we shouldn't be here at all." (29–30)

Here Margaret's aggressive displacement of the local environment reveals that behind her appeals to "America" and "family" lies a *völkisch* nostalgia for an abandoned white world in which the disruptive frequencies of a surrounding black culture sounded less perceptibly. She and Valerian want to expel these frequencies, to cleanse their digestive tracts of any obvious black influence. Their shared Eurocentrism translates plant production and food consumption into performative arenas wherein a common yearning to replace the local with the Northern can be enacted.

I next explore these palimpsestic machinations—which so overwhelm Margaret she must be reminded that "we are in the Caribbean"—before turning to the strategies by which the fugitive Son Green resists their completion. Focusing on *Tar Baby*'s association of Son with Brer Rabbit, I engage Morrison's folkloric source to show how food distribution in Valerian's home entrenches the social distinctions between his employers and employees. I also show how a nightly breaching disturbs this intimate spatial inequality, as Son arrives in the household, steals food, and later disrupts Valerian and Margaret's plans for the approaching Christmas festival. As the scene of Son's insistence that his hosts' extravagance depends on a lifelong underpayment of their neighbors, the meal on which we here focus might suggest a familiar catch phrase: guess who's coming to dinner.

In itself, the fact that *Tar Baby* describes Valerian and Margaret's lengthy plans for a ceremonial dinner but does not narrate its actual consumption recalls the similarly pivotal yet uneaten meal that concludes Stanley Kramer's famous 1967 film. Kramer's narrative of interracial love, in which Sidney Poitier's John Prentice enters a San Francisco mansion and asks for permission to marry his white fiancée, Joey Drayton (Katharine Houghton), is further summoned by the moment in *Tar Baby* when Valerian learns of his butler's ceramic skills and cries *"Sydney? A potter?"* (73). A hidden answer to the question that Stanley Kramer's film title poses, this shoehorned exclamation directs attention toward broader similarities between the casts of these two texts, which both include a retired white couple, a glamorous young woman everyone agrees to be beautiful, and black staff. In the figure of Son Green, who infiltrates Valerian's mansion in search not of marriage but of food, *Tar Baby* transcends such formal similarities to announce itself as a direct challenge to *Guess Who's Coming to Dinner*. This intruder, unlike Poitier's John Prentice, is less interested in African charity and scientific research than in escaping prison. He is, indeed, a man who asks as many questions as others ask of him.

Toni Morrison and Stanley Kramer make for unlikely bedfellows. The creative period culminating in Morrison's receipt of the Nobel Prize in 1993 coincided with the publication of a raft of critical works that almost universally dismissed Kramer's oeuvre as the embodiment of humanist cliché and integrationist condescension. It is hardly an exaggeration to say that, at the same time as novels like *Tar Baby* have been lifted above criticism, *Guess Who's Coming to Dinner* has been deemed beneath contempt. Outrage at the film on its release was not confined to Black Nationalist quarters; it was also articulated by that "quintessential historical document in the white phallocentric tradition . . . [of] liberal humanism," the *New York Times*.[33] Questioning whether Poitier's "brilliant, charming Negro" would consider marrying a "starry-eyed college senior," the *New York Times* review repeated objections raised in more radical quarters.[34] What, then, could be gained from comparing this premature epitaph for racism to a novel as keen to register the endurance of white supremacy as *Tar Baby*?

An answer to this question emerges from *The Devil Finds Work* (1976), James Baldwin's investigation of the cinematic representation of African Americans. Described by James Campbell as "personal reminiscence" and "ostensible subject" in equal part, this narrative exempts from its denunciation of *Guess Who's Coming to Dinner* Poitier himself, who had joined Baldwin both in the Freedom March of 1963 and at Martin Luther King's funeral five years later.[35] On other aspects of the film, however, Baldwin is unreserved. Reiterating the *New York Times*'s point, he observes that Prentice's parents "outrank their hosts, and might very well feel that the far from galvanizing fiancée is not worthy of their son" (75). Highlighting Kramer's representation of the maid Tilly, Baldwin addresses a concern to which his essays repeatedly return; he exposes her servility—also a characteristic of Uncle Remus—as the product of compensatory fantasies born of white racial anxiety. The fantastical aspects of Tilly's character surface as Baldwin observes: "And yet, black men have mothers and sisters and daughters who are not like that at all!" Baldwin thoroughly dismisses notions of kinship between the server and the served, insisting that "she assuredly does not love the white family so deeply as they are compelled to suppose" (72). Wholesale rejections like these, which demolish Kramer's characterization of the Drayton family's African American staff, validate our comparison between *Guess Who's Coming to Dinner* and *Tar Baby*. These stereotypical figures exist in such palpable contrast to those of *Tar Baby*—which clearly seeks to follow black servants into their own quarters, into their own lives—that Valerian's veiled utterance of Poitier's name becomes a sign of Morrison's ambition, not to refigure, but to transfigure Kramer's film. They reveal that similarities *Tar Baby* constructs with the cast of *Guess Who's Coming to Dinner* result from Morrison's disquiet with Kramer, from her wish to mutate his self-assured Draytons into the volatile Streets, his loyal Tilly into the angry if well-named cook Ondine, and the beautiful Joey into the beautiful, black Jadine.

This fractious intertextuality gains confirmation as *The Devil Finds Work* turns from Kramer's use of stereotype to his representation of landscape. To elucidate the land segregation on which the Draytons' palatial home is built, Baldwin analyzes one of the few scenes in the film in which the home's white occupants leave its four walls and enter downtown San Francisco. Baldwin pinpoints

> that lamentable scene in the city when [Spencer] Tracy tastes a new flavor of ice cream and discovers that he likes it. This scene occurs in a drive-in, and is punctuated by Tracy's backing his car into the car of a young black boy. The black boy's resulting tantrum is impressive—and also entirely false, due to no fault of the actor (D'Urville Martin). The moral of the scene is *They're here now, and we have to deal with them.* (76)

Here, through a compensatory naming of D'Urville Martin designed to correct his character's anonymity and absolve him from the scene's dubious implications, Baldwin redirects attention toward the man he deems auteur, Kramer, and the way he forces his cast into preconceived, stereotypical molds. Significantly, this dissection leads into Baldwin's discussion of Kramer's representation of landscape, his association of downtown San Francisco with black criminality, and the Heights with white gentility. From this discussion arises the incontrovertible moral: *"They're here now, and we have to deal with them."* Ventriloquizing a racial attitude he considered typical of bourgeois liberalism, Baldwin exposes consistencies between this 1960s stance and that adopted by Brer Fox, who "dealt" with the alien figure in his fields by constructing the Tar Baby. This premonition of invasion leavens the racialized stereotype of criminality personified by Martin with a further abjection, a further Othering, that renders this actor no less foreign in San Francisco than Brer Rabbit seems when caught in Brer Fox's fields of corn. Baldwin's denunciation of the hidden resonance that racial segregation sustains despite the antiracism Kramer's film espouses is bolstered as *The Devil Finds Work* proceeds to describe the Draytons' household in terms that not only recall "Tar Baby" but anticipate Valerian's palimpsestic estate. Valerian and Margaret's simultaneous dependence on and denial of the Caribbean reappears as Baldwin turns from the black criminality encircling the Draytons' home to the peripatetic status of those who, like Tilly, labor within it but return to their ghettos nightly. Inhabited by whites but managed by blacks, the

Draytons' mansion becomes for Baldwin a space that, by situating its laborers within range but out of sight, requires Poitier to embody saintliness and superhumanity before he can possibly be accepted. Baldwin cements such parallels by noting that the Draytons' home, like Valerian's, is built on land reclaimed from its original inhabitants. It is founded

> on the heights of San Francisco—at a time not too far removed from the moment when the city . . . reclaimed the land at Hunter's Point and urban-renewalized the niggers out of it. . . . And the black doctor [Sidney Poitier] is saying, among other things, that his presence in this landscape (this hard-won Eden) will do nothing to threaten, or defile it. . . . One can scarcely imagine striking a bargain more painless. (70)

And so we return once more to Brer Fox and Brer Rabbit's territorial battle. Here, as though inspired by the fact that brier must have proliferated before Brer Fox cut it back to the merest "patch," Baldwin's sympathies lie with those previous inhabitants whom land appropriation has forced into ever smaller racial enclaves. Although complicated by the fact that Poitier is here offered as a compromise rather than as an invader like Brer Rabbit, allusions to the folktale are sustained as Baldwin characterizes this particular "Eden" as no less "hard-won" and thus no less cultivated than Brer Fox's fields of corn. What this manufactured Eden signifies, then, is that a previous script has been buried beneath it; this script sustains it, just as nutrients injected into the soil by the humus of brier nourish the corn that replaced the weeds. In the process of this rhetorical exposure, Baldwin reveals the literally whitewashed mansion of *Guess Who's Coming to Dinner* to constitute another territorial palimpsest, another "parchment written upon twice," whose creation bears comparison with Valerian's estate. Just as this estate required Haitian laborers "to clear the land" and to fold "the earth where there had been no fold" (7), so the Draytons employ black staff who had once lived on the land where their palatial home now stands.

Many of Toni Morrison's novels are set in just such territories. As Barbara Johnson notes, a primary motive behind Morrison's oeuvre, one that shapes almost all her novels, is to recover historical moments and thus register that "there once was a *there* and now it is gone."[36] The interwar Harlem society of *Jazz* (1992), the postbellum black autonomy of *Paradise*—these abandoned moments, over which subsequent generations inscribe new scripts, are resurrected, thanks to Morrison's desire to wrestle back experiences displaced by the dominant American historical narratives. The forced removals described in the introduction to *Sula* (1973) exemplify the approach.

> In that place, where they tore the nightshade and blackberry patches from their roots to make room for the Medallion City Golf Course, there was once a neighborhood. It stood in the hills above the valley town of Medallion and spread all the way to the river. It is called the suburbs now, but when black people lived there it was called the Bottom.[37]

Sula's special relevance to this discussion lies in the way Morrison articulates its particular topological split in what appears to be the vocabulary of pork butchery. These introductory sentences not only manufacture a land division redolent of *Tar Baby* but also express this binary demarcation in the terms of a bodily amputation reminiscent of Doris Witt's recent exploration of the "metonymic possibilities" of chitterlings and other soul-food ingredients. If *Medallion* is a term sometimes used to describe expensive cuts of pork loin, then the part of *Sula*'s landscape reserved for black habitation—*Bottom*—recalls the "metonymic relationship" that, Witt suggests, leads from "soul food to chitterlings to blackness to filth" in dominant American culture. Reserving that section of the landscape signifying bodily functions for African American inhabitation, *Sula* not only carves its landscape into two but then attributes to its alienated islands qualities linking them to the rich and poor binary relations of American food distribution. Neither Witt nor Morrison accept this situation uncritically. By noting that the linking in white American culture of soul food with defecation situates the former not only as a "menace" but as an *internal* menace that threatens the "white man from inside," Witt illuminates the interdependency between Medallion and Bottom in *Sula*. Her interpretation also elucidates Valerian's reliance on black labor and reveals that the latter's ceaseless exclusion of nonwhite ingredients from his digestive tract must always be frustrated by the fact that even the "whitest" food he eats has passed through the black fingers of his cook, Ondine.[38]

For Morrison, meanwhile, biracial food distribution, which follows regional contours in *Sula* but exists in a single household in *Tar Baby,* is always seen as a fallible system; expensive foods are never necessarily better foods, and cheaper foods are never necessarily worse. For Morrison, as we will see, differences in income may lead to differences in the white and the black diet, but not necessarily to a superiority of the former over the latter; what some see as waste others see as edible, even as delicious.

There are many threads to this argument, the complexity of which arises from the rich intertextuality of Morrison's aesthetic. While we have so far traced *Tar Baby*'s allusions to "Tar Baby," *Guess Who's Coming to Dinner, Sula,* and even Roman feasts, our tour of such miscellany becomes simpler once we recognize that what all these different threads offer to Morrison is proof of the interdependency of the diets of rich and poor. Respectively juxtaposing brier with fields of corn, white affluence with black ghettos, orgiastic feasts with colonial starvation, and Medallion with Bottom, these varied threads place overfeeding and underfeeding in close proximity to each other and so confirm that hunger stems less from food shortage than from inequalities within our systems of food distribution. Morrison's allusions to these very different systems of food distribution prime the narrative for her dramatization of the inequality occurring on Valerian's estate, another world in which the hungry and sated coexist.

Son's arrival on the island and *Tar Baby*'s account of his undetected infiltration of Valerian's house at night initiate this dramatization. In these nocturnal invasions, Son seems to be repeating the actions of Brer Rabbit. *Tar Baby* describes his body as being as "lean as a runner's" (130), compares him to "a foraging animal" (104), and pictures him searching for a "hutch" (136). When Son leaves the jungle, enters a cultivated space, and steals food from it, he is clearly treading in Brer Rabbit's footsteps. He seems native to the brier and implicated in the jungle as it creeps "into Valerian and Margaret's seasoned and regulated arguments, subverting the rules" (67). His hunger is animalistic:

> [H]e was so tired in the day and so hungry at night, nothing was clear for days on end. . . . The first night he entered the house was by accident. The broken

pantry window where he was accustomed to look for food and bottled water was boarded up. He tried the door and found it unlocked. He walked in. There in the moonlight was a basket of pineapples, one of which he rammed into his shirt mindless of its prickers. He listened a moment before opening the refrigerator door a crack. Its light cut into the kitchen like a wand. . . . Three chicken wings were wrapped in wax paper. . . . He ate the bones even, and had to restrain himself from going right back and raiding the refrigerator again. (137–38)

In these burglaries Son steals foods that are portrayed as though they had merely been lying around Valerian's house. A complement to this seeming arbitrariness is the fact that among Son's bounty is a fresh pineapple. Son's apparent good fortune in discovering this fruit confirms that his bounty is dominated by foods that the owners of the household have rejected. Put another way, what Son steals consists at this point almost entirely of the "bottom" spurned by the estate's owners rather than the "medallion" they prize—consists of chicken wings rather than chicken breast and of the fresh pineapple that Margaret rejects, preferring it in its tinned form. Earlier in the narrative, however, an account of Ondine's assistant, the local Thérèse, casts a different light on these acts. Unbeknown to Son, Thérèse

knew of his presence twelve days ago long before he left the trail of chocolate foil paper. . . . Before that mistakable trail, he left the unmistakable one of his smell. . . . So a hungry man was on the grounds, or, as she said to Gideon, "Somebody's starving to death round here." . . . So she took to bringing two avocados instead of one and leaving the second one in the washhouse. But each third day when she returned it was still there, untouched by all but fruit flies. It was Gideon who had the solution: instead of fixing the sash on the window of the pantry as he was ordered, he removed one of its panes . . . soon they saw bits of folded foil in funny places and they knew he had gotten from the pantry chocolate at the very least. (104–5)

This passage suggests that the burglaries for which Son congratulates himself are actually encouraged by Thérèse and Gideon, who invite him into the house by removing a "window pane" and leaving the kitchen door unlocked. But it also indicates that Son's stealing of foods that Valerian and Margaret dislike has not come about accidentally but is a path down which he has been deliberately led. Before benefiting from the guidance of Thérèse and Gideon's invisible hands, Son concentrates his burglaries on "chocolate"—on the very lifeblood of Valerian's fortune, which he and his wife would hardly miss. After Thérèse and Gideon's intervention, however, Son is subtly guided away from this American commodity and toward the island's native produce. As the cited passage shows, Thérèse and Gideon not only leave chicken wings and fresh pineapple out for Son but also avocado, which they begin "leaving . . . in the washhouse." All three foodstuffs figure prominently in the diets of the estate's black staff but are never eaten by Valerian or Margaret. All three bear comparison to those Sethe steals from her employer in *Beloved*:

> None of the sausages came back. The cook had a way with them and Sawyer's Restaurant never had leftover sausages. If Sethe wanted any, she put them aside soon as they were ready. But there was some passable stew. . . . Had she been paying attention rather than daydreaming all morning, she wouldn't be picking around looking for her dinner like a crab. . . . Mr. Sawyer included midday dinner in the terms of the job—along with $3.40 a week—and she made him understand from the beginning she would take her dinner home.[39]

What enables these thefts to be defended, to be redeemed to the point where they cease to be thefts and can be presented instead as acts of redistribution, is more than Mr. Sawyer's prior awareness that Sethe intends to siphon from his stock. Instead, these redistributionist thefts are legitimized by the fact that they are of foods that, like those Thérèse and Gideon leave out for Son, might not otherwise be eaten. A critical distinction between what "the restaurant could not use" and the smaller category of foods that Sethe "would not" use effectively fills her haul with leftovers, with foods included within the restaurant clientele's definitions of waste but not within her own. This distinction concentrates Sethe's siphoning from the restaurant supplies on foods that, had she not taken them, would be thrown to "the four kitchen dogs waiting for scraps."[40] The innuendo of the "passable stew" renders this dish as invisible to Mr. Sawyer's eyes as fresh pineapple, avocados, and chicken wings are to the Eurocentric gaze of Valerian and Margaret Street. Because they concern foods considered edible by those who steal them but inedible by those who own them, these thefts become decriminalized. They become absolved, become stripped of opprobrium, not only to their perpetrators but also to notional "victims" like Mr. Sawyer, who turns a blind eye to Sethe's actions. Such indifference culminates in *Tar Baby* as Valerian, on discovering Son in his house, does little more than laugh and invite the thief to stay (128).

Crucially, however, even as Thérèse and Gideon encourage Son to steal foods that their white employer will not eat, they fail to follow their own advice. Discouraging Son from stealing chocolate and distributing avocados and pineapple to him instead, Thérèse and Gideon transgress this careful response to Valerian's binary distribution of food by appropriating an imported food—American apples—that is emphatically not "passable." The result of his wife's demand for an American variety for Christmas, these apples only reach the Caribbean after Valerian has alerted "a friend at customs." They are "contraband"; "only French-grown fruit and vegetables could arrive at" Dominique (108). Only because of this difference—only because they are cherished while the pineapple and avocado Son stole were rejected—can we begin to understand why Valerian responds to Thérèse and Gideon's theft, not by inviting them to stay in the guest bedroom, but by sacking them:

> "Gideon stole apples?" asked Son.
>
> "Yep." Valerian's back was to them. "I caught him red-handed, so to speak. Them, rather. She, Mary, had them stuffed in her blouse. He had some in each pocket. . . . I fired him. Her too." . . .
>
> Son's mouth went dry as he watched Valerian chewing a piece of ham . . . approving even of the flavour in his mouth although he had been able to dismiss with a flutter of the fingers the people whose sugar and cocoa had allowed him to grow old in regal comfort; although he had taken the sugar and cocoa and paid for it as though it had no value, as though the cutting of cane and picking of beans was child's play and had no value. (202–3)

Valerian's reassertion of ownership over the household's foods, his misnaming of Thérèse as Mary, and his violent response to her theft reinvigorate the hierarchy over which he presides. The striking contrast between Valerian's response to Thérèse and Gideon's theft and his benign neglect of Son's similar activities reveal that he is less concerned with justice than with protecting the distinctions between his diet and those of his staff. Rather as his wife's rejection of fresh pineapple seems related to the fruit's proliferation on the island, Valerian's disciplinary protection of these apples signifies a broader defense of the Streets' Eden, of their palimpsestic attempts to fabricate a temperate utopia on tropical soil. Yet, whereas Baldwin's commentaries reveal that Poitier's character fails to unearth the prior demographic on which the similarly palimpsestic *Guess Who's Coming to Dinner* unfolds, Son now makes good the foreboding of this film's title. When he learns of Valerian's action, his objective becomes a wholesale exhumation of the original script buried by both his host's greenhouse and the Christmas dinner arranged by his host's wife. Observing that two "people are going to starve so your wife could play American mama and fool around in the kitchen," Son transforms the dinner table into the scene of his polemic:

> Son's mouth went dry as he watched Valerian chewing a piece of ham, his head-of-a-coin profile content, approving even of the flavour in his mouth although he had been able to dismiss with a flutter of the fingers the people whose sugar and cocoa had allowed him to grow old in regal comfort; although he had taken the sugar and cocoa and paid for it as though it had no value, as though the cutting of cane and picking of beans was child's play and had no value; but he turned it into candy, the invention of which really was child's play, and sold it to other children and made a fortune in order to move near, but not in the midst of, the jungle where the sugar came from and build a palace with more of their labour and then hire them to do more of the work he was not capable of and pay them again according to some scale of value that would outrage Satan himself and when those people wanted a little of what he wanted, some apples for *their* Christmas, and took some, he dismissed them with a flutter of the fingers, because they were thieves. (204–6)

This speech is not so much an interior monologue as an interior diatribe; Son's repetition of certain phrases ("no value" concludes consecutive clauses, while the duplication of "a flutter of the fingers" enforces

Valerian's effete, deskbound life) signifies not only his passion but, potentially, that of his creator, Morrison. At the very least, Son's diatribe
seems motivated not just by his firsthand experience of his friends' plight
but by an authorial awareness that these friends are merely typical, are
merely representative of the undernourished millions in the world. Author
and character dovetail; as Son denounces Western capitalist practice, both
seem allied in the criticism of a global "scale of value" that, like Wright's
orphanage regime, distributes hunger as much as food to those who labor.

In this light, it is significant that Son's diatribe should also focus on the
principal ingredients of chocolate, the first food he stole from Valerian's
house. As tropical crops mainly eaten in the temperate North, "sugar
and cocoa" exemplify the continuing dependence of developing countries
on the export trade and thus the Manichean gulf in the world itself, its
cleaving into islands of rich and poor. The gulf between a food's place
of production and place of consumption is rarely so wide, geographically
and economically, yet so quickly sublimated into everyday mundanity
than when a citizen of the First World unwraps a bar of chocolate. That
Son has earlier been seen, in Valerian's house at night, doing exactly this
reminds us that chocolate, in this moment in *Tar Baby,* has been returned
home, has been returned to its point of production. Son's earlier stealing
of a chocolate bar at night in this way becomes associated with his scorn
for Valerian's greenhouse, with his scorn for Valerian himself, as another
act that ruptures this palimpsest to reveal the Caribbean soil beneath it.

The fact that chocolate is the first food Son steals from Valerian val-
idates his assertions of solidarity with Thérèse and Gideon, because it
reminds us that, like these thieves of American apples, he, too, has not
only lifted "passable" foods but also those items that the white resi-
dents of the house *would* miss. While the discrepancy in Valerian's responses to the thefts in his household confirms that he is unaware Son
stole chocolate, this particular crime is clearly of enormous importance
to Son himself and, in his diatribe, ceases to be a crime at all, becoming instead an act of reclamation, a redistribution of "cocoa and sugar"
from a vampiric white capitalism to the guts of a person affiliated with
neocolonial laborers. Through this announcement of a coalition between
African Americans and citizens of the developing world—the permuta-

tions of which reemerge in the conclusion—*Tar Baby* concludes, as we might have expected, in a very different manner than *Guess Who's Coming to Dinner*. Whereas the meal announced by the title of Kramer's film is served after the resolution of its plot, the Christmas dinner that Valerian and Margaret surround with such elaborate arrangements only occurs after Son, through his diatribe, initiates the dissolution of their Caribbean household. It is served only after Jadine leaves the island, only after Ondine has announced that Margaret tortured her son, only after Son's polemic—only after Valerian has been exposed as a tragic figure who has imprisoned himself in the palimpsestic Eden he so anxiously constructed.

Hunger Overcome?

It is common knowledge that those who work the hardest, and who complete the dirtiest jobs, are invariably paid the least and eat the cheapest foods. What is sometimes forgotten, however, is that cheap foods are not necessarily inferior foods. Rather, they have merely been rejected by the group holding the greatest purchasing power in any given society. This important distinction is often disguised by the fact that these rejections can be determined by nutritional or other health factors. One reason why fruits and vegetables marketed in Western supermarkets as "organic" cost more than those that are not is because they are said to contain far fewer harmful fertilizers and toxins. In other cases, notions of prestige and exclusivity cluster around foods and function, unassisted by health concerns, to prize certain items over others even when they are nutritionally identical. As we shall see, this latter phenomenon is exemplified by the way molasses, although neither less calorific nor more unhealthy than other sweeteners, long remained cheaper because of longstanding consumer preferences for the more "refined" staple of white sugar.

The fact that the price of all foods is determined by subjective cultural connotations as well as by objective nutritional factors means that, although the poorer characters of *Tar Baby* siphon "passable," or rejected, items from their rich employers, their diet does not automatically suffer in consequence. What makes a food more expensive, in the world of *Tar Baby*, does not necessarily make it better. The classic example by which

Morrison illustrates this is pineapple: Margaret eats it only when it comes packaged in tins, even though this more expensive version contains more sugar and fewer vitamins and is demonstrably inferior to the fruit growing for all and sundry on the island. Pineapple thus epitomizes the renegade means by which foods Valerian and Margaret consider to be waste often shed this inferior status, to become prized by the African American and Caribbean poor as luxuries in their own right.

Commentaries on African American cookery often stress such acts of revaluation, as is exemplified by Amiri Baraka's (Le Roi Jones) 1962 essay "Soul Food":

> Maws are things ofays seldom get to peck, nor are you likely ever to hear about Charlie eating a chitterling. Collards and turnips and kale and mustards were not fit for anybody but the woogies. So they found a way to make them taste like something somebody would want to freeze and sell to a Negro going to Harvard as exotic European spinach. . . . Did you hear of a black-eyed pea? (Whitey used it for forage, but some folks couldn't.) And all those weird parts of the hog? (After the pig was stripped of its choicest parts, the feet, snout, tail, intestines, stomach, etc., were all left for the "members," who treated them mercilessly.)[41]

Here, Baraka repeatedly turns prevailing food valuation on its head, so that foods "ofays seldom get to peck" are enlisted within an alternative system that installs them, instead, as delicacies. Baraka valorizes the transformative strategies by which African Americans in need have overhauled dominant systems of food assessment to salvage a usable cuisine from the most unpromising circumstances.

A similar note of triumph is sounded in Ntozake Shange's recipe "Pig's Tails by Instinct," as cited in the introduction, which also draws on these strategies of food transformation. Shange's talking recipe is based on an act of revaluation comparable to that of "Soul Food" because it centers on an ingredient—pig tails—that can be seen as a byproduct of the butchery trade, as a waste material commensurate with Sethe's "passable stew." The toughness of the tails is negotiated in the recipe's method, which advocates fast boiling until the meat falls "easily from the bones." Residual squeamishness is defeated, and new tastes achieved, via a method that prioritizes what Shange terms "pig extremities" over expensive cuts like bacon, pork shoulder, or pork chops. Shange's taste for this offal is so pronounced, she trails New York's five boroughs searching for a soul-food purveyor, finally finding a "calm I must attribute to the satisfaction of my ancestors" in a "small market" with "sawdust on the floor."[42] Like the British Asians who scour Bradford's supermarkets for *methi* leaves and ghee or the American tourists drawn to the burger outlets of European cities, Shange pursues a taste of home, the only difference being that she undergoes this characteristic expatriate experience without leaving the country of her birth. For Shange, immigration—which, Stuart Hall notes, "has turned out to be *the* world-historical event of late modernity"— becomes localized, transferred to a domestic scale.[43] Yet the symmetry between Shange's culinary quest and those of the truly expatriated is also a measure of the Othering of soul food, which ironically is often painted as more "foreign" and less American than pizza, frankfurters, bagels, and other dishes originally imported from Europe.

The aura of foreignness stubbornly surrounding soul food in dominant American culture demands that we return to the paradigm Doris Witt uncovers, which links the cuisine "to chitterlings to blackness to filth," since this associative string situates the ingredients Shange pursues not merely as a "menace" but as an *internal* menace able to threaten the "white man from inside." Witt's insight clarifies the cultural Othering of soul food, an Othering borne of a desire to obscure this cuisine's special role within precisely the same system of food distribution that gives rise to pizza and other Euro-American dishes. It reminds us that a pig whose hind quarters, when smoked, might yield a pizza's topping is often exactly the same pig for whose offal Shange travels up and down New York; although they derive from exactly the same source, these foodstuffs become subjected, once the abattoir's job is done, to an elaborate series of cultural associations that distance them from one another, granting bacon a normative culinary status while defaming pigs tails, and prizing gammon while devaluing chitterlings.

Only by acknowledging the complex processes involved in this subjectivization of food can we begin to appreciate the political and racial permutations at stake in *Tar Baby*'s consistent suggestion that the ingredients

Valerian cherishes and those he spurns spring from the same source. Again, pineapple provides Morrison with a lucid illustration of such subjectivization, because Margaret's curious preference for the canned version of the fruit is clearly not determined by its innate qualities. Instead, the fruit only becomes palatable to her after it has been assimilated into the same system of American capitalism from which she and her husband derive their wealth—only after it has passed along the conveyer belt, received the addition of sugar, and been encased in packaging that reassuringly suggests the tranquillity of home.

Similar implications arise in *Tar Baby*'s portrayal of the "contraband" apples that prompt Thérèse and Gideon's dismissal. Margaret's preoccupation with these fruits, like the high price Valerian is prepared to pay for them, stand in marked contrast to their actual appearance, as they are unloaded from ships also carrying "wilted lettuce, thin rusty beans and pithy carrots every month." Apples rank among this shoddy merchandise: they are a "hardship for the rich and the middle class, neither of whom would consider working a kitchen garden." They are "of no consequence to the poor who ate splendidly from their gardens, from the sea and from the avocado trees that grew by the side of the road" (108–9). Gardening subsequently effects in *Tar Baby* a radical alteration that supplants foods conventionally prized in the West with those that remain invisible to Valerian's Eurocentric gaze.

A fuller example of this phenomenon is provided in *Tar Baby*'s sketch of the Street family's ownership of a sweet factory in Philadelphia, a scene that concentrates on Valerian's uncles' response to his father's death.

> [T]he uncles gathered to steady everybody and take over the education of their dead brother's son since it was, they said, "self-understood" that he would inherit the candy factory. And just to show how much they loved and anticipated him, they named a candy after him. *Valerians*. Red and white gumdrops in a red and white box (mint-flavoured, the white ones; strawberry-flavoured, the red). Valerians turned out to be a slow but real flop, although not a painful one financially *for it was made from the syrup sludge left over from their main confection—Teddy Boys.*
>
> "What's the matter with them?" asked the uncles.

"Faggoty," said the sales reps. . . .

"But somebody's buying them," the uncles said.

"Jigs," said the salesmen. "Jigs buy 'em. Maryland, Florida, Mississippi. Close the line. Nobody can make a dollar selling faggot candy to jigs." . . .

But they didn't close it out. Not right away, at least. The uncles let the item sell itself in the South until the sugar shortage of the early forties and even then they fought endlessly to keep it on: they . . . held caucuses among themselves about whether to manufacture a nickel box of Valerians in Mississippi where beet sugar was almost free and the labour too. (47–48, emphasis added)

The rest of this chapter unpacks this extremely suggestive episode, in which a food eaten by African Americans ("Valerians") becomes disdained by whites in favor of a more expensive product ("Teddy Boys"). There is a great deal to unpack here, as Barbara Rigney points out in "Rainbows and Brown Sugar," an extensive discussion of Morrison's food imagery. Rigney notes: "[T]hese 'Valerians,' manufactured by Valerian Street's father . . . are . . . sickeningly sweet . . . metaphors for Valerian's own questionable masculinity and, presumably, for that of all white men. Black children will not buy them because the candies are 'faggoty.' " [44] This analysis is useful despite the textual errors it commits by attributing the Valerians to their namesake's father rather than to his uncles, and by stating that the children who refuse to buy Valerians are black when their race is not actually specified. It is crucial that we rectify the latter of these errors and recognize that the homophobic view positioning masculinity and homosexuality as mutually exclusive states is articulated by Morrison's characters rather than by Morrison herself. Only after this rectification can we see that this scene instead typifies Eve Sedgwick's thesis that what she calls "homosocial circles," such as the Streets' all-male board meeting, often invoke both homophobia and racism as ciphers by which they banish difference and solidify by an insisted conformity the cohesion of the group. [45] Bearing in mind Eve Sedgwick's discussion of such groups, homophobia here not only associates the odd choice of these despised consumers with naive effeminacy but also masks the threatening politics this choice summons. The tribute Valerian's uncles pay to his late father, which involves the industrial manufacture of red-and-white candy no less inanimate than the Tar Baby itself, opens unforeseen opportunities for black consumers to indulge in a politically strategic play upon the imagery of American patriotism. By swallowing the Valerians whole, by masticating these namesakes of a man who later so underpays his staff that they must steal food, these southern American "jigs" perform gestures of racial resistance and disrespect American patriotism, in a way that the uncles will inevitably find unpalatable. Thus, Valerian's uncles and their salesmen cannot conceivably welcome the success of their product among southern black customers but must invoke a set of prejudices that direct attention away from the unpatriotic implications this success heralds. Motivating their homophobia, then, is a desire to displace such implications under the discreet veil of a known sexual taboo that they can discuss more easily and even joke about.

By using homophobia to humiliate those they feel are humiliating Valerian, Valerian's uncles and their salesmen attribute the consumer choices made by these southern "jigs" less to perversity than to political radicalism. Unlike Thérèse and Gideon, these "jigs" do not transgress but transcend the binary food oppositions of dominant American culinary culture. Whereas Thérèse and Gideon's theft of apples confirms the higher value Valerian assigns to such American produce, these "jigs" collapse the structure of this normative evaluation by embracing a confection made from a "syrup sludge" left behind in the manufacture of the dearer Teddy Boys. A waste material "left over" from sugar processing, this "sludge" is blackstrap molasses—the same food Wright eats in the Memphis orphanage—and its favoring by these "jigs" is correspondingly comparable to Shange's favoring of pig tails over pork loin. Both decisions draw from radically new conceptualizations of taste. Both seem predicated on a wholesale reconstitution of Western food value, on a dramatic transformation of what is defamed into what is prized. And both choose historically cheap over historically expensive foods.

Admittedly, similar observations could well be made about chicken: Valerian and Margaret are partial to white breast meat, while Jadine (whose use of a personal pronoun tellingly accepts the racialization of these food connotations) asks Ondine: "Is there anything inside a chicken we don't eat?" (35). Yet I concentrate here on the binary relation between sugar and molasses both because *Tar Baby* itself concentrates on it and, more broadly, because these particular foods are saturated in the histories of industrialization, imperialism, and slavery. We have already seen that Western markets have long valued white sugar far more highly than brown molasses. We have noted that, as two products resulting from the arduous mixing and boiling of pulped sugar cane described in much African American literature, molasses was often consumed by those who performed such labor even as sugar was exported far away. A price hierarchy and color distinction in this way collaborated to create a situation wherein, as *Up from Slavery* and *American Hunger* testify, molasses came to be deemed appropriate for consumption by those who had picked, pulped, and boiled the cane. What must be stressed here, however, is that these binary systems and the racial designs they enforced were neither immanent nor innate but open to revaluation, to reinterpretations that, at their extreme, could even invert such cherished opposites. Again, in Washington's assertion that he found molasses "enjoyable" and in Bessie Smith's demand for a "pig foot and a bottle of beer," we have already encountered examples of these inversions, which demonstrate Shange's description of how what appear "arbitrary predilections of the 'nigra' " in fact constitute "symbolic defiance." In its description of southern "jigs" who actively prefer confectionery made with molasses to that made with refined sugar, however, *Tar Baby* delivers a scene that seeks to complete these strategies of food revaluation.

It seeks to complete these strategies because assumptions regarding the innate superiority of white sugar retain great resonance in Western cultures. The relegation of molasses beneath white sugar emerges, for example, from Neil Pennington and Charles W. Baker's *Sugar: A User's Guide to Sucrose,* which categorizes "the blackstrap . . . as a cattle feed . . . [also used] in the production of industrial alcohol, yeast, organic chemicals, and rum" (18–20). That *Tar Baby*'s black consumers favor a foodstuff still often thought of as unfit for human consumption reveals that their preference, like those of Booker T. Washington and Bessie Smith, can orchestrate a wholesale reconstitution of conventional Western food value. It reveals that the notions of purity and refinement to which scientific manuals on sugar still subscribe constitute, as Mary Douglas observes, a "relative idea" that "exists in the eye of the beholder."[46] Exposing this residual relativity, the decision of *Tar Baby*'s southern "jigs" discredits the binary opposition of sugar and molasses, implicitly insisting that this categorization has nothing to do with nutritional factors and everything to do with racial connotations. They expose the cheapness of molasses as a function of nothing more than what Paul Gilroy terms the "prestige attached to the metaphysical value of whiteness," of what Sidney W. Mintz calls the "symbolic linkage of whiteness to purity."[47] A choice that disturbs Valerian's uncles because it not only retrieves the edible from the putatively inedible but also then asserts the superiority of such waste thus consummates those strategies by which poorer cooks and consumers have reconstituted Western systems of food value. In this radical reconstitution, this wholesale inversion of prevailing food codes, *Tar Baby*'s southern consumers attribute to molasses all the prestige conventionally associated with sugar: they turn molasses into sugar, just as Shange effectively turns pig tails into bacon and, indeed, as *Beloved* turns brier into fruit:

> Stamp . . . stopped and backed up a bit to tell about the berries—where they were and what was in the earth that made them grow like that.
>
> "They open to the sun, but not the birds, 'cause snakes down in there and the birds know it, so they just grow—fat and sweet—with nobody to bother them 'cept me because don't nobody go in that piece of water but me and ain't too many legs willing to glide down that bank to get them. Me neither. But I was willing that day. Somehow or 'nother I was willing. And they whipped me, I'm telling you. Tore me up. But I filled two buckets anyhow. And took em over to Baby Suggs' house. It was on from then on. Such a cooking you never see no more. We baked, fried and stewed everything God put down here. Everybody came. Everybody stuffed. Cooked so much there wasn't a stick of kindlin left for the next day."[48]

What occurs here is almost by definition impossible: brier bears fruit. But by picturing this miracle, *Beloved* parallels the southern "jigs" of *Tar Baby,* vindicating their preference for a "sludge" expelled from one food system by imagining the Edenic berries that also lie beyond the white gaze, protected by a painful thicket of brier. The physical pain Stamp endures as the brier thorns cut him—so that the black of his skin and red of his blood mixes with the blackberries' intensely dark juice—betokens a natural equivalent of the experience American capitalism forces the "jigs" to undergo: both, it seems, must pass through an ordeal if they are to achieve an alternative to what Wright called "the culture that condemns" them.[49] Both *Beloved* and *Tar Baby* in this way retain faith in the possibility of total racial resistance: the fruition of brier, like the preference for molasses, undercuts America's white supremacist superstructure with premonitions of the course by which black hunger can be overcome. Whether by theft or by the transformation of waste, episodes throughout Morrison's oeuvre revel in the possibility that waste can be refashioned into food, that Brer Rabbit might stay at home and wait for the brier on his patch to blossom and bear fruit.

Morrison, then, shares with Shange and Baraka a desire to repudiate foregoing codes of culinary evaluation and to celebrate a resourcefulness she sees as inherent to soul-food cookery. What these celebrations of soul food often omit, however, is the limits to such resourcefulness. Although Morrison's novels elsewhere display an acute sensitivity to the fact that poverty always has the power to kill regardless of the ingenuity of the poor, this point becomes obscured, somewhat overshadowed in her enthusiastic portrayals of the transformative strategies of African American cooking. This is not to deny that many of these transformative strategies succeed. It is true that turnip tops and collard greens are highly nutritious and as good for the body as they are for this cuisine's much-vaunted "soul." It is equally true that the old Southern tradition of drinking "potlikker" enabled African Americans to gain as many nutrients from their vegetables as possible, and that, as Tracey Poe notes, poor black Americans in general have historically eaten more healthfully than whites on similarly low incomes.[50] But we must also remember that the oft-noted discrepancy between what tastes good to us and what actually *is* good for us influences soul food as much as any other cuisine; for every innovative treatment of healthy foods contained in this alternative culinary vocabulary, there exists a recipe for chitterlings, pork rind, or ham hocks. The chicken wings Ondine eats may be cooked in a more exciting way, employing more spices and stronger flavors than the chicken breast

Margaret eats, but this hardly prevents them from also containing far more saturated fat. The point is that Toni Morrison's celebration of the cooks who thus transform waste into food must be considered alongside Paul Gilroy's reminder that African Americans formed their culture under "the most difficult of conditions and from imperfect materials that they surely would not have selected if they had been able to choose."[51] If Morrison highlights means by which heroically ingenious cooks have initiated the process of overcoming hunger, the high infant mortality and low birthweight rates among African Americans today reveal that this battle remains unfinished.

The Negro question in the united States [*sic*] is the No. 1 minority problem in the modern world. It is No. 1 because if this cannot be solved, then there is no possibility of the solution of any minority problem anywhere. The fate of six million Jews in Europe, of perhaps twice or three times that number of individuals in the prison-camps of Russia, of Poles enslaved by Germans as a subordinate nation, . . . all this shows that here the world is not moving towards the peaceful enlightened solution of minority or national problems. It is doing the opposite.

The Negro problem becomes therefore a sort of touchstone. . . . The Negroes do not seek any special privileges, constitution or statehood. All they demand is freedom and equality. The world watches this extraordinary situation.

—C. L. R. JAMES, *American Civilization* (circa 1939–50)

Our challenge should now be to bring even more powerful visions of planetary humanity from the future into the present and to reconnect them with democratic and cosmopolitan traditions that have been all but expunged from today's black political imaginary.

—PAUL GILROY, *Between Camps* (2000)

Conclusion

WE CURRENTLY REMAIN TRAPPED in a world where the term *civilization* does little more than divide us. Saturated in Eurocentric racial ideology and infused with the history of the Crusades, *civilization* now seems to have outlived any useful function it once served, appearing tied inextricably to its notional opposite, barbarity, and to terrifying visions of transcontinental bipolarity, confrontation, and apocalypse. These problems were apparent long before September 11. Those concerned with Britain's colonization of India, the scramble for Africa, transatlantic slave trade, or Foucault's Great Confinement have long apprehended that Western civilization can refer merely to more lethal forms of savagery—to a newly efficient violence, inflicted on a grandly industrial, technological scale.

This violent background makes it surprising to recall that C. L. R. James, among the most prescient of twentieth-century intellectuals, included the term in the title of his study of U.S. society, *American Civilization*. James completed this work in the 1940s, years before Frantz Fanon's *The Wretched of the Earth* (1968) instigated the analysis of Western colonialism culminating in such seminal studies as Syed Hussein Alatas's *The Myth of the Lazy Native* (1977) and Edward Said's *Orientalism* (1978). But as a descendant of slaves and a historian of slavery who possessed an understanding of British imperial culture's white bias that was at once scholarly and personal, James was well primed to note the contradictions within the idea of civilization, to unlock its intrinsic tendency to displace to the subaltern the savagery it contained. We can understand James's choice of title only after *American Civilization* makes plain that he regards civilization less as an ideal that the United States has attained than as an unfulfilled ambition toward which it must work. *American Civilization* repeatedly figures the democratic promises of the American Revolution as worthy ideals, the consummation of which has been continually deferred—by Indian removal, by capitalist inequalities, and, especially, by the failure to extend these Constitutional guarantees to African Americans. Seen by James as the social group that has gained least from American democracy and so stands to gain most from its eventual completion, African Americans become a "touchstone," a barometer for the possibility of global democratic freedom. They lead the rest of the world—by which James means the disfranchised, hungry, and internally or externally colonized, all of whom avidly watch "this extraordinary situation" for clues toward attaining their own emancipations.

Once, ample evidence supported the consonance James identified between the domestic fight against Jim Crow and the international fight against colonialism and neocolonialism. Between the completion of *American Civilization* and the assassination of Martin Luther King Jr., African American activists were as assertively internationalist in their outlook as members of the Comintern. Although many still casually invoke Malcolm X's black nationalism and King's advocacy of nonviolent desegregation to epitomize the opposite extremes of 1960s black politics, the fact remains that both leaders were committed to a global solidarity that spanned the African Diaspora and reached well beyond it. Their commitment was reciprocated: as a banner of 1960s Jamaican agitation against "Babylon" neocolonialism insisted, "The Negro American's Struggle Is Our Struggle." Even as African students fully supported Malcolm X (el-Hajj Malik el-Shabazz) in his efforts to bring "the Afro-American's case before the United Nations," Pan-Africanism in general remained a vibrant political force.[1]

Somewhere along the line, these international links dissipated. Since the 1960s the disintegration of the domestic coalition between Jewish and black Americans has been paralleled by an erosion of the African American struggle's global alliances. Emphases on the astonishing ethnic differences, relentless barrage of information, and dizzying technological change that constitute postindustrial America have come to figure the nation as a microcosmic globe whose diversity leaves little mental space for the all too real world beyond it. Internationalism, when it has been advanced in new forms since 1970, has sometimes manifested a crude Afrocentrism that obfuscates socioeconomic difference and makes an essentialist racial commonality paramount. Among certain key commentators, only silence has greeted the militarization of America, and only silence has answered the increasingly violent anti-Americanism among those who once looked to the black struggle as a "touchstone." A global popularization of hip-hop has coincided with a marked increase in the isolationism of its lyrics, with a dramatic acceleration of that insularity Gilroy characterizes as the genre's "Americo-centric," even "ghetto-centric" gaze.[2] Thanks to these and other dispiriting developments, it has grown ever more difficult to imagine an African American Baptist minister influenced by Hinduism and Ghandian Satyagraha now rising to the eminence King once attained.

In this light, we need urgently to answer the utopian appeal that concludes Gilroy's *Between Camps* and "bring even more powerful visions of planetary humanity from the future into the present." As Gilroy suggests, we need to do far more than merely restore to the present the internationalist solidarity of the recent past. We must also embark on a transformative restoration of those futuristic conceptualizations, ex-pounded in much African American literature as well as the rhetoric of Martin Luther King, wherein the imagining of an enlightened utopia il-luminates the path present politics must follow. Thus, like James, Gilroy invokes a term (in this case, "humanism") that has become somewhat tar-nished in recent years (we earlier saw Michele Wallace castigating "liberal humanism" as a "white phallocentric tradition") and then revitalizes it by treating it less as an accomplished fact than as a future ambition. Both intellectuals vaunt the potential globalism of African American political culture; for both, the future is manifestly the source of freedom and other achievable utopias, and our task in the present is to draw it closer.

I suggest we can move toward these futuristic objectives, in the process restoring the internationalism of African American political culture, by returning to the statements on hunger that concern earlier portions of this book. A steady erosion of American internationalism has conspired with the anti-Americanism of the developing world—which sometimes fails to see past the International Monetary Fund to America's own traditions of political dissent—to hide the fact that African American literature and culture can help the world to abolish hunger. As I have argued through-out the preceding pages, an inescapable suggestion of the novels of Zora Neale Hurston, Richard Wright, and Toni Morrison is that malnutrition is preventable, is that hunger indeed can be overcome.

Their Eyes Were Watching God suggests this by imagining an achiev-able utopia, Eatonville, from which want is magically expelled. The co-incidence of this removal of hunger with the removal of a white authori-tarian presence from the town connects the two, implicating the latter in the former. A radical expulsion of racism elicits a domino-like collapse of hunger, producing an image of utopianism whose sustained negation of whiteness and want weaves both inextricably together.

American Hunger makes the same point more vigorously, as befits its original title. Throughout his autobiography, Wright insists that his child-hood and adolescent hungers invariably occurred in close proximity to a white "island" overflowing with food. Wright thus situates hunger as an immediately, easily solvable ordeal. Cooking a breakfast for his em-ployer's family, he encounters so much food—"eggs, bacon, toast, jam, butter, milk, apples"—that white diners use them as artillery in what we might now dub a "food fight."[3] Watching these makeshift missiles chart their trajectories across the table, Wright pictures himself as the captive audience of a decadent ceremony, the explicit message of which is that white Americans would rather ruin the food they will not eat than give it to their hungry black neighbors.

The adjacent worlds of plenitude and hunger described in *American Hunger* are forced into even closer proximity by *Tar Baby* and its representation of a Caribbean estate owned by whites but maintained by African Americans. By depicting such interior segregation, *Tar Baby* locates in the postcolonial Caribbean a system of racial demarcation redolent of the pre–Civil Rights South. Read in conjunction, the full narratives of *American Hunger* and *Tar Baby* thus promote an outward movement from the South to Chicago to the Caribbean, expanding the patterning of nutritional inequality from a regional to a national to an international plane. In conjunction, the Chicago sections of *American Hunger* and the island setting of *Tar Baby* suggest that late capitalist forms of labor exchange merely reproduce racial inequalities of the kind operating in Wright's interwar South. Late capitalism, *Tar Baby* implies, not only preserves the racial hierarchies of preceding economic systems but also supplements such stratification with the new legitimacy of an ostensibly deracialized, pseudoscientific system. Even in this post–Civil Rights context, the hungers of Son, Thérèse, and Gideon remain avoidable, since they, like the hunger of Richard Wright before them, could easily be satisfied if only their white employer threw open his larder doors.

All these authors employ distinctive fictional strategies, manufacturing distinctive narratives, distinctive plots, characterizations, and settings, yet these divergent routes ultimately usher each to a similar destination, to a comparable realization that hunger could be solved by a more equitable allocation of the American harvest.

On one level, this advocacy of a more equal distribution of food merely states the obvious. Wright's description of malnutrition, his placing his boyhood hunger in a society routinely producing a surplus harvest, merely anticipates the ideas of food entitlement that, at least since the publication of Amartya Sen's *On Economic Inequality* in 1973, have been widely accepted in scholarly circles. Similarly, Hurston's and Morrison's confirmation that hungry and sated Americans often exist in close quarters merely endorses Sen's lifelong dedication to those who, as in "the Bengal famine of 1943," "died in front of well-stocked food shops protected by the state."[4] In this respect, African American literature does little more than provide circumstantial evidence for what Maud Ellmann characterizes as Sen's central idea, his belief "that it is not the lack of food but the inability to purchase it that causes . . . catastrophes. People starve because they *have* no food, not because there *is* no food, and the problem, therefore, is 'entitlement' to food, rather than its notional availability."[5] While African American literature thus provides Sen with supporting evidence, he is hardly in need of such statistical confirmation. One sign of Sen's incredible success in convincing the intellectual world that hunger arises from inequalities in food entitlement is his Nobel Prize. Another is the fact that manuals for charities working on the frontline of hunger relief now routinely employ a Senian vocabulary, so that Oxfam's *Food Scarcity and Famine: Assessment and Response* (1992), for example, requires its readers to "consider whether food availability or people's entitlements to that food are more important."[6] A recent study insisting that past famines "occurred not only, or so much, because food was not available, but because poor people lost access ('entitlement')" to it corroborates the present dominance of Sen's ideas, confirming that African American literature's images of food inequality add to an already crowded, persuasive body of evidence.[7]

On another level, however, Hurston, Wright, and Morrison still have much to say to this situation. All too obviously the present ascendancy of Amartya Sen's theories of famine analysis has failed to rid the world of hunger. Total global nourishment remains elusive. Crucially, Liz Young attributes this continuing failure to a political situation in which we now know how to abolish famine but continue to lack the motivation. As the "main thesis" of her *World Hunger* (1997) insists, "hunger persists because the political will to eliminate it is lacking."[8] A sign of this failure of the West's collective "will" is surely that—decades after Martin Luther King suggested "a nation that continues year after year to spend more money on military defense than on programs of social uplift is approaching spiritual doom"—the current overseas economic aid budget of the United States remains a fraction of its defense budget.[9] Yet the seeds for this collective loss of will of the Western world are sown in the West itself. On a morning journey from suburb to central business district, many commuters pass through the blasted regions that are home to many of the eighteen million Americans who go hungry. But the millimeter gap of the car or train window through which these nourished Americans peer at their hungry fellow citizens is, it would seem, not a pane on reality so much as a television screen, which can be switched off at will. At the very least, commuters, turning back to the newspaper or to the road ahead, create a distance between themselves and those in need very like the gulf that lends legitimacy to First World inaction over Third World starvation. The American poor may be invisible, as Michael Harrington put it forty years ago, but theirs is also a created invisibility, a function of poverty's naturalization within a society that has eliminated alternatives to capitalism more thoroughly than any other, and it parallels how, amid our preoccupation with war, Third World starvation has likewise vanished.[10]

African American literature often makes the invisible visible. Like Ralph Ellison's *Invisible Man* (1952), who manifests himself through narrative, writing by other African Americans repeatedly collapses the distance between the underfed and the overfed, reminding its audiences that windows separating commuters from ghettos open on reality after all. What *Their Eyes Were Watching God, American Hunger,* and *Tar Baby* offer to Sen's economic explanation of famine is the ability to make nutritional inequality real, to populate the dry statistics of hunger analysis with the stories of the hungry. Through this dramatic capacity, this humanization of hunger, these novels regain their "touchstone" quality and illuminate paths by which we might yet reach a utopian future of universal satiety. The rhetorical brilliance and emotive appeal of *Their Eyes Were Watching God, American Hunger,* and *Tar Baby* can potentially renew the impetus of a campaign to combat hunger, adding to Amartya Sen's methods a political will that has hitherto been lacking.

The intimacy between want and satiety encountered in these texts establishes a resonant trope of the preventability of hunger less refutable than those invoked in nations where shortage has seemed either universal or the problem of a distant wilderness. Although you can plausibly blame hunger on nature if no food exists within fifty miles, you can hardly use such excuses if the hungry are forced, like Wright, to witness the fed throw their breakfast across the table. By juxtaposing the underfed and the overfed, these three narratives aid Sen's analysis because they tell human stories, human anecdotes that discredit any explanation of global famine in terms of natural catastrophe. Hurston's, Wright's, and Morrison's narratives send a signal out into the world, an insight into the economic context of hunger that holds special significance for those countries that, lacking America's spectacular abundance, have become targets of its capitalist rhetoric.

A Colonial Context

Comparisons between African American experiences and those of colonized peoples, although the inspiration for much compelling antiracist rhetoric, can be counterproductive. By invoking a phenomenon that arguably peaked a hundred years ago, such analogies often omit the modernity of African American life, the commercial success of its culture, its global influence, metropolitanism, and the new character of its violence and poverty. The internecine character of crime in American ghettos, to take one example, cannot be adequately considered if it is solely related to the explicitly revolutionary violence that, as though to fulfil Fanon's more dismal prophecies, has punctuated many countries' transition to post-colonial autonomy.[11] Outright starvation, to take another, features less prominently in African American than in other histories. African American history fortunately possesses no equivalent to the famines awaiting Native Americans on the frontier, which Dee Brown's history *Bury My Heart at Wounded Knee* (1991) classifies among the most deliberate, because they were preventable, in human history. Considered too economically useful to be jeopardized by the imposition of an unreliable diet, most African Americans may have been adequately nourished, in the slavery context, at the price of their humanity, but they were nourished nonetheless.

More significant for present concerns is the consensus among Hurston, Wright, and Morrison, who all suggest that the hunger African Americans *have* experienced has remained impermeable to what Maud Ellmann characterizes as the attempt to interpret "famine as a fluke of nature rather than a symptom of political inequities."[12] As a feat of rhetorical manipulation, the Malthusian, pre-Senian attribution of hunger to drought or famine has been pushed beyond the range of even the most pliant American racial apologist because of the pronounced visibility of the surrounding harvest. Want in America has been characterized by its proximity to a surfeit of food. One can hardly hope to legitimize hunger, to defend it as unavoidable, when its antidote remains within range.

Although concerned with general issues of inequality, Wright's essay "How 'Bigger' Was Born" (1940) reiterates this spatial intimacy, observing that American racism is distinguished by the fact that "the blacks were so *close* to the very civilization which sought to keep them out" (Wright's emphasis). This spatial intimacy, Wright suggests, differentiates what he terms the "program of oppression" implemented by white Americans against their black compatriots from projects pursued overseas. Unlike the strictures of official colonialism, this dynamic occurred "between people who were neighbors, whose homes adjoined, whose farms had common boundaries. . . . Had the Negro lived upon a common territory, separate from the bulk of the white population, this program of oppression might not have assumed such a brutal and violent form" (xiv). Since an equal intimacy between the overfed and the underfed is revealed in Sen's observations about those who "died in front of well-stocked food shops protected by the state," we must remain cautious about Wright's claim that this sheer closeness, this sheer Balkanization of inequality, is uniquely American. What really distinguishes the United States from colonial Ireland and India is that, for the majority of its population, such Balkanization was experienced, not as an exception to social norms, but as a commonplace event. Unlike the negotiable forms of nationalistic identification that often distanced colonizers from the colonized at least psychologically, both blacks and whites in the United States have long regarded themselves as American. Concentrated American spatial segregation, an intricate patchwork quilt of interlocking racial enclaves, has collaborated with this uniquely shared national identification to trap black and white together in a fractious dynamic from which, with the negligible exception of abortive repatriation schemes, escape routes have long been closed. The colonizer could always return home: yet to white and black Americans alike, those sites in which the violent flash points of race relations occurred *were* home. Experiences of inequality thus became domesticated for all its actors, acquiring an ordinary air. This explains the resigned cynicism with which Du Bois recalls his hunger in *Darkwater* (1898):

> I entered that broad and blatant hotel at Lake Minnetonka with distinct forebodings. . . . The long loft reserved for us, with its clean little cots, was reassuring; the work was not difficult,—but the meals! There were no meals. At first, before the guests ate, a dirty table in the kitchen was hastily strewn with uneatable scraps. We novices were the only ones who came to eat, while the guests' dining-room, with its savors and sights, set our appetites on edge! . . . It was nasty business. I hated it. (64)

A resigned cynicism that accepts hunger as an inevitable outcome of the hungering subject's classification on the wrong side of the racial partition produces this weary account. Du Bois's resignation to hunger arises from his recognition of its inevitability. His hunger may be less severe than those endured in India and Ireland, but it is also a more manifestly politi cized condition, because it has so irrefutably been caused by *someone* (whites) rather than *something* (nature).

To demonstrate these differences further, let us turn to those postcolonial experiences, in Ireland and in India, which, even now, are occasionally subjected to the legacy of Victorian laissez-faire assumption.

It has become something of a cliché to say that historians of Britain's involvement in Ireland often wear their political allegiances on their sleeves. The disclaimer with which Terry Eagleton begins his study of Irish literature, *Heathcliff and the Great Hunger* (1995)—"Irish cultural and historical writing are as much a minefield as the area they map, and for much the same reasons"—is in this respect standard (ix). Nowhere is such polarization revealed more clearly than when students and scholars of Irish history turn their attention to the famine of 1849. Nor does such subjectivity arise simply because the event was, as Eagleton remarks, "the greatest social disaster of nineteenth-century Europe" (23). The disaster also remains controversial because of a continuing scholarly disagreement about its precise causes. Some have explained the famine in terms of the "fluke of nature" theory, which Ellmann classifies as pre-Senian. Those advocating this approach have generally been reluctant to concede Westminster's promotion of Irish agricultural specialization, which encouraged dietary dependency on the potato. Others, meanwhile, concur with Ellmann by characterizing the "fluke of nature" theory as a smokescreen and by arguing that it was in fact the British Whig government's "economic policies . . . [that] exacerbated the privations they purported to be trying to assuage."[13] Characteristic of this alternative approach is Cecil Woodham-Smith's *The Great Hunger* (1962), still the best-known history of the famine, which vilifies the Whigs' inability to see beyond their ideological commitment to free trade and bring relief to Ireland sufficiently swiftly. Typically, such approaches accept that the fungus *Phytophthora infestans* was at the famine's root and, concentrating on this ecological disaster's aftermath, critique the flaws in Westminster policy. As a result, these explanations of the famine concentrate principally on the continuing of exports from Ireland. Again Woodham-Smith's account is exemplary:

> Forced by economic necessity to sell his produce [the Irish peasant] . . . was furiously resentful when food left the market towns under the eyes of the hungry populace, protected by a military escort of overwhelming strength. From Waterford, the Commissariat officer wrote to Trevelyan, on April 24, 1846, "The barges leave Clonmel once a week for this place, with the export supplies under convoy which, last Tuesday, consisted of 2 guns, 50 cavalry and 80 infantry escorting them on the banks of the Suir as far as Carrick."
>
> It was a sight which the Irish people found impossible to understand and impossible to forget. (76–77)

Like other historians of the famine, Woodham-Smith here concentrates less on the original cause of the famine than on the subsequent response of the British government. The question of "efficacy of action taken," as Cormác Oacute Gráda notes, remains central. Yet Oacute Gráda also points out that, even here, controversy reigns. Opinion on the Whig government's response "ranges from that caught in fiery nationalist John Mitchel's accusation that 'the Almighty sent the potato blight, but the English created the famine' . . . to William Wilde's claim that 'the most strenuous efforts which human sagacity, ingenuity and foresight could at the time devise were put into requisition.' " These continuing controversies free a middle ground to be claimed by the self-described "objective" historian. Oacute Gráda himself calls for a new and "full appraisal [of] . . . the issue of blame."[14] Even Terry Eagleton—whose critical technique is hardly famed for laying claim to the middle ground, a territory more often associated with liberalism than Marxism—adopts a deliberately neutral tone, echoing Oacute Gráda:

> There was no question of calculated genocide; and food imports, contrary to nationalist mythology, far outstripped exports in the Famine years. But neither was the Famine an act of God.[15]

Here, in the interests of balance, Eagleton provides the facts to an issue that he rightly describes as among the most contentious episodes in British imperial history: the continuing exportation of food from Ireland even at the height of its famine. Yet these exports—which, as Cecil Woodham-Smith suggests, Irish citizens "found impossible to understand and impossible to forget"—are here resolved into and dismissed by an equation that shows them to be far outweighed by imports. This equation is then pressed into the service of a refutation of the nationalist allegation of genocide; the balance sheet becomes evidence that this was not, after all, a rehearsal of the Holocaust.

At the same time, Eagleton's comments exemplify how the myriad inveiglements of Irish historiography encourage a skewed logic that designates certain "issues" to certain "groups" regardless of the actual point being made. The export question is characterized as the natural terrain of "nationalist mythology," and its discrediting, by extension, is seen as discrediting this particular faction. Eagleton presents his comment as evidence in favor of the British government's role, which he then scrupulously counterbalances with evidence against it. Yet, this comment also admits that exports, even at the height of the famine, continued. It sustains the view it purports to challenge. That is, Eagleton here supplies data suggesting that exports recorded on this balance sheet, like the ships sailing out of Limerick and Dublin harbors, were redeemed by the existence of those sailing *in*. Yet this position invites its own nationalist rebuke: that *no* ships should have been leaving these harbors, that *no* crops should have been exported at all, when those living near their place of production remained without food.

What these rather surprising negotiations delineate is the struggle that Amartya Sen's theoretical innovations continue to face if they are to wrestle the discursive vocabulary through which we understand famine away from laissez-faire assumption. Eagleton's commentary, by apparently accepting that imports may mitigate exports in times of food shortage, demonstrates that this vocabulary remains saturated in a Victorian ethos that holds that economies must recover by their own, capitalistic means if they are to become less vulnerable to future famine.

Sen repudiates laissez-faire assumption by emphasizing the ostensibly simple fact that money is often an unreliable mediator of access to food. As Sen notes: "Famines often take place in situations of moderate to good food availability, without any significant decline of food supply per head."[16] Elsewhere Sen reiterates this critical distinction by urging that, since "income is not desired for its own sake, any income-based notion of poverty must refer—directly or indirectly—to those basic ends which are promoted by income as means. Indeed, in poverty studies related to less developed countries, the 'poverty line' income is often derived explicitly with reference to nutritional norms."[17] Such insights position Oacute Gráda's statement that "the earnings gap between Britain and Ireland on the eve of the Famine was significant" as, in itself, sufficient evidence as to why British efforts to keep the Irish economy running as normal singularly failed to avert starvation.[18] They also discredit Eagleton's downplaying of the exportation of grain from Ireland, since they reveal that those imports whose sheer magnitude ostensibly nullified such exports actually helped maintain an economy that was itself responsible for pricing foods beyond the means of the poor. They explode the ideological foundations that supported British governmental attempts to present colonial famine as the growing pains of capitalism, which could be curtailed by a restoration of free trade via a renewed defense that guarded crops as though they were munitions.

Surprising as it may seem, however, this repudiation of laissez-faire assumption has also been advanced by *Their Eyes Were Watching God,*

American Hunger, and *Tar Baby.* By demonstrating that despite its abundance even American society has failed to banish hunger, these narratives anticipate Sen's entitlement approach and confirm that, like famines, hungers often take "place in situations of moderate to good food availability, without any significant decline of food supply per head." They consolidate this approach because, while those wishing to may still attribute distant famine to drought rather than to the economy, it is *impossible* to submit an equivalent explanation for, say, the hunger Du Bois experienced in "that broad and blatant hotel at Lake Minnetonka." It is precisely in the way these writers represent domestic black hunger as *so* avoidable, as *so* glaringly adjacent to a food surfeit, that we find evidence that "people starve because they *have* no food, not because there *is* no food, and [that] the problem, therefore, is 'entitlement.' "

In this way, these texts contribute to the realization, reached by diverse politicians and intellectuals following the Second World War but most fully expressed in the 1960s rhetoric of Martin Luther King, that the universal distribution of adequate nutrition is an achievable goal. Both domestically and internationally, these narratives have participated in the dawning realization across diverse discourses that our globe in fact possesses sufficient food for every man and woman on it. However unquantifiable their final influence may be, *Their Eyes Were Watching God* and *American Hunger* undeniably contributed to a new intellectual territory in which such pronouncements as the following can be made:

> If Western civilization does not now respond constructively to the challenge to banish racism, some future historian will have to say that a great civilization died because it lacked the soul and commitment to make justice a reality for all men. . . .
>
> Two-thirds of the peoples of the world go to bed hungry at night. They are undernourished, ill-housed and shabbily clad. . . .
>
> There is nothing new about poverty. What is new, however, is that we now have the resources to get rid of it. . . . [F]amine is wholly unnecessary in the modern world. Today, therefore, the question on the agenda must read: Why should there be hunger and privation in any land, in any city, at any table, when man has the resources and the scientific know-how to provide all mankind with the basic necessities of life?[19]

Because of its frequent representation of the abolition of hunger as an achievable goal, the African American literary tradition partly contributes to King's confident realization that "famine is wholly unnecessary in the modern world." Facilitating his assertion is *American Hunger*'s revelation that it is absurd to suggest to a black employee confronted by a "food fight" that his or her hunger is caused by natural catastrophe. Posthumously, King's ideas have also gained credence from representations in *Tar Baby*. Morrison's exposure of the abyss separating the diet of a rich employer and that of poor employees inside a single household endorses the suggestion in *Where Do We Go from Here?* (1967) that capitalism creates "a gulf between superfluous wealth and abject poverty" as wide as that which segregation imposed between black and white (217). No one has contributed more to achieving Martin Luther King's ambition of abolishing hunger than Amartya Sen. However, positions reached by these three very different African American writers, by unequivocally situating hunger as an avoidable condition, also add credibility to King's as yet unfulfilled objectives. Whereas Sen's theoretical contributions to understanding hunger are manifest, *Their Eyes Were Watching God, American Hunger,* and *Tar Baby* potentially assist him because they dramatize exactly what is at stake in his new economic philosophy. If Sen has helped acclimatize intellectuals globally to the possibility of malnutrition's total abolition, then the impetus to implement this project on the fullest possible scale is potentially reinvigorated by these African American writers, by their cast of hungry characters, and by their consistent imagining of a world without hunger.

A Domestic Context

Often, polemicists working toward King and Sen's goal of abolishing famine from the world have sought to maximize the emotive appeal of their rhetoric by focusing on hunger's physical victimization of children. Characteristically, this rhetorical concentration aims to profit from the perceived cultural assumption that such children embody an innocence that supersedes, or should supersede, race along with the notional economic failures of their nations or families. The purposefully emotive pamphlets of charity fundraising, for example, regularly display images of children that, it is hoped, will transcend entrenched notions of cultural difference and so activate Western audiences' latent sympathies for the hungers of distant lands. Although advocates of state intervention are concerned with domestic politics, they, too, often aim to mobilize their audiences by drawing attention to threats to children's presupposed innocence. A good example of this is Mike Davis's essay on the L.A. riots, "Los Angeles Was Just the Beginning" (1992), which attributes the uprising to the want experienced by the city's underclass:

> [The] nation's first multicultural riot was as much about empty bellies and broken hearts as it was about police batons and Rodney King. . . . At Christmas more than twenty thousand predominantly Latina women and children from throughout the central city waited all night in the cold to collect a free turkey and a blanket from charities. Other visible barometers of distress are the rapidly growing colonies of homeless compañeros on the desolate flanks of Crown Hill and in the concrete bed of the L.A. river, where people are forced to use sewage water for bathing and cooking. . . . Unlike the looters in Hollywood (some on skateboards) who stole Madonna's bustier and all the crotchless panties from Frederick's, the masses of MacArthur Park concentrated on the prosaic necessities of life like cockroach spray and diapers. . . . Meanwhile, thousands of saqueadores, many of them pathetic scavengers captured in the charred ruins the day after the looting, languish in County Jail, unable to meet absurdly high bails. One man, caught with a packet of sunflower seeds and two cartons of milk, is being held on $15,000 bail. (221–22)

Here Davis presents those unmet childhood needs—the lack of basic necessities, of "diapers," "milk," and clean water—as an especially outrageous social failure that only a more muscular governmental involvement can address. Davis's essay thus employs a distinctive symbolism, used incessantly in antihunger polemic, in which the stereotypically moonlike eyes and passive manner of the starving child fill our gaze in order to depoliticize malnutrition and establish it as a matter, not for ideology, but for a humanist morality considered universal.

As a rhetorical tradition, the invocation of youth in denunciations of hunger is old. Long before the erosion of welfare by Western governments, this form of symbolism was regularly incorporated into those late-nineteenth- and early-twentieth-century socialist polemics that originally helped to set this now-frayed safety net in place. Before the New Deal, revolutionaries and reformers alike often approached the hungering child in much the same manner as charities today: as a figure that embodied a ready-made and irrefutable appeal for Christian benevolence or socialism. Foremost among these reformers was Jacob Riis, whose special "sympathy" for "the cases of children and virtuous women," as characterized by Robert Bremner, is amply captured by some of his titles: *Children of the Poor* (1892), *Nibsby's Christmas* (1893), *Children of the Tenements* (1903), *Christmas Stories* (1923).[20] Among revolutionary texts that exploit the emotive potential of childhood hunger, we might include Frederick Engels's *The Condition of the Working Class in England* (1845), Jack London's *The People of the Abyss* (1903), even George Orwell's *The Road to Wigan Pier* (1937). The most comprehensive use of childhood hunger as a de facto argument in favor of revolution remains, however, John Spargo's *The Bitter Cry of the Children* (1906).

This polemic, completed shortly before Spargo embarked on a controversial transition from socialism to a role as an advisor to Woodrow Wilson, was published in response to the American press's questioning of statistics on child poverty submitted by Robert Hunter's *Poverty* (1904). It sought to defend Hunter's investigation and, in particular, to corroborate his estimation that "in normal times there are at least 10,000,000 persons in the United States in poverty," a statistic that lay at the root of most media criticisms of the work.[21] In the introduction to *The Bitter Cry of the Children*, Hunter praised Spargo's work as a potentially

> mighty factor in awakening all classes of our people to the necessity of under-
> taking measures to remedy the conditions which exist. The appeal of adults
> in poverty is an old appeal, so old indeed that we have become in a measure
> hardened to its pathos and insensitive to its tragedy. But this book represents
> the cry of the child in distress, and it will touch every human heart and even
> arouse to action the stolid and apathetic. (viii)

Hunter's implication here also informs much of Spargo's subsequent narrative, namely, that the American press criticized the statistical evidence of *Poverty*, rather than the precepts of its argument, because even the most avid advocate of unrestrained capitalism cannot justify childhood hunger. This perceived consensus between Right and Left stops *The Bitter Cry of the Children* from lengthily implicating the United States government in the hunger of its younger citizens, because Spargo assumes throughout that such implications muster widespread agreement. Rather than tackle economic theories outside this perceived consensus, Spargo concentrates on undermining the more insidious strategy, employed in right-wing quarters of the American media, of absolving such implications simply by refuting the evidence for the existence of such hunger. Thus, Spargo's approach becomes an exercise in statistical accumulation, of layering evidence upon evidence, in support of Hunter. A characteristic passage reads:

> [Hunter] has observed that poverty's misery falls most heavily upon the children, and that there are probably not less than from 60,000 to 70,000 children in New York city alone "who often arrive at school hungry and unfitted to do well the work required." By a section of the press that statement was garbled into something very different, that 70,000 children in New York city go "breakfastless" to school every day. In that form the statement was naturally and very justly criticized, for, of course, nothing like that number go absolutely without breakfast. It is not, however, a question of children going without breakfast, but of children who are *underfed,* and the latter word would have been better fitted to express the real meaning of the original statement than the word "hungry." Many thousands of little children go breakfastless to school at times, but the real problem is much more extensive than that and embraces that much more numerous class of children who are chronically underfed. (61–62)

The polemical intentions of these ostensibly objective sentences are betrayed only by the description of hungry children as "little," an emotive designation that not only recalls the sentimentality Charles Dickens engineered throughout *Little Dorrit* (1855–57) but also anticipates strategies employed in the fundraising publicity of the Children's Food Fund. As such, Spargo's writing here draws upon what might be termed an accepted stratification of want, which divides humans according to their perceived capacities for self-sufficiency and thus places the child at the head of an imagined hierarchy of need. When one considers that the perceived dependency of children that prioritizes them is also a dependency on those adults whose own needs are given secondary importance by this approach, such stratification of want becomes problematic. There is little point in ensuring that children receive proper nutrition if other aspects equally integral to their care cannot be adequately fulfilled because their parents remain hungry. Such contradictions emerge no less clearly in conventional Western television reporting of Third World famine. Here, cameras typically point at a child who has been isolated from others and, by these means, direct the gaze and thus the compassion of audiences away from those adults on whom such children depend. Often accompanying such news footage is a voiceover that appeals to notions of humanism by emphasizing the essential kinship between those who, bound into an unequal partnership by satellite, watch and those outside the West who are being watched. Although the relative invisibility of starving adults in such coverage immediately throws these appeals to kinship into question, potentially exposing such humanism as a premature deracialization, we cannot lightly dismiss the emotional resonance such footage stimulates in multiracial Western audiences. Joined together by a globalized economy whose benefits and hardships neither can control, televisual exchanges between starving subjects and sated Western viewers provide a forum in which the latter can complete a belated yet sincere admission of the privileges they enjoy. Like those of the readers of *The Bitter Cry of the Children,* the responses of viewers of famine news footage may be problematic; yet they are also responses that demonstrably save lives.

In itself, this fact demands that we approach *The Bitter Cry of the Children* as a text that does not necessarily share the special urgency its readers invest in childhood hunger but that manipulates such urgency to advance its own, socialistic objectives. As Hunter states, Spargo emphasizes childhood hunger not because he himself necessarily reserves a special sympathy for it, but because he realizes that even the most "stolid and apathetic" among his readers cannot hear "the cry of the child in distress" without it touching their "human heart[s]."

Yet the special urgency of childhood hunger also clarifies the ways by which, in the first half of *American Hunger,* Richard Wright strives to prompt his readers' outrage at the treatment he received when young. "I would feel hunger nudging my ribs, twisting my empty guts," remembers

Wright, evoking sensations that, he hopes to imply, no child should have to feel. "I would grow dizzy and my vision would dim. I became less active in my play," proceeds the narrative, incidentally demonstrating why Spargo characterizes malnutrition as an insurmountable obstacle to educational development.[22] *American Hunger,* having invoked the association between hunger and childhood in order to arouse a special sympathy in its audience, then channels this elicited compassion toward those caricatures of Negro boyhood for which white Southern culture reserved a certain indulgent affection. Having induced such compassion, however, Wright tests the extent to which it relies on its subject's incubation in prepubescence by initiating a chronological progression, preordained by the genre of the autobiography, toward that black masculinity for which white Southern culture, by contrast, reserved its most pressing anxieties. The conventional progressions of the autobiography genre thus enable Wright to erode and finally to expose the racial assumptions underpinning a sympathy he originally inspired by presenting himself as a hungry black boy. Having invited tears to fall at its personification of childhood helplessness, *American Hunger* implicates its readers in their own tears, asking what share of the American harvest they receive, in a narrative sequence that systematically replaces empathy with guilt, and sympathy with a restatement of social inequality.

James Baldwin—who once, when attempting to encapsulate the "mischief" of the author of *Native Son,* described Wright as a knowing "pickaninny"—exploits the same special sympathy for the tribulations of the young in *No Name in the Street* (1972).[23] In narrative moments such as the following rhetorical flourish, Baldwin associates this special sympathy specifically with hunger:

> America proves, certainly, if any nation ever has, that man cannot live by bread alone; on the other hand, men can scarcely begin to react to this principle until they—and, still more, their children—have enough bread to eat. Hunger has no principles, it simply makes men, at worst, wretched, and, at best, dangerous. (60)

No Name in the Street is not, however, a discussion of food and hunger and fails to expand on these tantalizing suggestions. Instead, Baldwin's narrative is a personal history of the assassinations of black leaders during the 1960s. It presents itself as an inside account of the violence of the time, of a violence that involved Baldwin so profoundly that his very clothes became "drenched in the blood of all the crimes of my country" (17). Narrating the victories, setbacks, and maneuvers of the Civil Rights and black nationalist movements, Baldwin positions himself as an elder who watches over these threatened yet youthful constituencies—who, indeed, recognizes the youth of its participants more readily than they themselves can. Of Malcolm X, Baldwin's principal memory is that he was "young and looked younger" (66); Medgar Evers has a "country boy preacher's grin" (100), while the youth of Martin Luther King Jr. is accorded similar emphasis.

No Name in the Street's manipulation of the cult of youth reaches an apotheosis as it turns to the killing of Black Panthers at the end of the 1960s. Baldwin laments the Oakland police force's shooting of the "unarmed black adolescent" Bobby Hutton as well as the way this attack, which *No Name in the Street* squarely positions as another assassination, traumatizes the surviving "comrade" Huey Newton. Youth subsequently becomes for Baldwin and his sister the single defining characteristic of the survivor Newton. For Angie Baldwin, Newton is simply "that nice boy," while for Baldwin himself, visiting him in the penitentiary, he is

> a hard man to describe. . . . Huey looks like the cleanest, most scrubbed, most well-bred of adolescents—everybody's favorite baby-sitter. He is old-fashioned in the most remarkable sense, in that he treats everyone with respect, especially his elders. . . . That day, for example, he was dealing with the press, with photographers, with his lawyer, with me, with prison regulations, with his notoriety in the prison, with the latest pronouncements of Police Chief Gain, with the shape of the terror speedily engulfing his friends and co-workers, and he was also, after all, at that moment, standing in the shadow of the gas chamber.
>
> Anyone, under such circumstances, can be pardoned for being rattled or even rude, but Huey was beautiful. (112–13)

Implied in this invocation of beauty is an emphasis on Newton's resemblance to an innocent child, which inexorably summons what Baldwin sees as American society's failure to allow this black boy a childhood.

Interestingly, however, this implication was echoed by the sympathy Newton and Bobby Seale extended to those even younger than they were. Early policies of the Black Panthers were principally concerned with issues facing schoolchildren, demanding, for example, a more adequate "education" able to expose "the true nature of this decadent American society."[24] Such rhetoric, when placed alongside Baldwin's emphasis on Huey Newton's youth, opens up two forms of distance, between the self-styled "elder" and young men, and between these young men and children. There emerges from Black Panther Party rhetoric that urgent and deliberately humanitarian desire to cure childhood hunger that also animates *The Bitter Cry of the Children* and *American Hunger*. As a declaration of 1969 stated:

> The Free Breakfast for School Children is about to cover the country and be initiated in every chapter and branch of the Black Panther Party. This program was created because the Black Panther Party understands that our children need a nourishing breakfast every morning so that they can learn.
>
> These Breakfasts include every nutrient that they need for the day. For too long have our people gone hungry and without the proper health aids they need. But the Black Panther Party says that this type of thing must be halted, because we must survive this evil government and build a new one fit for the service of all the people. . . .
>
> It is a *beautiful* sight to see our children eat in the mornings after remembering the times when our stomachs were not full. . . . At one time there were children that passed out in class from hunger, or had to be sent home for something to eat. But our children shall be fed, and the Black Panther Party will not let the malady of hunger keep our children down any longer. . . . *Hunger is one of the means of oppression and it must be halted.*[25]

I conclude this discussion of hunger and resistance in African American culture with a citation from Black Panther rhetoric for three reasons. I quote this rhetoric not to suggest a direct correlation between it and the speculations of African American literature, but to clarify further a mode of thinking about hunger and food that permeates much American culture. This polemic by the Black Panthers embodies both the simplicity and the complexity that, following Sen, we can identify in the positions *Their Eyes Were Watching God, American Hunger,* and *Tar Baby* advance on questions of inequality. Its objective of universal nutritional satiation is entirely consistent with these narratives since it, too, appears entirely achievable in a United States routinely producing a food surplus. Yet, as these three narratives also make clear, this simple objective remains frustrated, remains complicated by the lingering imprint of racial inequality on American social structures.

I also conclude with this quotation because, like *American Hunger*, it forces us to revise our understanding of hunger itself. If Wright's autobiography complicates conventional sociological characterizations of hunger as symptomatic of poverty, then the reorientation toward lived experience that this complication necessitates musters support in the Black Panthers' assessment that "hunger is one of the means of oppression." By characterizing hunger as a "means" rather than as a symptom or an end of "oppression," this statement of intent succinctly reiterates Wright's lifelong insistence that malnutrition, far from being a passive repercussion of poverty, actively manufactures its culture of debilitation, docility, and ignorance. The Black Panthers' restoration of this previously faceless measure of social failure into an ordeal that "our children" actually experience thus consolidates both the politicization and the centrality that hunger assumes in Wright's autobiography. Further, after prioritizing hunger, this rhetoric immediately proposes a solution to it as simple and achievable as that indicated in the joint expulsion of hunger and whiteness from Zora Neale Hurston's Eatonville. Proof that this text affirms both Wright's explicit and Hurston's implicit view of hunger as avoidable and politicized is, meanwhile, provided by the controversies that this scheme excited among political leaders. Only by understanding the affinity between emancipatory and nutritional demands can we explain Huey Newton's remark that the "survival program that seemed most laudatory— that of providing free breakfasts to schoolchildren—was pinpointed by J. Edgar Hoover as the 'real long-range threat to American society.' "[26] Such paranoia stemmed, not from the prospect of African American bodily nourishment per se, but from the possibility that such satiation would prompt interrelated calls for a psychological or political nourishment, provoking a collapse in the docility that, produced by hunger, had reconciled the poor to their penury. Hoover, in this sense, agreed with these black revolutionaries because he, too, saw that the abolition of nutritional hunger might facilitate an education, which in turn might facilitate the satiation of hunger's political counterparts. The fact that, in Hoover's shifting scale of national anxieties, the Black Panthers' breakfast scheme ranked higher than Vietnam and nuclear war provides the most eloquent evidence yet to support *American Hunger*'s suggestion that malnutrition is the cement that holds racial inequality together.

Finally, I conclude with this citation because it advocates its profound ambitions through cooking *and* writing. Into the voids of hunger and illiteracy, the Black Panthers' representation of cooking pours foods and words, filling an absence imposed from without. This text enlists the same dual cultural practice that carried the freed slave Abby Fisher to publishing renown in California. There is the same uniting of cooking and writing, the same alliance between stirring spoons and writing pens, which join to defeat hunger. On one level, cooking here produces breakfasts for hungry schoolchildren. It radically refuses an absence that it sees as entirely avoidable. But on another level, foods that these acts of cooking create are consumed not only by hungry schoolchildren but also by those readers who "digest" their polemical representation. *I* consume them, *you* consume them, *we* consume them because they have been represented in *words,* in *writing.* It is not just that cooking *is* a way of defying oppression: it is that this rhetoric, like Hurston's, Wright's, and Morrison's prose, says that it is. And it is through this statement—through this bid for publicity—that the Black Panthers, like many African American writers, support the worldwide project for abolishing hunger. They dramatize hunger, populate the statistics with firsthand experiences. They offer a way of regaining momentum, of restoring the impetus needed to implement Amartya Sen's ideas throughout the world. And in the process they remind us that, no matter how tarnished the idea of civilization may have become, the removal of hunger remains one measure of progress not contaminated by the awful legacy of race. Through these rhetorical means, through their ability to make the experience of hunger become potently immediate, Black Panther polemicists of the 1960s join Zora Neale Hurston, Richard Wright, and Toni Morrison as contributors, as emissaries to an intellectual movement that still seeks to resolve hunger's unnecessary presence on our ever more productive planet.

Notes

Introduction

1. Gates, *Signifying Monkey.*
2. Douglass, *Narrative of the Life,* 64, 48–49.
3. Plato, "Gorgias," 101.
4. Goody, *Cooking, Cuisine, and Class,* 98–118; Anderson, "Traditional Medical Values of Food," 80–91.
5. Morrison, "Cooking Out," 16.
6. Leeming, *James Baldwin.*
7. Washington, "A Letter to John Robert E. Lee," in *Booker T. Washington Papers,* 10:188.

8. Du Bois, "Education and Work," 575, 565.

9. West, "W. E. B. Du Bois: An Interpretation," in Appiah and Gates, *Africana*, 1,967–68.

10. Washington, "A Sunday Evening Talk," in *Booker T. Washington Papers*, 10:301–2.

11. Parts of the following argument were originally published in Andrew Warnes, "'Talking' Recipes: *What Mrs. Fisher Knows* and the African-American Cookbook Tradition," in *The Recipe Reader: Recipes in Cultural Context*, edited by Janet Floyd and Laurel Foster (London: Ashgate, 2003).

12. Zafar, "Signifying Dish," 250.

13. Smart-Grosvenor, *Vibration Cooking*, 6.

14. Bower, "Bound Together," 1.

15. Gronniosaw, *Narrative*, 10.

16. Gates, "Preface: Talking Books," in *Norton Anthology of African-American Literature*, xxxviii.

17. James Weldon Johnson, "O Black and Unknown Bards," in *Norton Anthology of African-American Literature*, 769.

18. Dunbar, "Possum," in *Selected Poems*, 64–65.

19. Shigley, "Empathy, Energy, and Eating," 130.

20. The status of Abby Fisher's work as the first cookbook to be published by an African American is proclaimed by the Applewood edition of *What Mrs. Fisher Knows*. However, Rafia Zahar challenges this status in forthcoming research, while in *Black Hunger* Doris Witt notes the existence of earlier recipes by African Americans.

21. Hess, "What We Know about Mrs. Abby Fisher and Her Cooking," in Fisher, *What Mrs. Fisher Knows*, 76.

22. Zafar, "Signifying Dish," 250.

23. Witt, *Black Hunger*, 23.

24. A useful discussion of the African American caricature in U.S. commercial advertising can be found at http://www.ferris.edu/news/jimcrow/tom (last accessed May 20, 2003).

25. Hess, *Carolina Rice Kitchen*, 111.

26. Shange, *If I Can Cook*, 75.

Eatingville

1. Hurston, *Their Eyes*, 196, 228.

2. Wright, "Between Laughter and Tears," 25.

3. Carby, *Cultures in Babylon*, 132, 157.

4. Bose, introduction to *Utopia*, vii.

5. Kumar, *Utopia and Anti-Utopia*, 30

6. Eagleton, "Utopia and Its Opposites," 34.

7. Bauman, *Socialism*, 14.

8. Baker, *Workings of the Spirit*, 97.

9. Hurston, *Dust Tracks on a Road*, 10; Rossi, "Bacon's Idea of Science," 13.

10. Bacon, "New Atlantis," 272–74.

11. McPhee, *Oranges*, 6

12. Smith, Plucknett, and Talbot, *Tropical Forests*, 98.

13. Defoe, *Robinson Crusoe*, 114.

14. Brown, *Bury My Heart at Wounded Knee*, 23–24.

15. Acclaim is usually accorded to the British naval surgeon James Lind, who, in a 1753 initiative that also inspired the nickname "limeys," recommended the distribution of citrus to all Royal Navy sailors. Yet many historians have also wished to bestow on Lind a further accolade for identifying the actual therapeutic benefits of citrus's antiscorbutic property. This is the position of Peter Kolchin's *American Slavery* (1993), which observes that, "unbeknownst to anyone" before the Revolutionary period, scurvy was caused "by a deficiency of vitamin C" (21). Yet it is hard to reconcile such observations with the fact that, although it predates Lind's discovery by over a century, Smith's *Generall Historie* proclaims "Oranges and Limons" to be an "undoubted remedie" for "Scurvie" (238).

16. Krumholz, "Ghosts of Slavery," 402.

17. Morrison, *Beloved*, 54.

18. Hurston, *Dust Tracks on a Road*, 18–19.

19. Murray, *Seven League Boots*, 100.

20. Genovese, *Roll, Jordan, Roll*, 363

21. Storace, "Scripture of Utopia," 64.

22. Washington, "Sunday Evening Talk," in *Booker T. Washington Papers*, 10:303.

23. B. Johnson, *World of Difference*, 60.

24. B. Johnson, *World of Difference*, 160–63.

25. Carby, *Cultures in Babylon*, 179.

26. Eagleton, "Utopia and Its Opposites," 34.

27. Baker, *Workings of the Spirit*, 88.

28. Hurston, *Mules and Men*, 274–75.

29. Hurston, *Mules and Men*, 186.

30. Wodrow, *Correspondence*, 149–50.

31. Steingarten, *Man Who Ate Everything*, 262; Zibart, Stevens, and Vermont, *Unofficial Guide to Ethnic Cuisine*, 333.

32. Poe, "Origins of Soul Food," 94.

33. Wright, *Eight Men*, 10.

34. Wright, *Eight Men*, 18.

35. Kanneh, *African Identities*, 65.

36. Toomer, *Wayward and the Seeking*, 123.

37. Gambrell, *Women Intellectuals*, 113, 115.

38. Hemenway, *Zora Neale Hurston*, 228–29.

39. Witt, *Black Hunger*, 176.

40. Gilroy, *Between Camps*, 117.

41. James, *Beyond a Boundary*, 7.

The Uses of American Hunger

1. Rampersad, note on the text, 487–88.

2. Rubin, "Self, Culture and Self-Culture," 789–96.

3. Mencken, "Negro Spokesman Arises," 188–90.

4. Rampersad, note on the text, 489.

5. Wright, "Book-of-the-Month Author," 1.

6. Wright, "How Richard Wright Looks at *Black Boy*," 3–4.

7. Wright, *Black Boy (American Hunger)*, 148, 453.

8. Cayton and Drake, *Black Metropolis*, 608–9; Poe, "Origins of Soul Food," 98.

9. Wright, "How Bigger Was Born," xiv.

10. Wright, introduction to *Black Metropolis*, xviii.

11. James, *American Civilization*, 234–35.

12. James, "Black Studies," 195–96.

13. Gilroy, *Black Atlantic*, 159.

14. Said, *Culture and Imperialism*, 61.

15. Dickens, *Oliver Twist*, 48.

16. Logan, *Betrayal of the Negro*, 52.

17. Foucault, *Discipline and Punish*, 308.

18. Hill, *Short-Term Influences on Hunger*, 10.

19. James, *Beyond a Boundary*, 7.

20. Shange, *If I Can Cook*, 17. Mathieson observes: "Those who fed the mill were liable, especially when tired or half-asleep, to have their fingers caught between the rollers. A hatchet was kept in readiness to sever the arm, which in such cases was always drawn in; and this no doubt explains the number of maimed

watchmen. The negroes employed as boilermen had a less exacting, but a heavier task. Standing barefoot for hours on the stones or hard ground and without seats for their intermissions of duty, they frequently developed 'disorders of the legs.' The ladle suspended on a pole which transferred the sugar from one cauldron to another was 'in itself particularly heavy'; and, as the strainers were placed at a considerable height above the cauldrons, it had to be raised as well as swung" (*British Slavery and Its Abolition*, 63).

21. Moody, *Slavery on Louisiana Sugar Plantations*, 50.

22. *Deadly Adulteration and Slow Poisoning*, 96. An American counterpart to this hysteria is "Impure Molasses Sold: The Board of Health Opens War on the Adulterated Article," *New York Times*, Dec. 7, 1900, 5.

23. Washington, *Up from Slavery*, 245, 10.

24. Washington, *Up from Slavery*, 246. Shange, *If I Can Cook*, 6.

25. J. L. S., *Sugar; How it Grows*, 6. Thomas Short similarly emphasizes the animal uses of molasses: "With the skimmings of the Juice of the Cane in the first and second Boilers, the Sugar-Makers feed their Swine and Poultry, which from its oiliness soon fattens them." See *Discourses on Tea, Sugar*, 80.

26. Williams, *Country and the City*, 12; Pennington and Baker, *Sugar*, 18–20.

27. Gilroy, *Between Camps*, 22

28. Faulkner, "Bear," 164.

29. Brown, *Bury My Heart at Wounded Knee*, 40.

30. Gates, *Figures in Black*, 93.

31. Witt, *Black Hunger*, 82, 86.

32. Marx, *Capital*, 55, 111.

33. Marx, *Capital*, 163; Wright, *Twelve Million Black Voices*, 25.

34. Foucault, *Discipline and Punish*, 166.

35. Douglass, *Narrative of the Life*, 52.

36. Gilroy, *Between Camps*, 203.

37. Thompson, "Where the West Begins," 157.

38. Gates, *Figures in Black*, 4.

39. Wright, "This, Too, Is America," 63.

40. Wright, *Native Son*, 166–67.

41. Karen Hess, "What We Know about Mrs. Abby Fisher" in *What Mrs. Fisher Knows*, 79.

42. J. B. Harris, *Iron Pots and Wooden Spoons*, 95–96; Ellison, *Invisible Man*, 215.

43. Wright, "*Black Boy* and Reading," 81.

The Blossoming of Brier

1. Throughout this chapter, "America" refers to the United States, while Morrison's fictional island is placed in the "Caribbean" region. I am aware that these designations raise many problems and use them only because of the lack of a geographically accurate adjective for the United States.

2. In this discussion, *Tar Baby* refers to Morrison's novel, "Tar Baby" to the folktale, and Tar Baby to the inanimate character itself. The following synopsis is consistent with the folktale presented in J. C. Harris, *Uncle Remus*.

3. Wright, *Black Boy*, 176.

4. Physician Task Force, *Hunger in America*.

5. E. M. Young, *World Hunger*, 25.

6. Morrison, *Tar Baby*, 8.

7. While the appearance of Jane Austen in this discussion of race and colonialism may seem surprising, Edward Said has persuasively argued that novels like *Mansfield Park* are "more implicated in the rationale for imperialist expansion than at first sight they have been" (*Culture and Imperialism*, 100).

8. A lineage tracing "Tar Baby" to the works of Thomas More is asserted in an 1892 review in *Punch*; see http://xroads.virginia.edu/~UG97/remus/punch.html (last accessed May 20, 2003). An attempt to attribute it to English West Country folklore can be found in the *North Carolina Journal of American Folklore* review; see http://xroads.virginia.edu/~UG97/remus/review.html (last accessed May 20, 2003). A scholarly article asserting an Indian provenance to the tale, meanwhile, is Cline, "Tar-Baby Story," 72–78.

9. "Review of *Uncle Remus and His Friends*," 19.

10. Twain, "Letter by Mark Twain to Joel Chandler Harris, August 10, 1881," in *Mark Twain's Letters*, 401.

11. Hemenway, "Introduction: Author, Teller, and Hero," 30–31; Werner, *Change Is Gonna Come*, 260–61.

12. Hemenway, "Introduction: Author, Teller, and Hero," 30–31. For refutations of the naiveté of "Tar Baby," see Levine, *Black Culture*, 131–32, and Baker, *Long Black Song*, 24–27.

13. Dorson, *American Negro Folktales*, 18; Brewer, *American Negro Folklore*, 4.

14. Hurston, *Mules and Men*, 89

15. Hurston, *Mules and Men*, 247

16. Dorson, *American Negro Folktales*, 18

17. Abrahams, *Deep Down in the Jungle*, 73.

18. Herskovitz, *New World Negro*, 175; emphasis added.

19. Herskovitz, *Myth of the Negro Past,* 255.

20. J. C. Harris, *Uncle Remus,* 57.

21. "Review of *Uncle Remus and His Friends,*" 19.

22. Werner, "Briar Patch as Modernist Myth," 155.

23. Hemenway, "Introduction: Author, Teller, and Hero," 30–31; Weatherford, "Tar Baby on the Soapbox,"923.

24. Morrison, *Sula,* 39.

25. Douglas, *Purity and Danger,* 38.

26. Morrison, *Playing in the Dark,* 72.

27. Willis, "Eruptions of Funk: Historicizing Toni Morrison," 34.

28. B. Johnson, *Feminist Difference,* 39.

29. Witt, *Black Hunger,* 80.

30. *Oxford English Dictionary* (Oxford: Clarendon, 1989), 11:95.

31. Hall, "Racism and Reaction," 25.

32. W. Johnson, *Soul by Soul,* 102.

33. Wallace, *Black Macho,* xviii.

34. Crowther, review of *Guess Who's Coming to Dinner,* 56.

35. Campbell, *Talking at the Gates,* 245.

36. B. Johnson, *Feminist Difference,* 75.

37. Morrison, *Sula,* 3.

38. Witt, *Black Hunger,* 86.

39. Morrison, *Beloved,* 189.

40. Morrison, *Beloved,* 127.

41. Baraka, "Soul Food," 102.

42. Shange, *If I Can Cook,* 9.

43. Chen, "Formation of a Diasporic Intellectual," 408.

44. Rigney, *Voices of Toni Morrison,* 86.

45. Sedgwick, *Between Men,* 1–20.

46. Douglas, *Purity and Danger,* 38.

47. Gilroy, *Between Camps,* 31; Mintz, *Tasting Food, Tasting Freedom,* 89.

48. Morrison, *Beloved,* 156.

49. Wright, *Black Boy (American Hunger),* 321.

50. Poe, "Origins of Soul Food," 91–108.

51. Gilroy, *Between Camps,* 12.

Conclusion

1. Malcolm X, *Autobiography,* 465.

2. Gilroy, *Between Camps,* 186.

3. Wright, *Black Boy (American Hunger)*, 175–76.

4. Sen, "Ingredients of Famine Analysis," 438.

5. Ellmann, *Hunger Artists*, 5–6

6. H. Young, *Food Scarcity and Famine*, 46–47.

7. Shaw, *U.N. World Food Programme*, 186.

8. E. M. Young, *World Hunger*, 2.

9. King, "Conscience and the Vietnam War," 32–33. The U.S. foreign economic aid budget for 1999 is given at $12.307 million and the defense budget for the same year at $348 billion in *Statistical Abstract of the United States: 2001*, 798, 261.

10. Harrington, *Other America*, 1–19.

11. For example, Fanon, "Colonial War and Mental Disorders," in *Wretched of the Earth*, 200–250.

12. Ellmann, *Hunger Artists*, 6.

13. Ellmann, *Hunger Artists*, 6.

14. Oacute Gráda, *Great Irish Famine*, 3–4.

15. Eagleton, *Heathcliff and the Great Hunger*, 24.

16. Sen, "Ingredients of Famine Analysis," 433–34.

17. Sen, "Capability and Well-Being," 41–42.

18. Oacute Gráda, *Great Irish Famine*, 15.

19. King, *Where Do We Go from Here*, 206.

20. Bremner, *From the Depths*, 69.

21. Spargo, *Bitter Cry of the Children*, 61.

22. Wright, *Black Boy (American Hunger)*, 16.

23. Baldwin's full description is "I always sensed in Wright a Mississippi pickaninny, mischievous, cunning, and tough." See Baldwin, *Nobody Knows My Name*, 148.

24. Foner, *Black Panthers Speak*, 2.

25. Foner, *Black Panthers Speak*, 168–69; emphases added.

26. Newton, *War against the Panthers*, 45.

Bibliography

Abrahams, Roger D. *Deep Down in the Jungle: Negro Narrative Folklore from the Streets of Philadelphia*. Chicago: Aldine, 1970.

Anderson, E. "Traditional Medical Values of Food." In *Food and Culture: A Reader,* edited by Carole Counihan and Penny Van Esterik, 80–91. London: Routledge, 1997.

Appiah, Kwame Anthony. "Battle of the Bien-Pensant." *New York Review of Books,* April 27, 2002, 41–45.

Appiah, Kwame Anthony, and Henry Louis Gates Jr. *Africana: The Encyclopaedia of the African and African-American Experience*. New York: Basic Civitas, 1999.

————, eds. *Dictionary of Global Culture*. London: Penguin, 1998.

Austen, Jane. *Mansfield Park*. London: Penguin, 1996.

Bacon, Francis. "New Atlantis." In *The Moral and Historical Works of Lord Bacon*, edited by Joseph Devey, 269–306. London: George Bell, 1874.

————. *The New Organon and Related Writings*. Edited by Fulton Anderson. New York: Bobbs-Merrill, 1960.

Baker, Houston A. *Long Black Song: Essays in Black American Literature and Culture*. Charlottesville: University Press of Virginia, 1972.

————. *Modernism and the Harlem Renaissance*. Chicago: University of Chicago Press, 1987.

————. *Workings of the Spirit: The Poetics of Afro-American Women's Writing*. Chicago: University of Chicago Press, 1991.

Baldwin, James. *The Devil Finds Work*. London: Joseph, 1976.

————. *Nobody Knows My Name: More Notes of a Native Son*. New York: Dell, 1961.

————. *No Name in the Street*. London: Corgi, 1973.

Baraka, Amiri (Le Roi Jones). "Soul Food." In *Home: Social Essays*, 101–4. New York: Morrow, 1966.

Barthes, Roland. "Toward a Psychosociology of Contemporary Food Consumption." In *Food and Culture: A Reader*, edited by Carole Counihan and Penny Van Esterik, 20–27. London: Routledge, 1997.

Bartram, William. *Travels of William Bartram*. Edited by Mark Van Doren. New York: Dover, 1955.

Bauman, Zygmunt. *Socialism: The Active Utopia*. London: Allen & Unwin, 1976.

Beeton, Mrs. *Mrs. Beeton's Cookery Book: A Household Guide All about Cookery, Household Work, Marketing, Prices, Provisions, Trussing, Serving, Carving, Menus, etc. etc.* London: Ward, 1901.

Benedict, Ruth. "Religion." In *General Anthropology*, edited by Franz Boas, 627–65. Boston: Heath, 1938.

Benghiat, Norma. *Traditional Jamaican Cookery*. Harmondsworth, Middlesex: Penguin, 1985.

Beverley, Robert. *The History and Present State of Virginia*. Edited by Louis B. Wright. Charlottesville, Va.: Dominia, 1968.

Bogle, Donald. *Toms, Coons, Mulattoes, Mammies, and Bucks: An Interpretive History of Blacks in American Films*. New York: Continuum, 1994.

Bose, Mishtooni. Introduction to *Utopia*, by Thomas More, vii–xiv. Ware, Herts: Wordsworth, 1997.

Bower, Anne L. "Bound Together: Recipes, Lives, Stories, and Readings." In

Recipes for Reading, edited by Anne L. Bower, 1–14. Amherst: University of Massachusetts, 1997.

Bradbury, Malcolm, and Richard Ruland. *From Puritanism to Postmodernism: A History of American Literature.* Harmondsworth, Middlesex: Penguin, 1991.

Bremner, Robert H. *From the Depths: The Discovery of Poverty in the United States.* New York: New York University Press, 1956.

Brewer, J. Mason. *American Negro Folklore.* Chicago: Quadrangle, 1968.

Brontë, Charlotte. *Jane Eyre.* London: Penguin, 1996.

Brown, Dee. *Bury My Heart at Wounded Knee: An Indian History of the American West.* London: Vintage, 1991.

Campbell, James. *Talking at the Gates: A Life of James Baldwin.* London: Faber & Faber, 1991.

Carby, Hazel. *Cultures in Babylon: Black Britain and African America.* London: Verso, 1999.

Cayton, Horace, and St. Clair Drake. *Black Metropolis.* London: Jonathan Cape, 1946.

Chen, Kuan-Hsing. "The Formation of a Diasporic Intellectual: An Interview with Stuart Hall." In *Black British Culture and Society: A Text Reader,* edited by Kwesi Owusu, 405–15. London: Routledge, 2000.

Cline, Ruth. "The Tar-Baby Story." *American Literature* 2 (1930): 72–78.

Cole-Hamilton, Isobel, and Tim Lang. *Tightening Belts: A Report on the Impact of Poverty on Food.* London: London Food Commission, 1986.

Crowther, Bosley. Review of *Guess Who's Coming to Dinner. New York Times,* December 12, 1967, 56.

Dampier, William. *A New Voyage round the World, describing particularly the Isthmus of America.* London: James Knapton, 1698.

Davis, Angela. "The Approaching Obsolescence of Housework: A Working-Class Perspective." In *Women, Race and Class,* 222–44. London: Women's Press, 1984.

Davis, Mike. "Los Angeles Was Just the Beginning: Urban Revolt in the United States: A Thousand Points of Light." In *Open Fire: The Open Magazine Pamphlet Series Anthology,* edited by Greg Ruggerio and Stuart Sahulka, 220–42. New York: New Press, 1993.

Deadly Adulteration and Slow Poisoning; or, Disease and Death in the Pot and the Bottle; in which the Blood-Empoisoning and Life-Destroying Adulterations of Wines, Spirits, Beer, Bread, Flour, Tea, Sugar, Spices, Cheesemongering, Pastry, Confectionary [sic]*, Medicines, &c. &c. &c. are laid Open to the Public.* London: Sherwood, Gilbert & Piper, 1829.

Dean, Mitchel. *The Constitution of Poverty: Towards a Genealogy of Liberal Government.* London: Routledge, 1991.

Defoe, Daniel. *Robinson Crusoe.* London: Penguin, 1985.

Dickens, Charles. *Little Dorrit.* London: Penguin, 1998.

———. *Oliver Twist.* London: Penguin, 1985.

Dorson, Richard. *American Negro Folktales.* Greenwich, Conn.: Fawcett Premier, 1967.

Douglas, Mary. "Deciphering a Meal." In *Food and Culture: A Reader,* edited by Carole Counihan and Penny Van Esterik, 36–54. London: Routledge, 1997.

———. *Purity and Danger.* London: Routledge, 1966.

Douglass, Frederick. *Narrative of the Life of Frederick Douglass, an American Slave, Written by Himself.* New York: Dover, 1995.

Du Bois, W. E. B. "Colonies and Moral Responsibility in Some General Problems of Education in Dependent Territories." *Journal of Negro Education* 15 (1946): 311–18.

———. *Darkwater: Voices from within the Veil.* Mineola, N.Y.: Dover, 1999.

———. "Education and Work." In *The Seventh Son: The Thought and Writings of W. E. B. Du Bois,* vol. 1, edited by Julius Lester, 558–76. New York: Random House, 1971.

Dunbar, Paul Laurence. *Selected Poems: Paul Laurence Dunbar.* Mineola, N.Y.: Dover, 1997.

Eagleton, Terry. *Heathcliff and the Great Hunger: Studies in Irish Culture.* London: Verso, 1995.

———. "Utopia and Its Opposites." In *Necessary and Unnecessary Utopias: Socialist Register 2000,* edited by Leo Panitch and Colin Leys, 31–40. Woodbridge, Suffolk: Merlin, 1999.

Ellison, Ralph. *Invisible Man.* Harmondsworth, Middlesex: Penguin, 1965.

———. *Juneteenth.* London: Hamish Hamilton, 1999.

———. *Shadow and Act.* London: Secker & Warburg, 1967.

Ellmann, Maud. *The Hunger Artists.* London: Virago, 1993.

Equiano, Olaudah. *The Interesting Narrative and Other Writings.* London: Penguin, 1995.

Fanon, Frantz. *The Wretched of the Earth.* London: Penguin, 1990.

Farley, Reginald, and Walter Allen. *The Color Line and the Quality of Life in America.* Oxford: Oxford University Press, 1989.

Faulkner, William. "The Bear." In *Go Down, Moses and Other Stories,* 135–236. London: Vintage, 1996.

Ferguson, Sheila. *Soul Food: Classic Cuisine from the Deep South.* New York: Grove, 1989.

Fisher, Abby. *What Mrs. Fisher Knows about Old Southern Cooking: Soups, Pickles, Preserves, etc.* Edited by Karen Hess. Bedford, Mass.: Applewood, 1995.

Fitchen, Janet M. "Hunger, Malnutrition, and Poverty in the Contemporary United States: Some Observations on Their Social and Cultural Context." In *Food and Culture: A Reader,* edited by Carole Counihan and Penny Van Esterik, 384–401. London: Routledge, 1997.

Foner, Philip S., ed. *The Black Panthers Speak.* New York: Da Capo, 1995.

Foucault, Michel. *Discipline and Punish: The Birth of the Prison.* Translated by Alan Sheridan. London: Penguin, 1991.

Frazier, E. Franklin. *The Negro Family in the United States.* Chicago: University of Chicago Press, 1947.

Gambrell, Alice. *Women Intellectuals, Modernism and Difference: Transatlantic Culture 1919–1945.* Cambridge: Cambridge University Press, 1997.

Gates, Henry Louis, Jr. *Figures in Black: Words, Signs and the "Racial" Self.* New York: Oxford University Press, 1987.

———. *The Signifying Monkey: A Theory of African-American Literary Criticism.* New York: Oxford University Press, 1988.

Gates, Henry Louis, Jr., and Nellie Y. McKay, eds. *The Norton Anthology of African-American Literature.* New York: Norton, 1997.

Genovese, Eugene. *Roll, Jordan, Roll: The World the Slaves Made.* New York: Pantheon, 1972.

Geras, Norman. "Minimum Utopia: Ten Theses." In *Necessary and Unnecessary Utopias: Socialist Register 2000,* edited by Leo Panitch and Colin Leys, 41–52. Woodbridge, Suffolk: Merlin, 1999.

Gidley, Mick, ed. *Representing Others: White Views of Indigenous Peoples.* Exeter: University of Exeter Press, 1992.

Gilroy, Paul. *Between Camps: Nations, Cultures and the Allure of Race.* London: Penguin, 2000.

———. *Black Atlantic: Modernity and Double Consciousness.* London: Verso, 1993.

Godden, Richard. "*Absalom, Absalom!* Haiti and Labor History: Reading Unreadable Revolutions." *ELH* 61 (3) (autumn 1994): 685–720.

Goody, Jack. *Cooking, Cuisine, and Class: A Study in Comparative Sociology.* Cambridge: Cambridge University Press, 1982.

―――. *The Domestication of the Savage Mind.* Cambridge: Cambridge University Press, 1977.

―――. *Food and Love: A Cultural History of East and West.* London: Verso, 1998.

―――. "Industrial Food: Towards the Development of a World Cuisine." In *Food and Culture: A Reader,* edited by Carole Counihan and Penny Van Esterik, 338–56. London: Routledge, 1997.

Gronniosaw, James Albert Ukawsaw. *A Narrative of the Most Remarkable Particulars in the Life of James Albert Ukawsaw Gronniosaw, an African Prince, as Related by Himself.* Leeds: G. Wilson, 1813.

Hakluyt, Richard. "A Discourse concerning Western Planting." In *Documentary History of the State of Maine,* vol. 2, edited by Charles Deane, 1–167. Cambridge, Mass.: John Wilson, 1877.

Hall, Stuart. "Racism and Reaction." In *Five Views of Multi-Racial Britain: Talks on Race Relations Broadcast by BBC TV,* 23–55. London: Commission for Racial Equality, 1978.

Harrington, Michael. *The Other America: Poverty in the United States.* Harmondsworth, Middlesex: Penguin, 1977.

Harris, Jessica B. *Iron Pots and Wooden Spoons: Africa's Gifts to New World Cooking.* New York: Fireside, 1999.

―――. *A Kwanzaa Keepsake.* New York: Fireside, 1998.

Harris, Joel Chandler. *Nights with Uncle Remus.* New York: Meredith, 1921.

―――. *Uncle Remus: His Songs and Sayings.* London: Penguin, 1986.

Hemenway, Robert. "Introduction: Author, Teller, and Hero." In *Uncle Remus: His Songs and Sayings,* by Joel Chandler Harris, 7–31. London: Penguin, 1986.

―――. *Zora Neale Hurston: A Literary Biography.* Urbana: University of Illinois Press, 1977.

Herskovits, Melville J. *The Myth of the Negro Past.* New York: Harper, 1941.

―――. *The New World Negro.* Bloomington: Indiana University Press, 1966.

Herskovits, Melville, and Frances Herskovits. *Dahomean Narrative: A Cross-Cultural Analysis.* Evanston, Ill.: Northwestern University Press, 1958.

Hess, Karen. *The Carolina Rice Kitchen: The African Connection.* Columbia: University of South Carolina Press, 1992.

Hickeringill, Edmund. *Jamaica Viewed: With All the Ports, Harbours, and Their Several Soundings, Towns, and Settlements.* London: John Williams, 1661.

Hill, Andrew John. "Investigation of Some Short-Term Influences on Hunger, Satiety and Food Consumption." Ph.D. diss., University of Leeds, Dept. of Psychology, 1986.

Hine, Darlene Clark, Elsa Barkly Brown, and Rosalyn Terborg-Penn, eds. *Black Women in America: An Historical Encyclopaedia.* Bloomington: Indiana University Press, 1994.

Hughes, Marvalene H. "Soul, Black Women, and Food." In *Food and Culture: A Reader,* edited by Carole Counihan and Penny Van Esterik, 272–80. London: Routledge, 1997.

Hunter, Robert. Introduction to *The Bitter Cry of the Children,* by John Spargo, vii–xii. New York: Johnson Reprint, 1969.

Hurston, Zora Neale. *Dust Tracks on a Road.* London: Virago, 1986.

———. *Go Gator and Muddy the Water: Writings by Zora Neale Hurston from the Federal Writers' Project.* Edited by Pamela Bordelon. New York: Norton, 1999.

———. *Jonah's Gourd Vine.* London: Virago, 1987.

———. *Moses, Man of the Mountains.* New York: Harper Perennial, 1991.

———. *Mules and Men.* New York: Harper Perennial, 1990.

———. "Spunk." In *Harlem's Glory: Black Women Writing 1900–1950,* edited by Lorraine Elena Roses and Ruth Elizabeth Randolph, 233–38. Cambridge, Mass.: Harvard University Press, 1996.

———. *Tell My Horse: Voodoo and Life in Haiti and Jamaica.* New York: Harper Perennial, 1990.

———. *Their Eyes Were Watching God.* London: Virago, 1986.

Jacobs, Harriet. *Incidents in the Life of a Slave Girl, Written by Herself.* Edited by Jean Fagan Yellin. Cambridge, Mass.: Harvard University Press, 1987.

James, C. L. R. *American Civilization.* Edited by Anna Grimshaw and Keith Hart. Cambridge, Mass.: Blackwell, 1993.

———. *Beyond a Boundary.* Durham, N.C.: Duke University Press, 1993.

———. "Black Studies and the Contemporary Student." In *At the Rendezvous of Victory: Selected Writings,* 186–201. London: Allison & Busby, 1984.

Jefferson, Thomas. *Notes on the State of Virginia.* Chapel Hill: University of North Carolina Press, 1955.

Johnson, Barbara. *The Feminist Difference: Literature, Psychoanalysis, Race, and Gender.* Cambridge, Mass.: Harvard University Press, 1998.

———. *A World of Difference.* Baltimore: Johns Hopkins University Press, 1987.

Johnson, Walter. *Soul by Soul: Life inside the Antebellum Slave Market.* Cambridge, Mass.: Harvard University Press, 1999.

Kanneh, Kadiatu. *African Identities: Race, Nation and Culture in Ethnography, Pan-Africanism and Black Literatures.* London: Routledge, 1998.

King, Martin Luther, Jr. "Conscience and the Vietnam War." In *The Trumpet of Conscience*, 21–34. New York: Harper Collins, 1987.

———. *Where Do We Go from Here: Chaos or Community?* New York: Bantam, 1967.

Kinnamon, Keneth. *The Emergence of Richard Wright: A Study in Literature and Society.* Urbana: University of Illinois Press, 1972.

Kohn, Marek. *The Race Gallery: The Return of Racial Science.* London: Jonathan Cape, 1995.

Kolchin, Peter. *American Slavery 1619–1877.* London: Penguin, 1993.

Krumholz, Linda. "The Ghosts of Slavery: Historical Recovery in Toni Morrison's *Beloved.*" *African American Review* 26 (1992): 395–408.

Kumar, Krishan. *Utopia and Anti-Utopia in Modern Times.* Oxford: Basil Blackwell, 1987.

Leeming, David. *James Baldwin: A Biography.* London: Michael Joseph, 1994.

Levine, Lawrence W. *Black Culture and Black Consciousness: Afro-American Folk Thought from Slavery to Freedom.* Oxford: Oxford University Press, 1977.

———. *The Unpredictable Past: Explorations in American Cultural History.* Oxford: Oxford University Press, 1977.

Lévi Strauss, Claude. *The Raw and the Cooked: Introduction to a Science of Mythology.* Translated by John Weightman and Doreen Weightman. London: Cape, 1970.

Logan, Rayford W. *The Betrayal of the Negro: From Rutherford Hayes to Woodrow Wilson.* New York: Da Capo, 1997.

Lovera, José Rafael. *Historia de la Alimentación en Venezuela: Con Textos Para su Estudio.* Caracas: Monte Avila, 1988.

Malcolm X. *The Autobiography of Malcolm X.* Harmondsworth, Middlesex: Penguin, 1968.

Marx, Karl. *Capital.* Edited by David McLellan. Oxford: Oxford University Press, 1995.

Mathieson, W. L. *British Slavery and Its Abolition.* London: Longmans, Green, 1926.

McPhee, John. *Oranges.* London: Penguin, 2000.

Mencken, H. L. *The American Language: An Inquiry into the Development of English in the United States.* London: Routledge & Kegan Paul, 1947.

———. "Negro Spokesman Arises to Voice His Race's Wrongs." In *The Impossible H. L. Mencken: A Selection of His Best Newspaper Stories,* edited by Marion Rodgers, 186–91. New York: Doubleday, 1991.

Mintz, Sidney W. *Sweetness and Power: The Place of Sugar in Modern Industry.* Harmondsworth, Middlesex: Penguin, 1986.

———. *Tasting Food, Tasting Freedom: Excursions into Eating, Culture, and the Past.* Boston: Beacon, 1996.

Moody, V. Alton. *Slavery on Louisiana Sugar Plantations.* New Orleans: Louisiana Historical Quarterly, 1924.

Morrison, Toni. *Beloved.* London: Vintage, 1997.

———. "Cooking Out." *New York Times Book Review*, July 10, 1973, 16.

———. "The Official Story: Dead Man Golfing." In *Birth of a Nation'Hood: Gaze, Script, and Spectacle in the O. J. Simpson Case,* edited by Toni Morrison and Claudia Lacour, vii–xxviii. London: Vintage, 1997.

———. *Paradise.* London: Vintage, 1999.

———. *Playing in the Dark: Whiteness and the Literary Imagination.* New York: Vintage, 1993.

———. *Sula.* New York: Plume, 1982.

———. *Tar Baby.* London: Picador, 1981.

Murray, Albert. *The Seven League Boots.* New York: Vintage, 1997.

Myrdal, Gunnar. *American Dilemma: The Negro Problem and Modern Democracy.* New York: Harper & Row, 1944.

Newton, Huey. *War against the Panthers: A Study of Repression in America.* New York: Harlem River, 1996.

Oacute Gráda, Cormác. *The Great Irish Famine.* Cambridge: Cambridge University Press, 1995.

Pennington, Neil L., and Charles W. Baker. *Sugar: A User's Guide to Sucrose.* New York: Van Nostrand Reinhold, 1990.

Philips, John Edward. "The African Heritage of White America." In *Africanisms in American Culture,* edited by Joseph E. Holloway, 225–39. Bloomington: Indiana University Press, 1991.

Physician Task Force on Hunger in America. *Hunger in America: The Growing Epidemic.* Middletown, Conn.: Wesleyan University Press, 1985.

Piven, Frances Fox, and Richard Cloward. *The New Class War: Reagan's Attack on the Welfare State and Its Consequences.* New York: Pantheon, 1982.

Plato. "Gorgias." In *Plato on Rhetoric and Language: Four Key Dialogues,* edited by Jean Nienkamp, trans. by Donald Zeyl, 85–164. Mahwah, N.J.: Lawrence Erlbaum, 1999.

Poe, Tracey N. "The Origins of Soul Food in Black Urban Identity: Chicago, 1915–1947." In *Food in the United States of America: A Reader,* edited by Carole Counihan, 91–108. New York: Routledge, 2002.

Rampersad, Arnold. Note on the text in *Black Boy (American Hunger): A Record of Childhood and Youth,* by Richard Wright, 487–89. New York: Harper Perennial, 1993.

———. Notes to *The Outsider* in *The Outsider,* by Richard Wright, 625–29. New York: Harper Perennial, 1991.

"Review of *Uncle Remus and His Friends.*" *New York Times,* December 18, 1892, 19.

Rich, Adrienne. *Blood, Bread and Poetry: Selected Prose 1979–1985.* London: Virago, 1987.

Rigney, Barbara. *The Voices of Toni Morrison.* Columbus: Ohio State University Press, 1991.

Ritzer, George. *The McDonaldization of Society.* Thousand Oaks, Calif.: Pine Forge, 2000.

Roses, Lorraine Elena, and Ruth Elizabeth Randolph, eds. *Harlem's Glory: Black Women Writing 1900–1950.* Cambridge, Mass.: Harvard University Press, 1996.

Rossi, Paolo. "Bacon's Idea of Science." In *The Cambridge Companion to Francis Bacon,* edited by Markku Peltonen, 1–24. Cambridge: Cambridge University Press, 1996.

Rubin, Joan Shelley. "Self, Culture and Self-Culture in Modern America: The Early History of the Book-of-the-Month Club." *Journal of American History* 71 (1985): 782–806.

S., J. L. *Sugar; How it Grows, and How it is Made. A Pleasing Account for Young People.* London: Darton & Clark, 1844.

Said, Edward. *Culture and Imperialism.* London: Vintage, 1994.

Seale, Bobby. *Barbeque'n with Bobby.* Berkeley, Calif.: Ten Speed, 1988.

———. *Seize the Time: The Story of the Black Panther Party.* London: Arrow, 1970.

Sedgwick, Eve Kosofsky. *Between Men: English Literature and Male Homosocial Desire.* New York: Columbia University Press, 1985.

Sen, Amartya. "Capability and Well-Being." In *The Quality of Life,* edited by Martha Nussbaum and Amartya Sen, 30–53. Oxford: Clarendon Press, 1993.

———. "Ingredients of Famine Analysis: Availability and Entitlement." *Quarterly Journal of Economics* 96 (1981): 433–64.

———. *On Economic Inequality.* Oxford: Clarendon Press, 1973.

Shange, Ntozake. *If I Can Cook / You Know God Can.* Boston: Beacon, 1998.

Shaw, D. John. *The U.N. World Food Programme and the Development of Food Aid.* Basingstoke, Hants: Palgrave, 2001.

Shigley, Sally Bishop. "Empathy, Energy, and Eating: Politics and Power in *The Black Family Dinner Quilt Cookbook.*" In *Recipes for Reading,* edited by Anne L. Bower, 118–31. Amherst: University of Massachusetts, 1997.

Short, Thomas. *Discourses on Tea, Sugar, Milk, Made-Wine, Spirits, Punch, Tobacco, &c. with Plain and Useful Rules for Gouty People.* London: Longman & Millar, 1750.

Smart-Grosvenor, Vertamae. *Vibration Cooking: Or the Travel Notes of a Geechee Girl.* New York: Ballantine, 1991.

Smith, John. *The Generall Historie of Virginia, New-England, and the Summer Isles.* In *The Complete Works of Captain John Smith,* 27–475. Chapel Hill: University of North Carolina Press, 1986.

Smith, Nigel, Donald Plucknett, and Jennifer Talbot. *Tropical Forests and Their Crops.* Ithaca, N.Y.: Comstock, 1992.

Spargo, John. *The Bitter Cry of the Children.* New York: Johnson Reprint, 1969.

Statistical Abstract of the United States: 2001. Austin, Tex.: Hoover's Business Press, 2001.

Steingarten, Jeffrey. *The Man Who Ate Everything, and Other Gastronomic Feats, Disputes, and Pleasurable Pursuits.* London: Headline, 1998.

Storace, Patricia. "The Scripture of Utopia." *New York Review of Books,* June 11, 1998, 64–69.

Thompson, Era Bell. "Where the West Begins." In *Harlem's Glory: Black Women Writing, 1900–1950,* edited by Lorraine Elena Roses and Ruth Elizabeth Randolph, 156–62. Cambridge, Mass.: Harvard University Press, 1996.

Toomer, Jean. *Cane.* New York: Norton, 1988.

———. *The Wayward and the Seeking: A Collection of Writings by Jean Toomer.* Edited by Darwin T. Turner. Washington, D.C.: Howard University Press, 1980.

Twain, Mark. *Mark Twain's Letters.* Edited by Albert Paine. New York: Gabriel Wells, 1917.

Walker, Alice. *In Search of Our Mothers' Gardens: Womanist Prose.* London: Women's Press, 1984.

———. *The Third Life of Grange Copeland.* London: Women's Press, 1985.

Wallace, Michele. *Black Macho and the Myth of the Superwoman.* London: Verso, 1990.

Washington, Booker T. *The Booker T. Washington Papers.* Vol. 10, *1909–11.* Edited by Louis Harlan and Raymond Smock. Urbana: University of Illinois Press, 1981.

———. *Up from Slavery.* Harmondsworth, Middlesex: Penguin, 1987.

Weatherford, Carole Boston. "Tar Baby on the Soapbox." *Callaloo* 14 (1991): 923.

Werner, Craig. "The Briar Patch as Modernist Myth: Morrison, Barthes and Tar Baby As-Is." In *Critical Essays on Toni Morrison,* edited by Nellie Y. McKay, 150–70. Boston: Hall, 1988.

———. *A Change Is Gonna Come: Music, Race, and the Soul of America.* Edinburgh: Payback, 2000.

Wheatley, Phillis. "From *Poems on Various Subjects, Religious and Moral.*" In *The Norton Anthology of African-American Literature,* edited by Henry Louis Gates Jr. and Nellie Y. McKay, 164–77. New York: Norton, 1997.

Williams, Raymond. *The Country and the City.* London: Chatto & Windus, 1973.

———. *Marxism and Literature.* Oxford: Oxford University Press, 1977.

Willis, Susan. "Eruptions of Funk: Historicizing Toni Morrison." *Black American Literature Forum* 16 (1982): 34–42.

———. *Specifying: Black Women Writing the American Experience.* Madison: University of Wisconsin Press, 1987.

Witt, Doris. *Black Hunger: Food and the Politics of U.S. Identity.* New York: Oxford University Press, 1999.

Wodrow, Robert. *The Correspondence of the Rev. Robert Wodrow, Minister of Eastwood, and Author of the History of the Sufferings of the Church of Scotland.* Edited by the Rev. Thomas McCrie. Edinburgh: Wodrow Society, 1842–43.

Woodham-Smith, Cecil. *The Great Hunger: Ireland 1845–1849.* London: Penguin, 1991.

Wright, Richard. "Between Laughter and Tears." *New Masses,* October 5, 1937, 25–26.

———. *Black Boy (American Hunger).* New York: Harper Perennial, 1993.

———. "*Black Boy* and Reading." In *Conversations with Richard Wright,* edited by Kenneth Kinnamon and Michel Febre, 81–82. Jackson: University Press of Mississippi, 1993.

———. "Book-of-the-Month Author Talks for AFRO." *Afro-American,* January 13, 1945, 1.

———. *Eight Men.* New York: Harper Perennial, 1996.

———. "How Bigger Was Born." In *Native Son,* i–xxvi. London: Jonathan Cape, 1970.

———. "How Richard Wright Looks at *Black Boy.*" *PM,* April 15, 1945, 3–4.

———. *Native Son.* London: Jonathan Cape, 1970.

————. *The Outsider*. New York: Harper Perennial, 1991.

————. "This, Too, Is America." *Tomorrow,* May 4, 1945, 63.

————. *Twelve Million Black Voices*. New York: Thunder's Mouth, 1995.

Young, E. M. *World Hunger*. London: Routledge, 1997.

Young, Helen. *Food Scarcity and Famine: Assessment and Response*. Oxford: Oxfam, 1992.

Zafar, Rafia. "The Signifying Dish: Autobiography and History in Two Black Women's Cookbooks." In *Food in the United States of America: A Reader,* edited by Carole Counihan, 249–62. New York: Routledge, 2002.

Zibart, Eve, Muriel Stevens, and Terrell Vermont. *The Unofficial Guide to Ethnic Cuisine and Dining in America*. New York: Macmillan, 1995.

Zwane, Benedict. "Overpopulation and Economic Growth in the Developing Countries." *Transition* 49 (1975): 53–63.

Index

Africa: and African American literary culture, 71, 130–31; and African American social conditions, 125–27, 166–67; folk cultures of, 128–30; Ghanaian cocoa production, 5–6. *See also* okra; "Tar Baby" folktale

African Diaspora. *See under* barbecue; cuisine

Afrocentrism, 167

American Civilization. See James, C. L. R.

American Dilemma (Myrdal), 51–52, 83, 87

American Hunger (*Black Boy*) (Wright), 4, 23, 168–69, 183–84, 186; and cooking, 118–22; and forgery, 113–19; and gender, 120–22; institutionalization in, 96–99; naming of, 80–84; and national